Community, Solidarity and Belonging

Levels of Community and Their Normative Significance

Despite the frequency with which the term 'community' is used, comprehensive explorations of the nature and value of community are rare. Whilst responding to this need, this book takes seriously the idea that community can be of different kinds and can exist at different levels, and that these levels and kinds may come into conflict with one another. It focuses on the question of what kind of community is valuable at the level of the state. It then explores the limits that ideals of political community place upon cultural diversity within the state, and the limits that, in turn, ideals of global community place upon the self-determination of political communities. This book will be of interest to students of political theory, philosophy and international relations.

ANDREW MASON is Professor of Political Theory at the University of Southampton. He is the author of *Explaining Political Disagreement* (1993), and editor of *Ideals of Equality* (1998).

Community, Solidarity and Belonging

*Levels of Community and
Their Normative Significance*

Andrew Mason

CAMBRIDGE
UNIVERSITY PRESS

CAMBRIDGE UNIVERSITY PRESS
Cambridge, New York, Melbourne, Madrid, Cape Town,
Singapore, São Paulo, Delhi, Mexico City

Cambridge University Press
The Edinburgh Building, Cambridge CB2 8RU, UK

Published in the United States of America by Cambridge University Press, New York

www.cambridge.org
Information on this title: www.cambridge.org/9780521637282

First published 2000

A catalogue record for this publication is available from the British Library

ISBN 978-0-521-63129-7 Hardback
ISBN 978-0-521-63728-2 Paperback

For Lynn

Contents

Acknowledgements

A number of people have helped me to write this book. Simon Caney, David Miller, Susan Mendus and John Tomasi criticized an early draft of it, and enabled me to see many of its weaknesses. Subsequent drafts of various chapters were revised in the light of suggestions and objections made by John Andrews, Richard Bellamy, Chris Brown, Matthew Clayton, Jonathan Dancy, Keith Graham, Brad Hooker, Dale Miller, Andrew Moore, David Owen, Bhikhu Parekh, Geraint Parry, Nick Wheeler and Andrew Williams. Roger Crisp and John Horton kindly agreed to read the whole of the penultimate draft of the book and their acute comments forced me to rethink a number of the issues. Many of the arguments were first tried out in 'Work in Progress' sessions held in the Philosophy Department at the University of Reading, which provided a supportive but rigorous environment to test and develop them. The book was completed whilst holding a Leverhulme Fellowship, and I would like to thank the Trust's Research Awards Advisory Committee for providing me with the freedom from teaching and administrative responsibilities which I needed in order to do so.

Introduction

'Community' is a term used with alarming frequency. People talk of international community, which some think has been made possible by the end of the Cold War; of national community, which politicians often promise to rebuild in the face of increasing crime and lawlessness or in reaction to the fear that it is being eroded by immigration; of the local or neighbourhood communities which are sometimes said to be threatened by gentrification or (like London's Docklands) redevelopment. Some also speak of the business community's attitude towards a rise in interest rates, or the gay community's support for legislation which equalized the age of consent for heterosexuals and homosexuals. Faced with this array of putative communities, it is hard not to become suspicious that the term is being used unreflectively, or that it is being used purely emotively, to induce support for social arrangements or policies which the speaker or writer happens to favour.

There is, no doubt, something in these suspicions. But they should not prejudice attempts to sort out from the mire of ordinary usage a coherent concept (or set of concepts) which may help to illuminate our linguistic practices and the nature of our social lives. If ordinary usage is to be trusted at all, it would appear that communities can be of different *kinds*. For instance, there may be religious communities, ethnic communities, national communities, moral communities or linguistic communities. Not only can communities be of different kinds they may also exist at different *levels*. So, for instance, it is possible in principle for there to be a religious community below the level of the state, involving just some of its citizens, or at the level of the state, involving all or the vast majority of its citizens and partially constituted by its major institutions, or above the level of the state, involving citizens from a number of different states.

These observations settle very little, if anything, about the nature of community, but nevertheless they indicate some of the difficulties of giving an analysis of community in general, and some of the limitations of such an exercise. For an analysis of community in general must in some way abstract from these different kinds of community; so too any account of the value of community in general must abstract from the value of different kinds of community. Although I think this sort of abstraction is worthwhile, it will leave partially unanswered questions about the nature and value of particular kinds of community at particular levels. Indeed one of the central questions for political philosophers is the following: what kind of community, if any, is valuable at the level of the state, and what steps, if any, may the state legitimately take to promote it?

This question provokes a barrage of others which are related to it. If the state can legitimately build some kind of political community, is it entitled to restrict the practices of communities below the level of the state in order to do so? (Note that I use the expression 'political community' to mean community at the level of the state, rather than to designate a particular kind of community.) What jurisdiction, if any, do international bodies, or other states, have in relation to the 'internal' affairs of a political community? For example, are they entitled to intervene in those affairs in order to promote some kind of community at the global level? In short, there are a variety of ways in which levels and kinds of communities can come into conflict with one another, and a host of questions about how, if at all, these conflicts should be resolved, in so far as it is within any individual's or group's power to do so.

During the 1980s a series of books and articles appeared which came to be referred to as communitarian,[1] and we might have expected them to provide some help with these questions. Communitarianism, however, was primarily a reaction to the perceived weaknesses of liberalism and there has been no systematic attempt within it to answer questions of the sort I have raised.[2] One striking omission from communitarian writings was any detailed or comprehensive exploration of the nature of community and its value. Unlike other central political concepts such as freedom, justice and equality, the concept of community has still not received the analytical attention it deserves.[3]

---

[1] The summary of the communitarian critique of liberalism which follows is indebted to S. Caney, 'Liberalism and Communitarianism: a Misconceived Debate', *Political Studies*, vol. 40, 1992, pp. 273–89. See also S. Mulhall and A. Swift, *Liberals and Communitarians*, revd edn (Oxford: Blackwell, 1996).

[2] Those who examine the debate between liberals and communitarians should not expect to find a set of doctrines that all communitarians endorse and which distinguish them from liberals. But they will find a family of more or less well-connected themes which communitarian writers draw upon, sometimes with different emphases. Even though the various criticisms of liberal theory display less unity than one might initially have expected, and despite the resistance several of those labelled as communitarians have shown to the term, there is some justification for grouping them together.

[3] The observation that 'community' has received relatively little careful attention was made by Raymond Plant, 'Community: Concept, Conception, and Ideology', *Politics and Society*, vol. 8, 1978, p. 78. It remains true. See also R. Goodin, *Reasons for Welfare: The Political Theory of the Welfare State* (Princeton, NJ: Princeton University Press, 1988), p. 71;

On many occasions communitarian theorists also seemed unclear about whether they thought political means should be used to protect or promote community of some kind at the level of the state, and even when they were unambiguous on this matter they often took up different positions among themselves. Alasdair MacIntyre has now said explicitly that he thinks community should be sought at the local level rather than above it.[4] Michael Sandel thinks that the defence of some principles of social justice, such as Rawls's Difference Principle, presupposes the existence of a 'constitutive' political community, that is, a political community in which citizens conceive their identity as defined to some extent by their membership of it.[5] But he appears sceptical about its practicality in modern states.[6] Michael Walzer's idea that justice within the state requires goods to be distributed in accordance with shared understandings presupposes that its citizens are part of a community, sharing a way of life in which goods have particular meanings.[7] Charles Taylor has expressed sympathy for the view that community is important at the level of the state: he has suggested that free regimes are unlikely to be sustainable in the absence of 'patriotic identification', that is, unless citizens identify with the polity's particular historical community, founded upon particular values.[8]

This book aims to make a contribution to the discussion of these issues. It provides an analysis of the notion of community, and explores its value. It then focuses on three inter-related questions which the concept of community raises for political philosophers: what kind of community, if any, is valuable at the level of the state, and what steps, if any, is the state entitled to take to protect or promote it? When political community of some valuable kind comes into conflict with the existence of communities below the level of the state, or the preservation of their current character, how should this conflict be resolved? When political community comes

---

J. Waldron, 'Minority Cultures and the Cosmopolitan Alternative', in W. Kymlicka (ed.), *The Rights of Minority Cultures* (Oxford: Oxford University Press, 1995), p. 95.

[4] A. MacIntyre, 'A Partial Response to My Critics', in J. Horton and S. Mendus (eds.), *After MacIntyre: Critical Perspectives on the Work of Alasdair MacIntyre* (Cambridge: Polity, 1994), pp. 302–3. MacIntyre assumes that a commitment to community at the level of the state is constitutive of communitarian thought and distances himself from communitarianism for that reason.

[5] See M. Sandel, *Liberalism and the Limits of Justice* (Cambridge: Cambridge University Press, 1982), especially pp. 79–82, 150.

[6] See Sandel, 'The Procedural Republic and the Unencumbered Self', in S. Avineri and A. de-Shalit (eds.), *Communitarianism and Individualism* (Oxford: Oxford University Press, 1992), pp. 26–7.

[7] See M. Walzer, *Spheres of Justice: A Defence of Pluralism and Equality* (Oxford: Martin Robertson, 1983), especially pp. 28–9.

[8] See C. Taylor, 'Cross-Purposes: The Liberal–Communitarian Debate', in his *Philosophical Arguments* (Cambridge, MA: Harvard University Press, 1995).

into conflict with the realization or promotion of a global community of some valuable kind, how should such conflict be resolved (assuming that the very idea of global community is intelligible)? My guiding assumption is that in order to understand the normative significance of community at the level of the state, we have to understand its relationship to community above and below it.

1.   The structure of the book

Part 1 of the book (comprising Chapters 1 and 2) attempts to unravel some of the complexities which surround the nature and value of community, in so far as it is possible to explore these issues in a general way. The discussion in these chapters forms the background against which subsequent arguments are developed, but those with less interest in the more general philosophical issues that I take up in them may prefer to move straight to Part 2.

In Chapter 1 I argue that the notion of community is fundamentally ambiguous. In political theory, and also in ordinary usage, the term is used to characterize two very different kinds of relationship. On the one hand, it is used to refer to groups whose members share values and a way of life, identify with the group and its practices, and acknowledge each other as members. I call this the ordinary concept of community. Versions of it have dominated much of recent Anglo-American political philosophy. On the other hand, 'community' is also used in a way that restricts its application to groups whose members are mutually concerned and do not exploit one another, or behave unjustly towards each other, at least not in any systematic way. I call this the moralized concept of community. I shall suggest that it is not uncommon for people to trade on this ambiguity by describing as a community in the moralized sense a set of social relationships which do not go beyond community in the ordinary sense. As a result, cynicism about the way in which the term may be used to dress up relationships which the speaker or writer happens to like, or which serve his interests, may sometimes be appropriate.

Chapter 2 explores the various sources and kinds of value that may be possessed by communities: it argues that community can have non-instrumental value in virtue of the cooperative activity which constitutes it, and that it may also possess considerable instrumental value because it can satisfy people's needs (or desires) to belong, or be recognized by others, and thereby help secure various other goods. I also address the question of whether the value possessed by a community can be, or must be, reducible to the value it has for individuals. I make no attempt to resolve that issue, arguing instead that it is not as important as it may appear. Much of what liberals, communitarians and others have wanted to say about the value of community, and its relation to other values, can be expressed whichever way we move on the question of whether the value of social phenomena is reducible without remainder.

The limits of any general examination of the nature and value of community become clear in Chapters 1 and 2. As I have already observed, community can in principle be realized at different levels and its value may in various ways be affected by the level at which it occurs. Not only might community be realizable at different levels, these levels might in various ways come into conflict with one another. Part 2 of the book explores the important question of what kind of community, if any, should be valued at the level of the state, and what sort of means might legitimately be used to sustain it in the face of conflict with communities below the level of the state.

Most liberals have thought that community at the level of the state could not be achieved without oppression, *if* community is understood to involve a commitment to some 'thick' conception of the good. Indeed Rawls denies that a society organized in accordance with the principles of justice he favours is a community, 'if we mean by a community a society governed by a shared comprehensive religious, philosophical, or moral doctrine'.[9] Many liberals have nevertheless thought that there is a notion of political community available to them, based upon the ideal of public justification. According to the dominant liberal conception, citizens form a political community when they identify with their major institutions because these institutions embody a commitment to principles which are justified to all. In its contractualist form, this generates a version of the moralized concept: citizens in such a community are mutually concerned because they possess a non-instrumental desire to justify their institutions to one another, and the institutions they favour are just because they are based upon principles that are justifiable to all.

In Chapter 3, I lay out the dominant liberal view of political community and explore its counterpart conception of how conflict between community at the level of the state and below it should be resolved. Liberals have sought to draw the legitimate limits of community below the level of the state in terms of respect for basic rights. At their most strident, they have claimed that any community's practices which violate basic rights should be ended, forcibly if necessary. As a result, liberals have sometimes been accused of cultural imperialism on the grounds that they seek to impose their principles on communities which do not share them, claiming that

[9] J. Rawls, *Political Liberalism* (New York: Columbia University Press, 1993), p. 40.

these principles are universally valid when they are in reality culturally specific. I explore the resources which liberalism can draw upon in making a case for the involvement of minority communities in the process of defining the basic rights and for showing greater forbearance when basic rights are being violated. I argue that liberals should accept that in practice the authority to adopt a set of proposed rights as basic depends upon that set's being the outcome of a political process in which everyone has a voice. When the outcome of that process is nevertheless the adoption of a set of rights which some reject, those rights should not automatically be forced upon dissenters; when doing so would lead to more injustice, or to a great sacrifice of other important values, then there are grounds for forbearance. Respect for communal autonomy also gives reason to allow minority communities to select any reasonable interpretation of the basic rights which they believe best suit their practices.

Chapters 4 and 5 subject the dominant liberal conception of political community to critical scrutiny. Chapter 4 considers what I call the republican challenge to it, viz., that we need to develop a thicker conception of community at the level of the state, based around the good of citizenship. According to one form of this challenge, citizenship involves special obligations, the fulfilment of which contributes to the good of citizenship and is necessary for the realization of political community, properly conceived. I consider whether the republican conception of political community can escape the liberal charge that such a community would be oppressive towards those who, quite reasonably, do not regard political participation as an essential ingredient of the good life. I argue that in at least one of its forms, the republican conception of political community is not vulnerable to this objection, for it claims merely that political participation is a possible ingredient of the good life.

In Chapter 5 I consider the different argument, developed by liberal nationalists, that the viability of the dominant liberal conception of political community depends upon the existence of a non-political unity such as that provided by a shared national identity. In consequence, this argument continues, liberals have favoured policies which are too permissive towards communities below the level of the state, because sustaining the shared national identity necessary for a viable political community may require a policy of assimilation which goes beyond what liberals have been willing to support. Liberals have generally objected to such a policy on the grounds that it poses an unjustifiable threat to individual liberty, but I argue that it need not do so.

In response to the liberal-nationalist, however, I suggest that the various benefits which he or she thinks are made possible by a shared national identity – stability, a politics of the common good and the kind of redistributive policies required by social justice – may be achievable in the absence of such an identity, provided that there is a widespread sense of belonging to the polity. As part of my response to the liberal-nationalist, I develop an ideal of inclusive political community, which I claim is a better regulative ideal than that provided by either the liberal or the republican conception. Citizens form an inclusive political community if they live in a polity governed by liberal institutions, and even those who do not endorse liberal principles have a sense of belonging to it. The idea is that those who reject liberal principles may nevertheless feel at home in such a polity, and identify with liberal institutions, because they have their own reasons for doing so, and because they are given a voice in the running of that polity. I go on to suggest how such a sense of belonging might be fostered by various forms of legal and political recognition and accommodation of cultural difference.

Chapter 6 addresses the question of whether these forms of legal and political recognition are likely to be sufficient to foster a widespread sense of belonging and argues that the educational system also has an important role to play. It suggests that multicultural education may be able to promote the mutual valuing of cultures, and in this way facilitate the changes in practices and institutions which seem necessary for such a sense of belonging to emerge. It distinguishes between two models of multicultural education, the neutralist and the pluralist model. The neutralist model requires that children be introduced to the ideas, practices and values of a number of different cultures, but insists that teachers should present them without judgement. The pluralist model also requires that children be introduced to a number of different cultures, but allows that schools may teach them from a particular evaluative perspective. I argue that the pluralist model is best suited to promoting an overall sense of belonging but only if it is constrained in various ways. Children must be taught in such a way that they become aware of themselves and each other as future fellow citizens of the particular liberal-democratic state in which they live, and each school's curriculum must be informed by a presumption of the value of other cultures. Schools must also be required to conform to liberal principles such as equality of opportunity, although within the bounds of reasonableness they should be allowed to interpret those principles to suit their practices.

The ideal of inclusive political community which I defend in Chapters 5 and 6 has an important regulative role. But the citizens of actual states rarely form communities that embody this ideal. To the extent that the boundaries of actual states do coincide with the boundaries of communities, these communities are likely to be communities in the bare ordinary sense of the term and many lack liberal institutions. Indeed some are committed to illiberal practices, and may even systematically violate basic rights. This raises the spectre of conflict between community at the level of the state, and global community, where the latter but not the former is understood as community in the moralized sense. So understood, global community is a vision of persons united together as participants in a way of life that enables them to be mutually concerned and enjoy just relationships with one another. It provides the focus for the chapters in Part III.

In Chapter 7, I defend the coherence of the ideal of global community and explore the apparent conflict between the realization or promotion of liberal conceptions of it and the existence of a plurality of political communities in the ordinary sense. If we suppose that respect for political community requires the adoption of a principle of non-intervention in the internal affairs of other states, then this appears to stand in the way of promoting global community between individuals, for it deprives any state of the warrant to act on behalf of those who are being oppressed in some other political community. In effect the principle of non-intervention resolves the conflict between liberal ideals of global community and political community in the ordinary sense in favour of the latter. I argue that, on the contrary, the principle of non-intervention should be reformed to allow 'humanitarian intervention' in some cases, and that the resolution of conflict between these ideals of global community and political community in the ordinary sense should favour the former more than current practice does.

In Chapter 8, I consider the possibility of systemic conflict between global community and a plurality of political communities in the ordinary sense. In particular, I focus on a long-standing controversy in international relations theory concerning whether the structure of the state system, i.e., the existence of a plurality of political communities in the absence of an overarching authority, places serious obstacles in the way of global community. Against those realists and neo-realists who maintain that it always does, I argue that under favourable circumstances it need not. I consider various accounts of what changes would need to occur for circumstances to be or become favourable, without attempting to defend any particular one of them.

Generally speaking, Part 2 of the book (Chapters 3–6) is concerned with political community in the moralized sense and its relationship to communities in the ordinary sense below the level of the state, whereas Part 2 (Chapters 7–8) is concerned with aspects of global community in the moralized sense and their relationship to political community in the ordinary sense.

2. The liberal–communitarian debate

Throughout Parts 2 and 3, I shall presuppose a liberal perspective. By 'liberalism', I mean a commitment to a set of individual rights which are to be given a high priority in the design of institutions and the choice of policies. I treat the question of what rights are included in this set as, within limits, a matter for discussion within liberalism. Some favour a limited set which is exhausted by a right to freedom of association (which they think implies a right of exit from a community) and a right against cruel or inhuman treatment. Others favour a more extensive set, involving rights to a variety of freedoms such as freedom of conscience and religious practice, freedom to engage in consensual sexual relationships, freedom of speech and expression, freedom of the person, and freedom from arbitrary arrest and seizure. In Chapter 3, I shall suggest that liberals should favour a relatively extensive list such as this one. But a commitment to even the restricted set might seem to beg a whole range of questions in relation to communitarian thought. Let me briefly survey the debate between so-called liberals and communitarians in order to make it clear why I start from the place I do.

Communitarians argued that liberals presuppose a conception of the self which separates it from its ends and attachments, whereas in reality we are constituted by those ends and attachments.[10] They argued that liberals ignore the fact that personal autonomy has various preconditions; people cannot develop the capacity to reflect and choose, nor possess a range of options from which to choose, unless they live in a culture which fosters that capacity[11] and sustains the social forms in which those options are embedded.[12] They argued that liberals underestimate the value of community; that liberals fail to appreciate the importance of a sense of belonging, and the virtues of citizenship, and fail to recognize the way in which talk of rights, rather than of responsibilities and duties undermines them.[13] They argued that the aspiration to create a universal political morality fails to appreciate that political morality must respond to our

---

[10] See, e.g., Sandel, *Liberalism and the Limits of Justice*, p. 150; A. MacIntyre, *After Virtue: a Study in Moral Theory* (Notre Dame, IN: University of Notre Dame Press, 1981), p. 220. This is a pervasive theme in communitarian writings. See Caney, 'Liberalism and Communitarianism', p. 274, note 3, for further references.

[11] See, e.g., C. Taylor, 'Atomism', in his *Philosophical Papers*: vol. II (Cambridge: Cambridge University Press, 1985), esp. pp. 190–1.

[12] See, e.g., M. Walzer, 'Justice Here and Now', in F. Lucash (ed.), *Justice and Equality Here and Now* (Ithaca, NY: Cornell University Press, 1996), esp. pp. 137, 148.

[13] See A. Etzioni, *The Spirit of Community* (New York, 1993); D. Selbourne, *The Principle of Duty* (London: Sinclair-Stevenson, 1994).

shared traditions of thought and practice, or our shared understandings, and cannot transcend them.[14]

Much of the debate between liberals and communitarians now seems misconceived.[15] It is not obvious what is meant by the idea that the self is constituted by some of its ends and attachments. Communitarians often seem to hold back from claiming that the self is *wholly* constituted by some or all of its commitments.[16] But if they make the weaker claim that the self is only partially constituted by those commitments, then this leaves space for the idea that there is some aspect of the self which is not socially constituted, and makes it unclear how the communitarian conception of the self differs from that which many liberals seem to have advocated or presupposed.[17]

Perhaps the communitarian idea is that the liberal conception of the self fails to appreciate that people are unable to hold up their deepest commitments to critical scrutiny: a deeply religious person, for example, is unable to subject his core religious beliefs to rational assessment. But this is questionable in a number of ways. It is not clear that most people are in general engulfed by their particular ends and attachments in the way that this thesis would require. As Will Kymlicka suggests, for many it is part of their self-understanding that they can hold up their particular ends and attachments to critical scrutiny – one at a time, at least – and imagine themselves with different ones.[18] We can be gripped by particular commitments, and possess a deep attachment to particular individuals, groups or ends, manifested in an unwillingness to question those attachments, but we nevertheless generally retain the freedom to subject these commitments to critical scrutiny if we so choose. (This is not to deny that as the inheritors of particular cultural outlooks, some social forms may not represent meaningful choices for us, and that we may lack the re-

---

[14] See Walzer, *Spheres of Justice*, e.g., pp. 8–10; A. MacIntyre, *Whose Justice? Which Rationality?* (London: Duckworth, 1988), esp. chs. 1, 18, 20; R. Rorty, *Contingency, Irony, and Solidarity* (Cambridge: Cambridge University Press, 1989), esp. ch. 3.

[15] For a sustained argument for this conclusion, see Caney, 'Liberalism and Communitarianism'. For other arguments for much the same conclusion, see also J. Feinberg, *The Moral Limits of the Criminal Law*, vol. 4, *Harmless Wrongdoing* (New York: Oxford University Press, 1988), ch. 29A; A. Buchanan, 'Assessing the Communitarian Critique of Liberalism', *Ethics*, vol. 99, 1989, pp. 852–82; W. Kymlicka, *Liberalism, Community and Culture* (Oxford: Oxford University Press, 1989), chs. 4–5; S. Benn, *A Theory of Freedom* (Oxford: Oxford University Press, 1988); A. Ryan, 'The Liberal Community', in J. W. Chapman and I. Shapiro (eds.), *NOMOS*, vol. 35, *Democratic Community* (New York: New York University Press, 1993), pp. 91–114.

[16] See Sandel, *Liberalism and the Limits of Justice*, p. 150; 'The Procedural Republic and the Unencumbered Self', p. 23; C. Taylor, *Sources of the Self: The Making of the Modern Identity* (Cambridge: Cambridge University Press, 1989), p. 27.

[17] Kymlicka, *Liberalism, Community and Culture*, pp. 55–6.

[18] *Ibid.*, pp. 57–8.

sources to reflect upon them in a fully intelligent way.[19] They are not, as Bernard Williams would say, real options for us.[20])

Even if it were true that most of us are engulfed by our commitments, it is not obvious that liberals need deny that this is so. It would not, by itself, be sufficient to undermine the idea that it is valuable and important for people to subject their deepest commitments to critical scrutiny, not all at once of course, nor within a short space of time. Liberals can also recognize that autonomy of this kind is, in various ways, a cultural achievement and has various preconditions: that individuals are not born with a capacity to reflect and choose, and need to be brought up in some environment which fosters it; that they cannot exercise this capacity unless they are provided with a relatively secure range of culturally defined options.

Even if liberals have sometimes underestimated the importance of a sense of belonging, the virtues of citizenship, and community in general, this is not the result of a deep theoretical deficiency within liberalism. Liberals can recognize that people have a need to feel that they belong to some larger group or enterprise, and that polities will be enduring, stable and vibrant only if their citizens have a healthy sense of civic responsibility. Even liberals committed to the importance of political neutrality can accept that it is legitimate for the state to fund communal goods and projects. For example, they can argue that the principles which govern our major institutions ought to be neutral between reasonable views of the good life, but allow that particular policies not essentially concerning matters of justice may legitimately be designed to promote an ideal of the good life provided that they are the outcome of a neutral political procedure.[21] For the same reason, liberals need not be committed to always favouring policies which promote personal autonomy when there is a conflict between it and communal goods and projects.

Liberals would be well advised to reject the idea that our political morality must be bound by our own particular community's traditions of thought and inquiry, at least if that is taken to imply that these traditions are incommensurable with those of other communities. Alasdair MacIntyre would argue that there is no alternative but to accept the idea that different conceptions of justice and practical rationality are part of incom-

---

[19] See D. Archard, 'Autonomy, Character and Situation', in D. E. Milligan and W. W. Miller (eds.), *Liberalism, Citizenship and Autonomy* (Aldershot: Avebury, 1992), pp. 166–7.
[20] B. Williams, 'The Truth in Relativism', in his *Moral Luck: Collected Papers 1973–1980* (Cambridge: Cambridge University Press, 1981).
[21] See B. Barry, *Justice as Impartiality* (Oxford: Oxford University Press, 1995), p. 143; cf. Rawls, *Political Liberalism*, pbk. edn, p. 214; T. Nagel, *Equality and Partiality* (New York: Oxford University Press, 1991), p. 160.

mensurable traditions because he thinks it is apparent that they do not share standards of assessment. I doubt that this view can be sustained.[22] But in any case, since MacIntyre allows that a particular socially embodied tradition may nevertheless show itself to be superior in virtue of solving the problems it encounters, he must leave it open whether liberalism can triumph in this way. At least, he has not yet said enough to show that liberalism, when it is conceived as a tradition, cannot do so.

Consider the different idea, to be found in Michael Walzer's writings, that the distribution of goods in a community should reflect its shared understanding of the meaning of those goods. As I have argued, however, people may be members of a number of different kinds of communities at different levels, and these may have different shared understandings. Which of these shared understandings is privileged in justifying our political morality? The answer to this question may seem obvious: as Walzer in effect argues, our political morality should reflect the shared understandings of our *political* community.[23] But modern liberal democracies are characterized by massive disagreements about what principles should govern our basic institutions. It is far from clear that there are shared understandings other than at a very abstract level, and even at that level we tend to find convergence on principles (for example, that people should be treated as equals) rather than 'meanings' of goods. Moreover, as Ronald Dworkin has pointed out, the very idea that our political morality should simply reflect our shared understanding of the meanings of goods violates the widespread practice of worrying that our political community's shared understandings may be deeply mistaken and as a result we may be deeply confused about what justice requires.[24]

More could be said, and has been said, on these issues. But it is not clear that the issues which remain are any longer helpfully framed in terms of a conflict between liberals and communitarians. The central questions I shall be addressing, concerning the nature and value of community, the kind of community which is valuable at the level of the state, and what limits, if any, it places on communities above and below this level, arise for so-called liberals and so-called communitarians, and their answers to these question are unlikely to place them on different sides of a single fence. The liberal–communitarian debate has left as its legacy a variety of questions and concerns which need further exploration, but little is to be gained by seeing them as dividing theorists into two mutually exclusive camps. The liberal–communitarian debate is, in vari-

---

[22] See my 'MacIntyre on Liberalism and its Critics: Tradition, Incommensurability and Disagreement', in Horton and Mendus (eds.), *After MacIntyre*, especially pp. 230–8.

[23] Walzer, *Spheres of Justice*, pp. 28–9.

[24] See R. Dworkin, *A Matter of Principle* (Oxford: Oxford University Press, 1985), p. 219.

ous ways, relevant to answering these questions about the nature and value of community, and the proper relationship between the different levels and kinds of community, but it does not take us very far in doing so.

It might nevertheless be thought that in presupposing a liberal perspective, I am starting out too far along the path which the liberal–communitarian debate has led us. But I have defined 'liberalism' in a very broad way, as a commitment to a set of individual rights which are to be given a high priority in the design of institutions and the choice of policies. Although not uncontroversial, this is a fairly mild assumption:

(i)   Within limits, it is consistent with different accounts of what individual rights are included in this set. Although in Chapter 3 I give reasons for adopting a relatively extensive set, I do not begin with the assumption that we should do so. Throughout the book, I shall also try to remain neutral on the question of whether individuals have various 'economic' rights, for instance to a certain minimum level of need satisfaction. (Indeed I shall try to avoid the question of whether social justice may require redistribution of wealth, nationally or internationally, although I believe that it does.)

(ii) It is consistent with one or more of a number of different accounts of how these rights are to be justified, each starting from different premises. For example, some might take the view that they specify the preconditions for agency, whilst others might even argue that they are justified by the value and importance of community.[25] Some may employ a utilitarian or consequentialist style of justification, whilst others appeal to deontological premises. These justifications may meet, or aim to meet, more or less demanding standards. For instance, some will claim that these rights cannot reasonably be rejected in the light of the arguments for them, whilst others will think that any justification that can be given of them will fall short of the rigour required for that to be the case. By endorsing these rights, one is not committed to a form of foundationalism which has it that they can be justified by deduction from some set of self-evident premises, and nor is one committed to rejecting an anti-foundationalist epistemology.

(iii) It is consistent with different accounts of the scope of these rights: some may regard all of these rights as universal, as applicable in all times and places; others may regard them all as culturally specific; some may think that they are a mixture of the universal and culturally specific.

[25] See Buchanan, 'Assessing the Communitarian Critique', for an illustration of how individual rights might be justified by appeal to the value and importance of community.

(iv) It is consistent with the idea that communities, as well as individuals, are the bearers of rights, and that these rights may *sometimes* be more important than the rights of individuals. Indeed, it is consistent with the idea that communities may have value which cannot be reduced to the contribution they make to the lives of individuals.

 (v) It is consistent with various doctrines that are sometimes distinguished from liberalism: for example, libertarianism, various forms of socialism, nationalism and conservatism.

(vi) It is consistent with the idea that individuals have various social responsibilities and duties in addition to their rights.

(vii) It is consistent with the idea that these rights can reasonably be interpreted differently. Individuals, starting from their own beliefs, and those norms and beliefs they must accept on pain of unintelligibility, may without inconsistency reach different interpretations of these rights. So, for example, there may be reasonable interpretations of the right to freedom of expression which permit restrictions on pornography or the mocking or ridiculing of sacred texts, and reasonable interpretations which do not. (Liberalism, as I define it, is also consistent with the idea that even though these rights can reasonably be interpreted differently, there is a single best interpretation of each of them which the balance of reasons supports.)

(viii) It is consistent with the idea that rights are practically relevant only in societies where there is some degree of disharmony. It need not deny the claim that rights-talk would be redundant in any society where there was superabundance of resources, or in which everyone was perfectly altruistic.

Part 1

Community and its value

1 The nature of community

There is a range of disputes over what kind of social relationships can be communities.[1] Some argue that communities have to be face to face, whilst others allow that they may unite those who do not know each other. Some maintain that members of a community must inhabit the same locale, whilst others allow that they may be geographically dispersed. Some argue that communities must involve relationships of a certain moral quality, e.g., where exploitation is absent, whilst others allow that feelings of solidarity may be sufficient, even if these feelings rest upon illusions or misconceptions about the moral character of the relationship.

These disputes, coupled with the sheer variety of its ordinary and theoretical uses, can give rise to the worry that 'community' is employed by people simply to commend the social arrangements they happen to favour. If so, the term would have no shared descriptive meaning, and there might be no properties common to those things which are labelled communities.[2] More cynically, it might be thought that the term 'community' is often applied to a group in order to divert attention from the deep divisions within it and thereby serve the interests of its dominant class. I shall try to answer some of these worries, although not by supplying precise necessary and sufficient conditions for the proper use of 'community' since I am sceptical about the value of attempts to do so. I shall also suggest that confusion can be created by failing to distinguish between two concepts of community which play different roles in ordinary usage (and which are partly distinguished in terms of these roles), but which both have descriptive content. The main purpose of this chapter is to clarify: to make sense of the variety of usages of the term 'community', and to remove some of the confusions that surround them.

---

[1] This chapter extends my argument in 'Two Concepts of Community', in N. Snow (ed.), *In the Company of Others: Perspectives on Family, Community, and Culture* (Lanham, MD: Rowman and Littlefield, 1996).

[2] Raymond Plant surveys some reactions of this kind in 'Community', esp. pp. 79–80.

1.   Is community an essentially contested concept?

One proposal which might seem to promise an account of why the term 'community' is used so widely, and why disputes over its proper use occur and persist, is the idea that it expresses an essentially contested concept.[3] What are essentially contested concepts? W. B. Gallie introduced the notion by saying that they are concepts whose nature it is to be open to endless dispute, and listed a number of criteria which needed to be satisfied by a concept in order for it to be essentially contested.[4] An essentially contested concept is appraisive: it accredits a valued achievement. This accredited achievement is complex, i.e., made up of a number of different elements. These elements can reasonably be weighted differently, and disputes arise over the proper application of the concept when people do so. Those who give a particular weight to the elements acknowledge that others weight them differently. Furthermore, the accredited achievement admits of unpredictable modification in the light of changing circumstances.

As examples of essentially contested concepts, Gallie gives the concepts of democracy, social justice, work of art and a Christian life. Consider his reasons for classifying the concept of democracy as essentially contested. It accredits a valued achievement since democracy is widely regarded as a valuable form of government. This achievement is internally complex, Gallie claims, because it makes reference to three elements: the power of the people to choose and remove governments; equality of opportunity to attain positions of political leadership and responsibility; active participation of citizens in political life at all levels. These elements can be, and are, weighted differently by contestants. Furthermore, the concept of democracy is open in character because 'democratic targets will be raised or lowered as circumstances alter'.[5]

Gallie might have added (in the way others have since done) that concepts are essentially contestable not just because people can reasonably attach different weights to the elements which make up the achievements they accredit, but also because these elements may be interpreted

---

[3] Raymond Plant, Harry Lesser and Peter Taylor-Gooby explore this idea and give it a qualified endorsement in their *Political Philosophy and Social Welfare* (London: Routledge and Kegan Paul, 1980), ch. 9. Michael Taylor expresses deep scepticism about it, and deems it to be unworthy of discussion: see his *Community, Anarchy and Liberty* (Cambridge: Cambridge University Press, 1982), p. 26, note 17.

[4] See W. B. Gallie, 'Essentially Contested Concepts', *Proceedings of the Aristotelian Society*, vol. 56, 1955–6, 167–98. Those sympathetic to the notion of an essentially contested concept have included William Connolly, *The Terms of Political Discourse*, 2nd edn (Oxford: Martin Robertson, 1983); Steven Lukes, *Power: A Radical View* (London: Macmillan, 1974); and Susan Hurley, *Natural Reasons: Persons and Polity* (Oxford: Oxford University Press, 1989).   [5] Gallie, 'Essentially Contested Concepts', p. 186.

differently; for example, Gallie's analysis of the concept of democracy invites the observation that what counts as having the power to choose and remove governments, what counts as equality of opportunity to attain political positions, and what constitutes active participation in political life, are all matters of reasonable dispute. So one essentially contested concept is related to a group of other concepts whose proper uses are themselves contested, perhaps also essentially.

The notion of an essentially contested concept has been subject to considerable criticism. The most important challenge maintains that to classify a concept as essentially contested is to imply that there is no correct interpretation of it, which appears to lead into the mire of relativism.[6] I have tried to answer this objection elsewhere, so here I will merely sketch a response: essentially contested concepts are open to a number of reasonable interpretations, but this does not mean that all these interpretations or conceptions are equally good or correct; some may be better than others, and one particular conception may be the best of the lot.[7] If one particular conception is the best, someone who disagrees when confronted by the good arguments in favour of it need not be unreasonable, though they are mistaken.

Is community an essentially contested concept, i.e., a concept of which there are a number of reasonable conceptions, with its being a matter of political dispute which of them is the best? And, if so, can this at least partially account for the extensive use made of the concept, and for the disputes over the nature of community? This suggestion has some plausibility. The concept of community often seems to be used to represent a valued achievement. It is complex because it involves a number of different elements: for example, shared values, participation in a shared way of life, identification with the group and mutual recognition. People interpret these elements differently, or weight the presence or absence of them differently, and hence disagree over what counts as a community. Although this explanation may seem as if it has some power, I do not think that it captures the way in which the term 'community' functions in ordinary usage. My point is best made by considering a worry that Gallie expressed about his initial criteria for marking off essentially contested concepts: that they may fail to distinguish genuine essentially contested concepts from terms that conceal two different concepts, disputes over which are simply the result of confusing these concepts.[8]

Gallie argues that we can distinguish essentially contested concepts

---

[6] Brian Barry was one of the first to voice this sort of worry, in his review of Lukes's *Power*. See 'The Obscurities of Power', *Government and Opposition*, vol. 10, 1975, pp. 250–4.
[7] See my *Explaining Political Disagreement* (Cambridge: Cambridge University Press, 1993), ch. 2.   [8] See Gallie, 'Essentially Contested Concepts', p. 175.

from ambiguous terms by employing a number of further criteria, the most important of which are that an essentially contested concept must be derived from an original exemplar whose authority is recognized by all the contestants, and that continuous competition between rival users of the concept must make probable or plausible the claim that the original exemplar's achievement has been sustained or developed in an optimum fashion.[9] Can a plausible case be made for saying that the concept of community is derived from an original exemplar in this way? Raymond Plant, Harry Lesser and Peter Taylor-Gooby suggest that although there is no *single* exemplar which inspires the contestants, there are different exemplars to which they appeal.[10] For example, some hark back to the Greek *polis* as the paradigm of community, others to the feudal village; and some have in mind a vision that has not yet been unrealized. But this would not satisfy Gallie that the concept is essentially contested as opposed to radically confused; it would leave open the possibility that those who appealed to different exemplars simply had different concepts of community.[11]

Perhaps the problem lies in Gallie's conditions for distinguishing essentially contested concepts from ambiguous terms. Perhaps these are too restrictive and there need only be an area of agreement on what counts as a community, or on what fails to count as a community, in order to justify the claim that people share the same underlying concept. I think Gallie's conditions are too restrictive, but I doubt whether it is possible to show that the term 'community' is univocal on any plausible set of more permissive conditions. It is employed to express two different concepts of community, and confusion can be created by failing to distinguish them. Only one of these concepts is essentially contested. This is what I shall argue in the next four sections.

2.   The ordinary concept

On both concepts of community I shall distinguish, a community differs from what I call a mere society or association.[12] A mere association consists of people who interact with one another primarily on a contractual basis, in order to further their own self-regarding interests.[13] Accord-

---

[9] *Ibid.*, p. 180.

[10] See Plant *et al.*, *Political Philosophy and Social Welfare*, p. 209. See also Plant, 'Community', pp. 84–5.

[11] Plant *et al.* seem to recognize this point when they say that '[t]his feature of community would make it perhaps more radically contested than any other central social and political concept' (*ibid.*, p. 210) but do not in my view fully appreciate its implications.

[12] This is similar to John Rawls's notion of a private society: see J. Rawls, *A Theory of Justice* (Cambridge, MA: Harvard University Press, 1971), p. 521.

ing to what I shall call the ordinary concept or ordinary sense, a community differs from this, for it is constituted by a group of people who share a range of values, a way of life, identify with the group and its practices and recognize each other as members of that group. This concept of a community is to be found, at least implicitly, in a considerable amount of recent Anglo-American political philosophy.[14] Let me clarify some of the elements involved in it.

What is a *group of people*? In the relatively broad sense I intend, a group is a collection of individuals who either act together, or who cooperate with one another in pursuit of their own goals, or who at least possess common interests.[15] Communities in the ordinary sense are a sub-set of groups: all communities are groups, but not all groups are communities.

When the individual members of a group genuinely act together (as opposed to merely coordinate their actions in response to each other), they have goals and perform actions which are not reducible to the goals or actions of those individuals considered separately, even though the group does not exist independently of its having individual members.[16] Consider a mundane example. When a number of individuals together lift a heavy object, then if there is an action performed that can be correctly described as the lifting of that object (and there seems no good reason to deny that there is such an action), then it must be attributed to the group constituted by those individuals, for there is no individual member of the group who lifts the object. The members of this group may also share goals or purposes the specification of which makes an ineliminable reference to the group; each individual may want it to be the case that *the group* lifts the heavy object, and each may see himself as contributing to the realization of this goal by cooperating with the others. (There are also cases where a group performs an action which could not even in principle be performed by an individual – consider the way in which a group of jazz

[13] See Ferdinand Tönnies, *Community and Association*, trans. C. P. Loomis (London: Routledge and Kegan Paul, 1955).

[14] See, for example, Feinberg, *Harmless Wrongdoing*, pp. 101–5. Many political philosophers seem to presuppose this concept, though it is difficult to be sure because they often do not provide an account of what they mean by 'community'. See, for example, Robert Nozick, *Anarchy, State, and Utopia* (Oxford: Blackwell, 1974), especially pp. 307ff.; Marilyn Friedman, 'Feminism and Modern Friendship: Dislocating the Community', *Ethics*, vol. 99, 1989, pp. 275–90 (reprinted in P. Weiss and M. Friedman (eds.), *Feminism and Community* (Philadelphia, PA: Temple University Press, 1995)); MacIntyre, *After Virtue*, especially pp. 204–5, 233.

[15] See L. May, *The Morality of Groups: Collective Responsibility, Group-Based Harm, and Corporate Rights* (Notre Dame, IN: University of Notre Dame Press, 1987), esp. pp. 29–30.

[16] Here I am indebted to Keith Graham's work: see especially K. Graham, *The Battle of Democracy: Conflict, Consensus and the Individual* (Brighton: Wheatsheaf, 1986), pp. 103–8.

musicians might have a musical conversation, where the conversation itself was a constitutive part of the piece of music that they played.[17])

Some genuine cases of acting together presuppose a matrix of social practices and institutions, such as when a jury finds in favour of a defendant. Juries are part of a legal system which defines the rules under which they operate. Under those rules the action of finding in favour of a defendant could not be properly attributed to all or even some of the jurors considered simply as individuals. This can be seen most clearly in cases where the decision of a jury is not based upon a unanimous vote; in such cases it is the jury which finds the defendant innocent, not some sub-set of them, and if we focus on the individual jurors alone, the action of finding in favour of the defendant will be unattributable.

We might express some of these points by saying, as Keith Graham does, that some groups are collectives, and that

although they consist of nothing over and above individuals in certain relations, it is not *as* individuals but only as members of the collective in question that those individuals have any role in the process which constitutes that collective's deliberating and acting.[18]

Some but not all communities are constituted as collectives, i.e., as the subjects of goals, decisions and actions.

What is *a way of life* and what is it for members of a group to share one? A way of life is a set of rule-governed practices, which are at least loosely woven together, and which constitute at least some central areas of social, political and economic activity. Members of a group share a way of life when they participate with each other in such a set of practices. One way of life may be 'nested' in another, and a person may therefore be a participant in several. The boundaries between different ways of life may be hard to draw and inherently imprecise.

Does the fact that communities are partly constituted by shared ways of life mean that members of a community must always share a culture? The term 'culture' has many different meanings, but in at least one of its main senses today it is used to refer to a way of life which is informed by a set of interconnected traditions of thought and inquiry. Understood in this way, members of any community which involves a way of life of this general kind will share a culture. Cultures too can overlap or exhibit a nested character, and persons may participate in more than one at the same time.[19]

[17] See D. Brudney, 'Community and Completion', in A. Reath, B. Herman and C. Korsgaard (eds.), *Reclaiming the History of Ethics: Essays for John Rawls* (Cambridge: Cambridge University Press, 1997), p. 397.
[18] Graham, *The Battle of Democracy*, p. 103.
[19] See J. Charvet, 'What is Nationality, and Is There a Moral Right to National Self-Determination?', in S. Caney, D. George, and P. Jones (eds.), *National Rights,*

A way of life necessarily involves cooperative activity; the practices which make up a way of life are rule-governed so their very existence relies upon participants cooperating with one another in abiding by those rules. The participants need not value cooperation for its own sake, however. Duelling, for example, might be an essential element in a shared way of life that is informed by a particular conception of honour. It would rely upon the cooperation of participants in abiding by the rules governing duels, but they would not need to value cooperation for its own sake. Sometimes, however, the full achievement of the goods which are internal to a practice may require the participants to do so – some team sports, such as football, and some musical forms, such as certain kinds of jazz, are arguably of this kind.

To *identify* with a group and its practices (in the relevant sense) is to commit oneself to it in a way that normally involves endorsing its practices and seeking to promote its interests, whilst regarding one's well-being as intimately linked to its flourishing. In order for a person to be able to commit herself to a group and its practices, she must be able to perceive them as valuable, whether instrumentally or non-instrumentally, and see her concerns reflected in them. A person's identifications need not be wholly non-voluntary, and may involve an element of choice; someone may decide to commit herself to a group's goals and practices because she regards them as valuable and sees her concerns reflected in them.

According to my account, identifying with a group need not involve making what Margaret Gilbert has called a joint commitment. A joint commitment is a commitment of two or more people that is not simply the sum of the independent personal commitments of those people, and cannot be unilaterally rescinded.[20] The paradigm case of a joint commitment is a promise or agreement to do something together, for example, go for a walk. Gilbert, however, thinks that the class of joint commitments is much larger than promises and agreements, and includes cases where people have a mutual understanding that they will each do something, perhaps created simply by past practice, for example, the fact that they have for years gone for a walk together on a Sunday afternoon.[21] When a person identifies with a group and its practices, she makes a personal commitment to it, but she need not make a joint commitment with its other members. In order for a member of a group to make a joint commitment with its other members, there needs to be some mutual

---

International Obligations (Oxford: Westview, 1996), p. 63.

[20] See M. Gilbert, *Living Together: Rationality, Sociality, and Obligation* (Lanham, MD: Rowman and Littlefield, 1996), esp. pp. 10–11, 364–8.

[21] Gilbert, *Living Together*, pp. 364–8. Although I agree with Gilbert that joint commitments can arise in the absence of explicit promises or agreements, it can be hard to tell whether they have been made, since it can be hard to know whether there is a mutual understanding of the right kind.

understanding that being a member of that group, and participating in its practices, involves incurring such a commitment. That understanding need not be present in a community, and is not implicit in the very idea of identification as I have presented it.[22] The practices which are constitutive of ways of life will often create joint commitments amongst their participants, but this will depend upon the nature of those practices and the understandings which govern participation in them.

It is worth distinguishing between a person's identity and her identifications. It may be that a person's actual identifications are based on illusions or misconceptions, and that she would identify with a different group were these illusions and misconceptions to be shattered. In such circumstances, we might justifiably say that her true identity was different from what her actual identifications would lead one to expect, and that she would discover her true identity if she rid herself of the illusions and misconceptions. Marxists have said something of this kind about membership of the working class[23] – many people whose identity is constituted by their membership of the working class do not identify with it as a result of misconceptions about their real interests.[24]

Some have gone further than this. They have regarded a person's identity as an objective phenomenon, constituted (at least in part) by her membership of some group, where that membership obtains in a way that is *wholly* independent of her, or indeed anyone's, belief that it obtains, but have seen identification as a merely subjective phenomenon, dependent solely upon what commitments she makes. (Race, gender or ethnicity have sometimes been thought to be part of a person's identity in this sense.) For some purposes, this distinction may also be worthwhile, but it needs to be handled with care for at least two reasons.[25]

First, there needs to be clear grounds for holding that a person does

---

[22] Gilbert gives a different proposal for how we should unpack the notion of identification which does essentially involve the idea of a joint commitment: see *Living Together*, ch. 16. Gilbert would, I think, agree that the ordinary notion is so vague that it allows for either my or her analysis, even if she would also maintain that her analysis is more fruitful.

[23] For an illuminating discussion of Marx's views on these matters, see K. Graham, *Karl Marx, Our Contemporary* (Hemel Hempstead: Harvester Wheatsheaf, 1992), sections 2.4–2.5, 4.3.

[24] The relevant sense of identity here is that of *social* identity. My social identity may change whilst I remain essentially the same person. Indeed as Bernard Williams points out, we need such a distinction to make sense of the possibility that a member of a culture might *herself* experience a loss if that culture were destroyed: '[i]f, for instance, native Americans on reservations are conscious of the loss of an identity, they are conscious precisely of their own loss' (B. Williams, 'Identity and Identities', in H. Harris (ed.), *Identity: Essays Based on Herbert Spencer Lectures Given in the University of Oxford* (Oxford: Oxford University Press, 1995), pp. 8–9).

[25] For further discussion, see R. Hardin, *One for All: The Logic of Group Conflict* (Princeton, NJ: Princeton University Press, 1995), pp. 6–10.

belong to some group in such a way that it is appropriate to regard it as contributing to her identity even if she does not identify with it and could not be brought to do so. To give a hackneyed example, the fact that a person belongs to the class of people with brown hair does not mean that she is a member of that group in a sense that is relevant to her identity on any sensible view of what that involves. To make out a case that belonging to some class of people is relevant to a person's identity in the objective sense will require a defence of the idea that this is an important fact about her, even if she does not think it is and indeed could not necessarily be persuaded that it is. This claim may be sustainable in a number of cases, but it will always be potentially problematic. Second, we should beware of moving illegitimately from the premise that a person has some objective identity to the conclusion that a person *ought to* identify with the group of people who share that identity. (In some cases there may be reasons for a person *not* to identify with the commitments of the group that constitute her identity in this sense; think of someone whose identity is partly constituted by his membership of some white-supremacist organization.)

The fact that individuals identify with the same group does not guarantee *mutual recognition*, for someone who identifies with a group may be regarded by others as an outsider. A group of people constitute a community of the ideal type only when each recognizes the other as belonging to it. (Note that recognition can be compatible with forms of rejection – members of a community can only regard someone as a traitor to it if they recognize them as a member.) Members of a group may operate with formal or informal criteria for determining who is, and who is not, a member of that group, and these criteria can be many and various. Obvious possibilities are ethnicity, birthplace, religious affiliation, dress and participation in certain practices or rituals. Satisfying some of these criteria will be a non-voluntary matter: a person either does or does not satisfy them and cannot choose to do so. Satisfying others will be a matter of what a person achieves, and hence she may have a degree of control over whether or not she does so. Failures of mutual recognition may occur either when there is disagreement over whether someone meets an agreed set of criteria for membership of the group, or when there is (implicit or explicit) disagreement over the criteria themselves.

My account of community in the ordinary sense does not specify precise necessary and sufficient conditions for a group to be a community in this sense, for example, it does not say exactly how far values need to be shared, or how encompassing its common way of life must be. Community comes in degrees, and the ordinary concept of community is inherently vague. Its application requires a judgement about whether members of a group share enough values, whether they participate in a way of life that is sufficiently encompassing, whether they identify sufficiently strongly with the group, and whether there is sufficient agreement amongst them concerning who counts as a member of the group. For this reason not much is to be gained by trying to specify precisely the degree of shared values or the extent of a shared way of life that needs to be present in order for a group of people to count as a community in the ordinary sense.

Since 'community' in the ordinary sense involves four different elements, viz. sharing values, a way of life, identifying with the group and its practices, and recognizing each other as members of the group, we might distinguish *aspects* of community from *degrees* of community. A particular group may exhibit aspects of community if, for example, they share values and a way of life, but there is little or no identification with the group and its practices. Whenever one or more of the elements that make up community in the ordinary sense is present, then the relevant group contains some aspect of community; it exhibits degrees of community-ness only if all four elements are present to some extent.

In this light consider the question of whether there is a Muslim community in Britain, as opposed to a larger Asian community including Sikhs and Hindus, and as opposed to smaller Muslim communities in Bradford, Leeds and other cities or regions. One crucial issue here is how individuals regard themselves. For example, do Muslims living in Britain think of themselves as part of an Asian community in Britain, or perhaps as part of a Muslim community in Britain, or as part of a Muslim community in (for example) Bradford? Or all three? The answers to these questions are further complicated by the fact that identifications are dynamic and changing. They are, at least in part, responses to the particular contexts in which individuals find themselves and are forged in the light of interactions with those they encounter in these contexts.[26] So, for example, Muslims in Britain may come to think of themselves as part of a single community in response to the way in which a particular issue bears upon them as a group, such as the publication of Salman Rushdie's *The Satanic Verses*.

This much is clear. The concept of community has blurred boundaries. A group of people may exhibit degrees or aspects of community without fully exemplifying one. In consequence there may be many cases where it

---

[26] See A. O. Rorty, 'The Hidden Politics of Cultural Identification', *Political Theory*, vol. 22, 1994, p. 158; K. Anthony Appiah, 'Identity, Authenticity, Survival: Multicultural Societies and Social Reproduction', in A. Gutmann (ed.), *Multiculturalism: Examining the Politics of Recognition* (Princeton, NJ: Princeton University Press, 1994); T. Modood, *Not Easy Being British: Colour, Culture and Citizenship* (London: Trentham Books, 1992).

is impossible to say definitively that some group constitutes, or does not constitute, a community. So long as we are aware of the factors that are involved in classifying a group as a community in the ordinary sense – shared values, a shared way of life, identification with the group and mutual recognition – not much is to be gained from an extended discussion of whether enough of these are present, and to a sufficient degree, amongst (say) Muslims in Britain or Muslims in Bradford, or both.

3. The moralized concept

The second concept of community, I shall call the moralized concept. According to it, a community is not just a group of people who share a range of values and a way of life, identify with the group and its practices, and recognize each other as fellow members. In order for a group to constitute a community in the moralized sense, two further conditions need to be met. First, there must be solidarity between its members. 'Solidarity' is a multiply ambiguous notion, but in the sense I intend it consists in mutual concern: minimally this means that members must give each other's interests some non-instrumental weight in their practical reasoning.[27] (In what follows I shall use the expressions 'solidarity' and 'mutual concern' interchangeably.) Second, there must be no systematic exploitation or (on some versions) no systematic injustice.

Like my account of community in the ordinary sense, however, this account does not provide a precise list of necessary and sufficient conditions for a group to be a community in the moralized sense. Like the ordinary concept, the moralized concept allows for degrees of community-ness. Aspects of community in the moralized sense may also be present even when community (in that sense) as a whole is not realized to any degree; for example, the members of a group may be mutually concerned even though some of them exploit the others. (According to some notions of mutual concern, genuine concern will be impossible in the presence of exploitation. But I do not myself think that it is a conceptual truth that exploitation is inconsistent with genuine concern: a person may have beliefs about others that makes him think he is not exploiting them and which can allow his concern for them to be genuine even whilst he is exploiting them.)

The moralized concept of community is to be found particularly in the socialist tradition. John Baker, for example, gives expression to it when he

---

[27] There is also another sense of solidarity in which 'solidarity with a group' simply means identifying with that group. Solidarity in this sense does not entail solidarity in my sense, although there may be some connections between the two in practice: see section 4 of this chapter.

writes that 'there can be no genuine sense of community between de-grader and degraded or exploiter and exploited – these relationships mock the very idea of community'.[28] In a similar vein, John MacMurray maintains that in community 'each . . . acts, and therefore thinks and feels for the other, and not for himself', and are related to one another as equals: 'equality and freedom are constitutive of community; and the democratic slogan, "Liberty, equality, fraternity", is an adequate defini-tion of community – of the self-realization of persons in relation.'[29] But the moralized concept is not restricted to socialist theory, for there are liberal, feminist, and conservative variants which provide their own dis-tinctive interpretations of what counts as solidarity, exploitation or injus-tice.[30]

The way in which different ideological perspectives may involve differ-ent conceptions of exploitation or injustice is obvious enough, but per-haps it is less clear how they may involve different conceptions of solidar-ity. One way in which these conceptions may diverge is by taking different approaches to the question of whether a welfare state, funded through compulsory taxation, can be an expression of genuine solidarity. So, for example, some right-wing libertarians will take the view that when the taxes necessary to fund a welfare state have to be forcibly extracted, then paying them cannot constitute an expression of mutual concern. They might maintain that mutual concern requires charitable giving, and argue that a welfare state is unnecessary where that concern exists, and indeed is likely to undermine rather than foster it. Others may believe that wide-spread support amongst citizens for a welfare state which is designed to meet each other's basic needs can sometimes be regarded as an expres-sion of their mutual concern, for example, when they can be seen plaus-ibly as 'conditional altruists', who are willing to donate only when they have the assurance (provided by compulsory taxation) that others will do so as well.[31]

There may also be disagreement amongst left-liberals and socialists about how much inequality of condition is compatible with mutual

---

[28] John Baker, *Arguing for Equality* (London: Verso, 1987), p. 35.

[29] J. MacMurray, *Persons in Relation* (London: Faber and Faber, 1961), p. 158. MacMurray in effect equates concern for the other with complete self-sacrifice.

[30] The notion of solidarity can also function in different ways that cut across ideological conflicts. In some variants of the moralized concept, each member of a community must be concerned for the others simply because they are members of the same group. According to other variants which have more cosmopolitan leanings, each member of a community must be concerned for the others because they are fellow human beings (or perhaps fellow sentient creatures) whom he or she happens to be in a special position to help, not essentially because they are members of the same group.

[31] See D. Miller, *Market, State and Community: Theoretical Foundations of Market Socialism* (Oxford: Oxford University Press, 1989), ch. 4.

concern. Some will argue that genuine mutual concern between citizens merely requires a commitment to meeting each other's basic needs where feasible. Others will argue for a more demanding conception which requires an intolerance of inequality except when it is licensed by something similar to John Rawls's difference principle: citizens would have to be unwilling to be better off unless this somehow improved the condition of the worst off.[32] Thomas Nagel in effect proposes a somewhat weaker requirement for mutual concern than willing acceptance of the difference principle, for he appears to think that the best off might properly be said to be concerned for the plight of the worst off even when they accepted benefits which had the effect of worsening the position of the worst off, provided the benefits were sufficiently large.[33] But he also concedes that genuine mutual concern might require 'the development of a general reluctance on the part of members of the society to be conspicuously better off than others'.[34]

It should be uncontroversial among those of different ideological persuasions that what counts as concern (and hence mutual concern) depends on the nature of the relationship involved. Consider, for example the non-communal relationship between doctor and patient.[35] Whether a doctor is genuinely concerned for her patients depends upon (amongst other things) the attention she gives them, the care with which she considers different possible courses of action, and her willingness to give time when needed. In professional roles such as these, concern can exist in the absence of any particular feelings: a concerned doctor need not

---

[32] Plant objects to the idea that community might be created amongst citizens by realizing the difference principle. He argues that in Rawls's theory the difference principle is justified in terms of the idea that it would be chosen by rationally self-interested individuals in the original position, and hence does not manifest mutual concern (see Plant, 'Community', p. 105). It is true that Rawls does justify the difference principle in this way, but his theory is multifaceted and the difference principle receives other kinds of justification. Indeed Brian Barry argues that Rawls's theory is an incoherent mixture of 'justice as impartiality' and 'justice as mutual advantage', where the latter is represented in Rawls's idea that in the original position the parties are to pursue their own conceptions of the good unconstrained by considerations of fairness (see B. Barry, *Theories of Justice* (Hemel Hempstead: Harvester-Wheatsheaf, 1989), ch. 4).

[33] See Nagel, *Equality and Partiality*, p. 73.

[34] *Ibid.*, p. 126. Some socialists may go further than Nagel or Rawls does, arguing that even the operation of the difference principle is compatible with a gross disregard for the welfare of fellow citizens. G. A. Cohen's discussion of that principle, for example, raises doubts about the appropriateness of regarding the talented as concerned for the worst off if the talented *make it the case* that the position of the worst off could not be improved unless they become better off, by refusing to work harder without incentives. See G. A. Cohen, 'Incentives, Inequality, and Community', in G. B. Peterson (ed.), *The Tanner Lectures on Human Values*, vol. XIII (Salt Lake City, UT: University of Utah Press, 1992).

[35] Naomi Scheman makes the following points in more detail in 'On Sympathy', *The Monist*, vol. 62, 1979, p. 322 (reprinted in her *Engenderings: Constructions of Knowledge, Authority, and Privilege* (New York and London: Routledge, 1993), esp. pp. 13–14).

even particularly like her patients. What it is to have and express concern for a friend will be different from this: it may require sympathetic identification, experiencing another's feelings as if they were one's own. Likewise, what counts as concern in a communal relationship will depend on the nature of the community, for example, its size and what binds it together.

4.   Are the two concepts really distinct?

The ordinary and moralized concepts of community are both employed in ordinary discourse and in theoretical contexts but are rarely distinguished.[36] They are distinguishable, however.[37] A group of people might count as a community in the ordinary sense but not the moralized sense. They might share values and a way of life, identify with the group and its practices, and regard each other as members, whilst systematically exploiting one another. Imagine, for example, a plantation where the work is done by slaves, and they are managed by overseers. Suppose that these slaves suffer from an unlikely form of false consciousness in which they share the values of their owners – for example, think that their proper role is to work hard as slaves so that their owners can prosper from their efforts – and, like their owners and the overseers, identify strongly with the plantation and the way of life in which they participate. According to most

---

[36] Elizabeth Frazer and Nicola Lacey make a related distinction between descriptive and ideological senses of community: see Elizabeth Frazer and Nicola Lacey, 'Blind Alleys: Communitarianism', *Politics*, vol. 14, 1994, p. 76; see also their *The Politics of Community: A Feminist Critique of the Liberal-Communitarian Debate* (Hemel Hempstead: Harvester-Wheatsheaf, 1993), pp. 141, 153.

[37] St Augustine implicitly acknowledged the existence of two different concepts of community in the *City of God*, where he discusses the notion of a people, and a people is taken to be a political community. Augustine is concerned with Cicero's definition of a people as the coming together of a considerable number of men who are united by a common agreement about what is right and by shared interest, and with his definition of a commonwealth as the affairs of a people (see Cicero, *On the Commonwealth*, trans. by G. H. Sabine and S. B. Smith (New York: Macmillan, 1976), p. 128; St. Augustine, *City of God*, trans. H. Bettenson (Harmondsworth: Penguin, 1984), p. 73. In Cicero's dialogue these definitions are put in the mouth of Scipio). It becomes clear that what Cicero really means is that a people is a group of men united (in part) by what *is* right, for he argues that where there is injustice, there is no genuine people; in effect the notion of an unjust people is a contradiction in terms (Cicero, *On the Commonwealth*, p. 225). St. Augustine concludes that according to Cicero's definitions of a people and a commonwealth, there never was a Roman commonwealth: the Romans did not constitute a people because they did not serve God and in consequence justice did not exist in their souls (Augustine, *City of God*, bk. XIX, sect. 21). But he proposes an alternative definition of a people as 'the association of a multitude of rational beings united by a common agreement on the objects of their love', and argues that on this definition the Romans were a people, for it allows that a people might be united by the wrong objects of love and hence be unjust (Augustine, *City of God*, p. 890).

conceptions of justice and exploitation, it will follow that the slave owners exploit the slaves and act unjustly towards them. The group they together form could count as a community in the ordinary sense but not on any reasonable version of the moralized conception.[38] How widespread cases of this kind are thought to be will depend upon one's conception of justice and exploitation. Orthodox Marxists believe that members of a capitalist society cannot constitute a community because such a society is essentially exploitative. And some radical feminists take the view that members of a patriarchal society cannot constitute a community since the relations between men and women in such a society are inherently exploitative and unjust.[39]

The two concepts of community I claim to have distinguished are related in some obvious ways and this may raise worries about whether they really are distinct. Members of a community in the moralized sense, like members of one in the ordinary sense, share values, a way of life, identify with the group, and acknowledge each other as members. More worryingly perhaps, members of a community in the ordinary sense will often be mutually concerned, which means that there is even greater overlap between what I am regarding as the two different concepts. But the presence of mutual concern in a community in the ordinary sense is not sufficient to make it a community in the moralized sense, since the absence of exploitation and systematic injustice is also required. Furthermore, there is no reason to think that there is a *general* tendency for members of a community in the ordinary sense to be mutually concerned: whether solidarity arises will depend on the nature of the community and its practices, and how members of the community conceive of the group and its relationship to its individual members. If members of a community regard personal need as a manifestation of weakness, they may not value practices of mutual aid and may lack anything recognizable as concern for other members. If the members of a community in the ordinary sense suppose that the prosperity of the community is wholly or partly independent of the prosperity of their individual members, they

---

[38] In this context consider Eugene Genovese's willingness to describe plantations in the Old South as communities: 'Paternalism created a tendency for the slaves to identify with a particular community through identification with its master . . . The slave owners had to establish a stable regime with which their slaves could live. Slaves remained slaves . . . And blacks remained rigidly subordinated to whites. But masters and slaves, whites and blacks, lived as well as worked together. The existence of the community required that all find some measure of self-interest and self-respect' (E. Genovese, *Roll, Jordan, Roll: The World the Slaves Made* (New York: Pantheon Books, 1974), p. 6). Genovese here uses 'community' in the ordinary rather than the moralized sense.

[39] Indeed this is the source of many feminists' reservations about community in the ordinary sense. See Frazer and Lacey, *The Politics of Community*; and the papers by Weiss and Friedman in Weiss and Friedman (eds.), *Feminism and Community*.

may be concerned about the prosperity of that community and have little (if any) non-instrumental regard for the well-being of its other members.

Some communitarians will reply that members of a community in the ordinary sense *must* always be mutually concerned since membership of such a community always generates special obligations to attend to each other's welfare, and motivates them to meet those special obligations. If each member of a community is under an obligation of this kind and motivated by it, then even communities in the ordinary sense will be marked by mutual concern. This would not mean that the ordinary concept of community collapses into the moralized concept, but it would mean that there was more overlap than describing them as two different concepts would seem to permit.

What underpins the idea that membership of a community generates special obligations to fellow members? The line of thought here is usually that these obligations in some way arise out of each person's constitutive attachment, or commitment, to that community.[40] When discussing national communities, for example, Yael Tamir maintains that 'deep and important obligations flow from identity and relatedness'.[41] But it is implausible to suppose that membership of each and every community, whatever the particular nature of its bond, generates special obligations to attend to the well-being of other members. Even if we accept that special obligations are generated automatically by membership, this is not enough to determine the *content* of these obligations. The content of these obligations must depend, at least in part, on the nature of the particular community, taking into account its way of life or traditions; if the obligations are generated by a constitutive attachment or commitment to it, then the content of these obligations will have to cohere with its traditions and practices. Membership of a community whose traditions accept that personal need diminishes individual well-being, but then regard it as a form of weakness, could not by itself generate special obligations to promote the well-being of fellow members. It is only membership of communities which have a tradition of promoting each other's welfare which can plausibly generate special obligations to do so.

The same sort of remarks apply to the idea that communities generate special obligations between members to meet each other's needs because

---

[40] For example, Jack Crittenden writes: 'Communal obligations arise out of the members' concern for the welfare or well-being of all other members, and that concern arises out of the members' own sense of identity.' See J. Crittenden, *Beyond Individualism: Reconstituting the Liberal Self* (New York: Oxford University Press, 1992), p. 131.

[41] Y. Tamir, *Liberal Nationalism* (Princeton, NJ: Princeton University Press, 1993), p. 99. Richard Rorty suggests that we can have obligations to others simply in virtue of our identification (what he calls our sense of solidarity) with a group to which we all belong: see Rorty, *Contingency, Irony, and Solidarity*, p. 195.

membership involves making what Gilbert calls a joint commitment. Even if being a member of a community is necessarily to make a joint commitment (something I denied in section 2), the content of that commitment will be determined by the mutual understandings around which it is formed, and these may not involve any thought that those in need will be looked after.

Special obligations to promote the well-being of fellow members of a group, or meet their needs, can in some cases be derived from general duties. Robert Goodin, for example, argues that special obligations arise from assigned responsibilities: they are 'merely devices whereby the moral community's general duties get assigned to particular agents'.[42] But this approach could not justify the idea that all communities generate special obligations to look after each other, and Goodin does not intend it to do so. Some communities (for example, some religious communities) are geographically dispersed, and there is no reason to suppose that assigning special obligations to their members will be the most efficient way of discharging general duties. The distinction between the ordinary and moralized concepts remains intact. The concepts cannot be even partially bridged by the implausible idea that communities always generate special obligations amongst their members to give priority to each other's needs.

5.   The different roles played by the two concepts

The two concepts of community I have distinguished are perhaps best contrasted in terms of the role they play in our language and social life, and these different roles provide part of the justification for claiming that there really are two different concepts at work there. The ordinary concept often plays an explanatory role: since it centrally involves the idea of identification, one of its main roles is in explaining people's allegiances and hence their behaviour. When we classify a group of people as a community, we do so at least partly because the individual members identify with the group. A correct understanding of people's identifications clearly is of great importance in explaining their behaviour and their general orientation to the world. In particular, it helps us to understand phenomena such as alienation, social cohesion and social conflict.[43] Tariq

---

[42] R. Goodin, 'What is So Special about Our Fellow Countrymen?', *Ethics*, vol. 98, 1988, p. 678.

[43] For one way of approaching the explanation of these phenomena which is based upon the importance of identification, and which uses the tools of rational choice theory, see Hardin, *One for All*.

Modood, for example, argues that one reason why social theorists in Britain were taken by surprise by the Muslim reaction to Salman Rushdie's *The Satanic Verses* was because they failed to recognize the enormous importance of religious commitment to many Asians living there. According to Modood, some theorists mistakenly thought that because the wider society identified Muslims as Blacks, it was this category which would need to be employed to explain their behaviour.[44] Arguably there is a Muslim community in Britain but no Black community which includes Asians, and we have to appeal to membership in the Muslim community to explain the force of religious commitments to Muslims living in Britain.

The ordinary concept of community also has an important role to play in evaluative contexts: identifying with a group and the forms of cooperative activity involved in a shared way of life are often valuable for various reasons which we shall consider in Chapter 2. So normative questions about when and how communities should be given special protection, about the kind of jurisdiction a community should have over its members, and about whether community is something to be pursued at the level of the state, inevitably appear on the political agenda, and are fertile ground for political philosophers. Indeed some of them will preoccupy me in Part II of this book. But they are not involved in the very identification of a group as a community.

The moralized concept of community mainly plays a critical role (although it too can play an explanatory role[45]) – it is used primarily in order to condemn social and political arrangements or praise them. Some social relationships are described as communal in order to commend them, whereas others are described as lacking in community in order to condemn them, and to hold up an alternative model as a vision of something better. William Morris, for example, criticizes capitalism and argues that a truly communal life requires the elimination of the capitalist: 'the capitalist or modern slave-owner has been forced by his very success . . . to organize his slaves, the wage-earners, into a co-operation for production so well arranged that it requires little but his own elimination to make it a foundation for communal life . . .'[46] The communal life is one which

---

[44] See Modood, *Not Easy Being British*, especially pp. 54–5.
[45] The notion of solidarity which is central to the moralized concept gives that concept an important explanatory role too: 'Solidarity is . . . a way of being interested in what is happening to one's fellow group members, and from it springs the capacity to act as a group' (May, *The Morality of Groups*, p. 40). So group behaviour may sometimes be best explained in terms of the solidarity characteristic of community in the moralized sense.
[46] A. L. Morton (ed.), *The Political Writings of William Morris* (London: Lawrence and Wishart, 1979), p. 177.

involves brotherhood and cooperation rather than 'selfish greed and ceaseless competition'.[47]

Marx also employs a version of the moralized concept of community to criticize relations under capitalism (and earlier forms of social and economic organization), in particular the way in which the state becomes an 'illusory community', and to sketch an alternative vision:

> The illusory community [*Gemeinschaft*], in which individuals have up till now combined, always took on an independent existence in relation to them, and was at the same time, since it was the combination of one class over against another, not only a completely illusory community, but a new fetter as well. In the real community the individuals obtain their freedom in and through their association.[48]

Marx argues that only communist society is a true community, and only in a true community is personal freedom possible for all.[49]

Only the moralized concept of community is genuinely essentially contested. The ordinary concept does meet a number of the criteria for being essentially contested, however. It accredits a valued achievement. It is internally complex because it makes reference to a number of different elements: shared values, an encompassing way of life, identification with the group and mutual recognition. It is open to different interpretations, for these elements might reasonably be weighted differently by different people. But it is not essentially contested because the very identification of community in the ordinary sense is not a site of political controversy. People disagree about whether communities in this sense should be given special protection, whether they should be allowed to coerce their individual members to conform to traditions, and whether the practices they contain are desirable or not. But there are rarely serious disputes over

[47] Morton (ed.), *Political Writings of William Morris*, p. 171. See Caroline McCulloch, 'The Problem of Fellowship in Communitarian Theory: William Morris and Peter Kropotkin', *Political Studies*, vol. 32, 1984, pp. 437–50, for a fuller discussion of Morris's conception of community.

[48] Karl Marx and Friedrich Engels, *Collected Works*, vol. V (London: Lawrence and Wishart, 1976), p. 78 (from *The German Ideology*, written in 1845–6). There are problems with describing Marx as an advocate of the moralized concept of community. As is well known, Marx at best had an ambivalent attitude towards morality, and sometimes seems to have regarded all morality as ideological. In some broad sense of 'moral', however, it is hard to escape the idea that Marx's vision of communism, in which community is to be realized, is a moral vision. It is also hard to escape the conclusion that (despite his protestations to the contrary) Marx is committed to the idea that capitalist society is unjust, although some have tried.

[49] For more comprehensive discussions of Marx's conception of community, see Brudney, 'Community and Completion'; D. Archard, 'The Marxist Ethic of Self-realization: Individuality and Community', in J. D. G. Evans (ed.), *Moral Philosophy and Contemporary Problems* (Cambridge: Cambridge University Press, 1987); Graham, *Karl Marx, Our Contemporary*, pp. 31–2.

whether some group of people constitute a community in the ordinary sense: that is usually granted for the sake of argument.[50]

Whether some political concept is contested depends upon particular historical and political circumstance, not just its nature. For example, Terence Ball points out that: '[t]he now ubiquitous disputes about the meaning of "democracy", for instance, are of relatively recent vintage, while the once-heated arguments about "republic" have cooled considerably since the late 18th century.'[51] The ordinary concept of community could become essentially contested, but it is not at the moment. We might say that it is essentially contest*able*, meaning that it is by its very nature open to different interpretations, but not essentially contest*ed*, since it is not currently the site of political controversy over its proper application.

The moralized concept of community is genuinely essentially contested, however. The identification of community in the moralized sense is a site of political controversy because it incorporates other moral notions – solidarity, exploitation or justice – each of which receives a number of reasonable interpretations. (I do not deny that what counts as a reasonable interpretation may itself be a matter of reasonable dispute: there is often no neutral standpoint from which to draw the distinction between reasonable and unreasonable conceptions of justice and the like, but that is not to say there is no right or wrong way of drawing it.)

For example, socialists such as Morris and Marx see the relationship between capitalist and worker as fundamentally exploitative, and appear to think that the abolition of private ownership of the means of production would end all exploitation. Some feminists, however, would disagree and argue that men might continue to exploit women even after capitalism had been transcended, because, for instance, women might continue to perform unremunerated work for men in fulfilling their familial obligations.[52] Different theories of exploitation thereby generate different conceptions of the moralized concept of community. (For some ways in which the notion of solidarity may become a site of ideological conflict, see section 2 of this chapter.)

In subsequent chapters, I shall employ liberal versions of the moralized concept. The versions I employ are liberal because they are committed to conceptions of justice which recognize a range of individual rights of the sort described in the Introduction, and give these rights a high priority in

---

[50] There are some disagreements of this sort: for example, people do sometimes disagree over whether there is a gay community in the ordinary sense, or a community of womankind. But these disputes are not widespread.

[51] Terence Ball, *Transforming Political Discourse* (Oxford: Blackwell, 1988), p. 14.

[52] See Christine Delphy and Diane Leonard, *Familiar Exploitation* (Cambridge: Polity, 1992).

the design of institutions and the choice of policies. I do not assume that all non-liberal versions of the moralized concept are unreasonable, but I do suppose that they are less defensible than liberal ones in polities which contain a range of different ways of life. As I pointed out in the Introduction, however, liberalism as I conceive it in this book is not as contentious as it may seem because it leaves open a series of questions about how these rights are to be justified and (within limits) their precise nature and significance, and is compatible with perspectives which are sometimes contrasted with liberalism, for example, many forms of socialism, feminism and conservatism.

Theorists sometimes employ both notions of community I have distinguished. Marx is an example. He sometimes refers to feudal villages as if they were communities, apparently employing community in the ordinary sense, but on other occasions regards these villages as illusory communities, apparently employing the term in the moralized sense (albeit from a non-liberal perspective). In *The German Ideology*, he refers to 'the previous substitutes for community' (particularly the state as conceived by the Hegelians) and 'the illusory community'.[53] Yet in other writings he also refers to villages in nineteenth-century India as communities. He deplores the loss of an ancient form of civilization under British colonialism, whilst emphasizing the oppressiveness of these village communities: 'we must not forget that these idyllic village communities, inoffensive though they may appear, had always been the solid foundation of oriental despotism . . . these little communities were contaminated by distinctions of caste and by slavery . . .'[54] There is nothing wrong with employing both senses of community, but it would be confused to suppose that community in the moralized sense is more of a community or a more authentic or real community than community in the ordinary sense.[55]

The ambiguity in the idea of community might also make us wonder whether it is common practice to trade on it by correctly describing a group as a community in the ordinary sense, but implicitly claiming for it

---

[53] Marx and Engels, *Collected Works*, vol. v, p. 78.

[54] Karl Marx and Friedrich Engels, *Selected Works*, vol. I (Moscow: Foreign Languages Publishing House, 1962), pp. 350–1 (the passage is taken from an article on British rule in India, originally published in the *New York Daily Tribune*, 25 June, 1853).

[55] Indeed versions of the moralized concept are often introduced by the phrases 'genuine community' or 'real community'. Penny Weiss, for example, writes that 'families are not necessarily real communities' and that 'their failure to be real communities is tied to their inegalitarianism' (see Weiss and M. Friedman (eds.) *Feminism and Community*, p. 8). In her editorial introduction, she tends to move unreflectively between ordinary and moralized senses of community. Communities in the ordinary sense are real communities, they are just real communities in a different sense to communities in the moralized sense.

the moral qualities of community in the moralized sense when they are in reality lacking. 'Community' might then function in a way that is in some respects similar to Ernest Gellner's not entirely imaginary concept of 'boble'. 'Bobility' is used either to characterize people who display various virtues such as courage or generosity, or to characterize people who merely hold a certain social position or office. Gellner proposes that

Bobility is a conceptual device by which the privileged class of the society in question acquires some of the prestige of certain virtues respected in that society, without the inconvenience of needing to practice it, thanks to the fact that the same word is applied either to practitioners of those virtues or to occupiers of favoured positions.[56]

If 'community' does sometimes function in a similar way, it may serve the ideological purpose of diverting attention from the relationships of exploitation that exist within a way of life.

6.   Must communities be face to face?

One issue that has frequently divided writers on community is the question of whether communities must be face to face. Even those who have been willing to describe larger groups as communities have often thought that they are communities only in an extended sense, because they have supposed that the paradigm of a community is a small group, members of which are personally acquainted with one another.[57] The question of whether communities must be face to face can be raised in relation to communities in either of the two senses I have distinguished.

What reasons could there be for supposing that community in the ordinary sense must be face to face? One thought might be that a community requires a degree of intimacy which is possible only when those concerned know each other personally. My account of the ideal type of community in the ordinary sense does not include or entail this idea, however, and ordinary usage, which, for example, licenses the description of nations as communities, provides no warrant for it. Are there any theoretical reasons for insisting that community in the ordinary sense must be face to face?

It is perhaps possible to construct an argument for that conclusion,

---

[56] E. Gellner, 'Concepts and Society', in Brian Wilson (ed.), *Rationality* (Oxford: Blackwell, 1970), pp. 41–2.

[57] For example, Michael Taylor writes: 'It seems to me that we should want to say that, other things being equal, a group of individuals amongst whom relations are to some extent mediated is to that extent less of a community than a group in which relations are relatively direct' (Taylor, *Community, Anarchy and Liberty*, p. 28). He concludes that for this, and other reasons, communities must be relatively small (*ibid.*, p. 32).

based on the supposition that community is what prevents alienation. It would run as follows. When people are unknown to each other, they must always relate to one another via a description, for example, Sam's father or the owner of the factory, whereas when they know each other personally they can also relate to each other directly, without needing to pick out each other as occupants of roles, or by using other descriptions. But this means that the relationships between people who do not know each other personally must always be mediated or indirect. If relationships are always mediated or indirect, then they must, to some degree, involve alienation, and any degree of alienation is incompatible with genuine community.[58] The problem with this argument, however, is that it is unclear how someone might defend its fundamental premise, i.e., that when one individual always relates to another via a description which singles out one aspect of her being, rather than at least sometimes directly in her full personhood, they must be alienated from each other to some extent.[59]

There is no good reason for insisting that communities in the ordinary sense must be face to face. Even if face-to-face relations are qualitatively different, it would be an act of pure stipulation to insist, in the face of ordinary usage, that we should mark this distinction by reserving the term 'community' solely for face to face relations. It is possible for a group to constitute a community in the ordinary sense if they share values, a way of life, identify with the group, and have some means of deciding whether a person is a member of that community, without each needing to know the others. These conditions can be satisfied by large groups as well as small ones; there is no conceptual or empirical reason for resisting this conclusion.[60] In this context it is illuminating to consider Benedict Anderson's notion of an imagined community.[61] By an 'imagined community' Anderson does not mean an imaginary community. Imagined communities are real enough, but their existence depends upon people conceiving

---

[58] This argument is perhaps connected with the idea, sometimes attributed to the German Romantics (such as Herder and Schiller), that community involves the whole man: see Raymond Plant, *Community and Ideology: An Essay in Applied Social Philosophy* (London: Routledge and Kegan Paul, 1974), pp. 16–17; Robert Nisbet, *The Sociological Tradition* (London: Heinemann, 1967), p. 47. But Herder at least was happy with the idea that individuals could exist in an integrated form in nations, which clearly are not face to face.

[59] See Iris Young, 'The Ideal of Community and the Politics of Difference', in Linda Nicholson (ed.), *Feminism/Postmodernism* (London: Routledge, 1990), p. 315. Young argues that even personal relationships are necessarily mediated.

[60] Daniel Bell distinguishes between communities of place, communities of memory and psychological communities. In his terminology, to think that all communities must be face to face is to think that they must all be psychological communities, and to ignore the possibility of communities of place and memory. See D. Bell, *Communitarianism and its Critics* (Oxford: Oxford University Press, 1993), pp. 14, 124ff., 170ff.

[61] Benedict Anderson, *Imagined Communities: Reflections on the Origin and Spread of Nationalism*, rev. edn (London: Verso, 1991), pp. 5–7.

of themselves as related to one another. People who have never met can do this by subsuming their relationship to each other under some description, for example, compatriot, fellow Sikh. Mutual recognition of this kind can be secured in various ways (for example, by dress, attendance at ceremonies, participation in rituals) and does not require personal acquaintance.

What of community in the moralized sense: must it be face to face? It might be thought so on the grounds that solidarity of the appropriate sort is possible only in small groups. Jack Crittenden argues that when 'the community has grown too large, the strain on mutual concern and obligations would be great' and asks rhetorically, 'Could one feel obligations to persons that one had never met?'[62] Stanley Benn argues that sympathetic identification is impossible in large groups: 'Communitarian ideals . . . require more than a concern for well-being, for that can be too impersonal. They call for *sympathetic* concern, a caring for the other "as if it were oneself", for some measure of identification with the fate of the other.'[63] Benn maintains that communitarian ideals – what he calls comradeship, for example – may be instantiated in 'a moderately large kibbutz, an extended family, or even a regiment'[64] but cannot reliably extend much further. But he gives us no good reason for restricting communitarian ideals to relationships where caring for others (which would seem to require some degree of physical proximity), as opposed to mere concern for another's well-being (where physical proximity is unnecessary), is a real possibility. Solidarity, i.e., mutual concern, is what matters here. As I claimed in section 3 of this chapter, it can take different forms depending on the nature of the relationship, so what it amounts to may vary depending on group size. Although mutual concern in a small group may require 'a caring for other as if it were oneself', mutual concern in the context of a larger association, such as the nation, is not so demanding. If so, community in the moralized sense may extend beyond those who are immediately acquainted with one another, perhaps as far as the nation state,[65] and perhaps even further to the world as a whole.

7.   **Conclusion**

The main purpose of this chapter has been clarificatory. I hope to have shown that the notion of community is ambiguous: the ordinary concept of community picks out groups whose members share values and a way of life, identify with the group and its practices, and recognize each other as

[62] Crittenden, *Beyond Individualism*, p. 134.
[63] Benn, *A Theory of Freedom*, p. 223.   [64] *Ibid.*
[65] See S. A. Schwarzenbach, 'On Civic Friendship', *Ethics*, vol. 107, 1996, pp. 119–24.

members. The moralized concept requires that the relationships between members of a community be non-exploitative or just, and that mutual concern exist between them. The moralized concept is inherently perspectival in the sense that there can be different versions of it, animated by different conceptions of exploitation, justice and mutual concern. (But this is not to deny that some of these conceptions may be better than others, or that there may be a conception of each that is the best.) Both of the concepts of community I have distinguished are perfectly legitimate. Whichever we employ, we need to recognize that the concept of community is broad and inherently fuzzy. It applies (potentially at least) to a wide variety of groups. It comes in degrees, and aspects of community may be realized even when community as a whole is not. In Chapter 2, I shall explore the different sources of value of community in both its senses.

2   The value of community

Both of the concepts of community I distinguished in Chapter 1 play an evaluative role: each picks out a worthwhile type of social relationship. But why do these relationships have value and what sort of value do they possess? Although I have touched upon these questions, in this chapter I propose to explore them in more depth. This requires me to draw some distinctions in value theory, between what I call individualist and collectivist accounts of the value of social phenomena, and between something's being instrumentally valuable, non-instrumentally valuable or a necessary condition of achieving some other value. Having made these distinctions, I apply them to the case of community.

1.   Some preliminary distinctions

Let me begin by distinguishing between individualist and collectivist accounts of the value of social relations and social entities, such as communities. Individualist accounts hold that the value of social relationships or other social phenomena is always reducible without remainder to the value they contribute to the lives of individuals. On this view, the value of a community has to be understood in terms of its contribution to the lives of members and non-members. In contrast, collectivist accounts of value allow that the value of a social phenomenon may not be reducible to the value it contributes to the lives of individuals. Donald Regan, for example, maintains that a community contributes to the value of the universe in which it occurs and its value is over and above the value it has for its members.[1] (Note that a collectivist about the value of social phenomena can accept that they are in some sense nothing but relationships between individuals, but argue that value can emerge from these relationships which cannot be reduced to the way these relationships enhance the lives of individuals.)

[1] See D. Regan, 'Authority and Value: Reflections on Raz's *The Morality of Freedom*', *Southern California Law Review*, vol. 62, 1989, p. 1047.

When assessing the value of community, it is also important to distinguish between instrumental and non-instrumental value, and to contrast that distinction with a more problematic one between intrinsic and extrinsic value. When something has non-instrumental value, it has value as an end in itself (and is valuable for its own sake in that sense), whereas when it has instrumental value, it has value as a means to something else. (The very same thing can of course possess both instrumental and non-instrumental value.) The distinction between intrinsic and extrinsic value is sometimes thought to coincide with that between non-instrumental and instrumental value, but they are different.[2] In order to bring out their differences, let me simply stipulate that intrinsic value is value which something possesses in virtue of its intrinsic properties, where its intrinsic properties are those which do not depend, even in part, on the existence or nature of anything else. In contrast, something which is extrinsically valuable has that value in virtue of its extrinsic properties, i.e., those properties which depend, at least in part, on the existence or nature of something else. These two distinctions – between instrumental and non-instrumental value on the one hand, and intrinsic and extrinsic value on the other – do not map on to each other, for something may have extrinsic but non-instrumental value: for example, something may have value because it is rare or unusual, but still be non-instrumentally valuable in virtue of its rarity or unusualness.[3]

Any moral theory which attributes value to persons, characters, actions or collectivities needs to recognize that there is non-instrumental value. Not everything could (logically) be of merely instrumental value. But it is a matter of controversy within value theory whether anything has intrinsic value. For example, those who believe that the value of a thing always depends upon its relationship with other things might seem to be committed to denying the very existence of intrinsic value.[4] (Even those who allow that some things are intrinsically valuable may think that they are few in number: Kant, for example, believed that only a good will is unconditionally valuable, which seems to imply that only it is intrinsically

---

[2] For the importance of keeping these two distinctions apart, see C. Korsgaard, 'Two Distinctions in Goodness' in *Creating the Kingdom of Ends* (Cambridge: Cambridge University Press, 1996).

[3] In 'Two Distinctions in Goodness', Korsgaard is particularly interested in the idea that something may possess non-instrumental but extrinsic value because its value depends upon the fact that it is desired or the object of a rational choice.

[4] This is a trickier question than it might appear, however. For it might be the case that the value of a thing is always *affected* by its context (and in this sense always depends upon its relationship to other things), but that when it possesses value, that value nevertheless *derives* from its intrinsic properties, in which case (according to my definition of intrinsic value) it would possess intrinsic value. See also note 11 below.

valuable.[5]) I shall not concern myself with the question of whether community has intrinsic value, for I do not want to beg the question of whether anything at all has intrinsic value. Instead I shall focus on the more practically relevant question of whether community has instrumental value, non-instrumental value, or both, and I shall use the expression 'valuable for its own sake' to mean non-instrumentally valuable.

The distinction between instrumental value and non-instrumental value is not exhaustive. Something may have value without being instrumentally or non-instrumentally valuable, in virtue of being a necessary condition for the achievement of something which possesses either instrumental or non-instrumental value.[6] So, for example, someone might hold that a culture has value because it supports a range of goods, thereby supplying a necessary condition of autonomous choice, without supposing that the culture has either instrumental or non-instrumental value of its own.

The way in which something may be a necessary condition for the *achievement* of something else that is valuable needs to be contrasted with the way in which something may be a necessary condition of something else's *being* valuable. So, for example, we might say that a condition of the value of a beautiful painting is that it be viewed.[7] Or, as Joseph Raz maintains, that a condition of the value of autonomy is that it be exercised in pursuit of the good.[8] Critics have argued that Raz's position is incoherent because he claims that autonomy is non-instrumentally valuable but possesses that value only when exercised in pursuit of the good.[9] But Raz's position is perfectly coherent.[10] According to his view, autonomy would seem to be extrinsically valuable because it is valuable only under certain conditions.[11] But it does not follow that it cannot therefore also be non-instrumentally valuable. We should not suppose that anything which

[5] See Korsgaard, 'Two Distinctions in Goodness', pp. 256–9.
[6] See A. Moore and R. Crisp, 'Welfarism in Moral Theory', *Australasian Journal of Philosophy*, vol. 74, 1996, p. 609.
[7] Korsgaard, 'Two Distinctions in Goodness', pp. 264–5.
[8] J. Raz, *The Morality of Freedom* (Oxford: Oxford University Press, 1986), pp. 380–1.
[9] R. P. George, *Making Men Moral: Civil Liberties and Public Morality* (Oxford: Oxford University Press, 1993), p. 175. Cf. Regan, 'Authority and Value', p. 1084.
[10] Unfortunately, Raz uses 'intrinsic' to mean 'non-instrumental'. If his position is to be stated coherently, he needs to distinguish between intrinsic and non-instrumental value.
[11] Again, however, this is a difficult issue. Even though on Raz's account autonomy is valuable only under certain conditions, it might be argued that it is still properly regarded as intrinsically valuable under those conditions, on the grounds that the value it then possesses is due solely to its intrinsic properties. The fact that autonomy's value is *affected* by the conditions under which it appears does not show that it cannot be the case then when it has value, that value *derives* from its intrinsic properties. According to this sort of view, the intrinsic value of a thing may vary from one context to another. Jonathan Dancy explores this possibility in his 'Value and Intrinsic Value' (unpublished paper).

is extrinsically valuable must be non-instrumentally valuable: that would be to confuse non-instrumental value with intrinsic value.

The fact that something can be non-instrumentally valuable but only under certain conditions or in certain contexts shows that it is wrong to suppose that if something is non-instrumentally valuable, it must possess that value in all contexts in which it appears. Something may be non-instrumentally valuable but only possess that value under certain conditions. Evaluative properties display at least a modest holism: what counts as an evaluatively relevant property, and the way in which it is evaluatively relevant, sometimes depends upon what other properties are present.[12]

2.   Individualist and collectivist accounts of value

Individualist accounts of value have obvious appeal: how could there be a residue of value when, on a collectivist account, we subtract the ways in which a community enhances the lives of individuals from the full value of the community? In principle, however, there are at least two possible ways in which a collectivist account might try to make space for the idea that there is such a residue.

The first involves maintaining that a social relation or other social phenomenon may have value which cannot be reduced either to its value for individuals[13] or to its value for a group. Although this position may be logically consistent, it is hard to motivate.[14] Some endorse a related view in environmental ethics, viz. that the natural environment has value independently of its actual or possible effects on sentient creatures (or even groups of them), and hence that its value is not exhausted by its benefits to such individuals (or groups). That view can be motivated by an appeal to intuitions, for example, the intuition that some value would be lost if the natural environment were destroyed even if nobody was there to enjoy it and (for whatever reason) no one would enjoy it in the future.[15] But it is hard to see how the view that some social relations or

---

[12] Christine Korsgaard shows that Kant's theory presupposes a modest holism of this kind: 'it allows us to say of certain things that they are valuable only under certain circumstances, or valuable only when certain other things are true or present, without forcing us to say that these kind of things must be valuable merely as instruments' ('Two Distinctions in Goodness', p. 270). Jonathan Dancy defends a thorough-going holism about moral properties in his *Moral Reasons* (Oxford: Blackwell, 1993), esp. ch. 4.

[13] In the sense I intend, something may have value *for* an individual even if they do not value it and do not appreciate its value for them.

[14] Regan seems to advance some such view: see 'Authority and Value', p. 1047.

[15] This is the intuition exploited by the 'last man' argument. See R. Sylvan (Routley), 'Is There a Need for a New, an Environmental, Ethic?' in M. E. Zimmerman (ed.) *Environmental Philosophy: From Animal Rights to Radical Ecology* (Englewood Cliffs, NJ: Prentice Hall, 1993), pp. 16–17.

other social phenomena have value independently of the benefits they provide to individuals or groups could be made plausible. The mere assertion that they add value to the universe in which they occur is not enough to do so.

A more attractive collectivist account would hold that a social relation or social phenomenon could have value for a group that does not reduce to its value for the individual members of that group. Consider an example which might be thought capable of establishing that conclusion, even if it was not originally designed to do so. In an attempt to persuade his critics of the value of communal self-determination, Michael Walzer asks us to imagine that a group of revolutionaries come to power in a country called Algeria, with the aim of creating a democratic and secular state with equal rights for all.[16] Things go badly wrong, and the regime that results is a brutally repressive military dictatorship, which denies citizens civil and political liberties, and returns women to religious subordination. More fantastically, Walzer then asks us to suppose that the Swedish government possesses a chemical which, if introduced into the Algerian water supply, would turn all Algerians into Swedish-style social democrats, wiping out of their minds their own culture, leaving them with no sense of loss, and creating in them the knowledge, ability and cultural background necessary to make such a system work for them.

Walzer asks whether there would be any objection to introducing this chemical and concludes that there would, because 'the historical religion and politics of the Algerian people are values for the Algerian people'.[17] Walzer might be thought to be drawing upon an intuition which could support a collectivist account of value: the value of self-determination *for a people* is such that it could not be reduced, say, to the value that the preservation of their culture, religion and the like has for them considered as individuals. But there is a lot going on in Walzer's example, and it cannot lend unambiguous support to a collectivist account of value. For example, a defender of an individualist account might argue that it would be wrong to introduce the chemical because it would be a violation of the personal autonomy of those whose minds were thereby manipulated. This would not refute a 'collectivist' analysis of Walzer's example, but it does show that the intuitions which underlie the response he invites us to give need not be collectivist in nature.

Charles Taylor defends a collectivist account by arguing more gen-

---

[16] M. Walzer, 'The Moral Standing of States: A Response to Four Critics', in C. Beitz, M. Cohen, T. Scanlon, and A. J. Simmons (eds.), *International Ethics: A Philosophy and Public Affairs Reader* (Princeton, NJ: Princeton University Press, 1985), pp. 233–4.
[17] *Ibid.*, p. 234.

erally that part of what makes some goods such is that they are enjoyed with other people and they can only be enjoyed in social relations.[18] Membership in a community could be regarded as a good of this kind. Taylor means to distinguish goods which, for contingent reasons, we can enjoy only with other people – so called public goods – from those goods which for conceptual reasons cannot be had separately for part of what *makes* them goods is that they are enjoyed together.[19] The latter are surely important, but Taylor is mistaken in thinking that individualist accounts cannot make sense of them. Individualist accounts can maintain that the value of these goods is reducible to the contributions they make to the lives of those who acquire them. Even if part of what makes something a good is that it is enjoyed with other people (and in that sense it is irreducibly social because it cannot be obtained separately), we are not thereby committed to giving a collectivist account of its value.[20] This does not show that Taylor's analysis of these goods is mistaken, but it does show that he has not defeated an individualist account of them.

Nor is a collectivist account of value entailed by the idea that communities or social relations more generally are prior to individuals. There are at least two different sorts of claims here, and they can come in different versions. According to the first type of claim, social relations are an empirical precondition of individuals: as a matter of fact individuals can acquire the capacities essential to their natures only through interaction with other people. So, for example, it might be argued, as Taylor does, that individuals can acquire their capacity to reason, or their capacity for self-direction, only in relationship to others.[21] The second type of claim maintains that social relations are logically or conceptually prior to individuals. For example, it might be argued that individuals could not even in principle acquire the capacities essential to their natures in the absence of social relations. Some have thought that Wittgenstein's discussion of the nature of rule-following provides some support for this idea, for it might be taken to show that it makes no sense to say that someone is following a rule – part of what it is to think – unless their behaviour is

---

[18] Taylor appears to endorse collectivism in the following sentence: 'Some things have value to me and to you, and some things essentially have value to us' (Taylor, 'Cross-Purposes', p. 190). See also 'Irreducibly Social Goods' in his *Philosophical Arguments*.

[19] Taylor, 'Cross-Purposes', pp. 190–1.

[20] Moore and Crisp reach the same conclusion: see their 'Welfarism in Moral Theory', pp. 610–11. In 'Irreducibly Social Goods' Taylor characterizes one set of goods which he believes cannot be captured by an individualist account as goods 'that incorporate common understandings of their value' (*Philosophical Arguments*, p. 140). Again, however, it is hard to see why the value of these goods can not be reduced to the value they have for individuals. [21] See Taylor, 'Atomism'.

placed in the context of a community's practices.[22] Or it might be argued that persons are constituted, in whole or in part, and in some sense which stands in need of elucidation, by their social relationships. Several of those labelled as communitarians have advanced such a view, for example Michael Sandel, Alasdair MacIntyre and Charles Taylor.

It is not clear, however, that any of these versions of the idea that the community is prior to its individual members is strictly inconsistent with an individualist account of value. Even if individuals could not in practice exist in the absence of community, we might suppose that the value of community is nevertheless reducible to its value for individuals, for example, its contribution to individual well-being. Causal priority does not entail moral or evaluative priority: perhaps persons cannot exist in the absence of chains of carbon atoms, but it would not follow that chains of carbon atoms had evaluative primacy. Even if collectives or social relations were *ontologically* prior to individuals, in the sense that individuals could not exist even in principle in the absence of social relations, it would not follow that they were prior morally or evaluatively speaking. It is not a general truth that if X is constituted by Y, then Y is the most basic unit from all points of view. Suppose, for example, that a drawing is at one level of description constituted by a set of pencil marks on a piece of paper, characterizable solely in terms of the spatial positions of those marks, and their intensity, sharpness etc. It does not follow that these pencil marks, and the vocabulary used to describe them, are basic from the point of view of aesthetic appraisal. Similarly, even if an individual is constituted by their social relations, it does not follow that those social relations and the language we use to describe them are the most basic unit from an evaluative point of view.

It is hard to motivate collectivist accounts of value by an appeal to intuitions. But it is also hard to refute them, for they need not display any obvious incoherence. In their most plausible variants, however, they do not pose the threat to liberal values that some have feared. Collectivist accounts of the value of community have often been treated with suspicion because they have been associated with intolerance and fanaticism, for example, the view that 'deviants' are like the diseased part of an organism and need to be excised, or the view that a person should always be prepared to sacrifice himself for the community, especially the nation, whenever it is under threat. But a collectivist about the value of commu-

---

[22] See, for example, S. Kripke, *Wittgenstein on Rules and Private Language* (Cambridge, MA: Harvard University Press, 1982). Kripke's account has been much criticized, however, both as an interpretation of Wittgenstein and in its own right. Influenced by Kripke, Philip Pettit has argued that the identity of the rules a person is following is fixed by communal interactions, and that in practice thinking is so constituted that it supervenes on these interactions: see Philip Pettit, *The Common Mind: An Essay on Psychology, Society, and Politics* (Oxford: Oxford University Press, 1993).

nity need not regard a community as analogous to a living organism in which each part plays a necessary role in its functioning, so we have been given no reason to suppose that they cannot take a tolerant attitude towards non-conformists.

Nor are collectivist accounts of the value of community committed to either of two other extreme views: that the value of an individual life is reducible to its contribution to the life of the community; that the part of the value of a community which cannot be reduced to its value for individuals is greater than the value of the life of some individual. Since collectivists about value can reject these views they need not endorse the idea that an individual should sacrifice himself for his community whenever this is necessary to relieve a threat to it.[23] Reasonable collectivists will acknowledge that some of the value of a community consists in its contribution to the lives of individuals, members or non-members. Even if there is a residue of value when we subtract the value a community contributes to the lives of individuals from its overall value, it is not clear why we should suppose that this residue is more important, or should be given greater weight, than the value it provides for individuals.[24] Faced with the demise of a community, it is the suffering and deprivation of individuals in various ways which concerns us, and which is of overriding importance, not the loss of any residue of value which cannot be understood in these terms.[25]

Provided individualists about value acknowledge that there are goods of the kind which Taylor identifies, i.e., goods which are such that part of what makes them goods is that they are enjoyed with others, and provided collectivists about value do not give overwhelming importance to that part of the value of social relations or social phenomena which they claim is not reducible to value for individuals, then not much turns on whether we endorse a collectivist account of the value of community or an individualist one. So I shall remain neutral on the question.

---

[23] It is true that in practice collectivists have thought that the value of a collectivity as such is often so great that it does justify such a sacrifice. And that has sometimes been the point of affirming a collectivist account. But since collectivists are not committed to this view, it is best regarded as a dispute within a collectivist account of value, rather than a dispute between the individualist and collectivist about value.

[24] Roger Crisp reaches a similar conclusion in relation to the idea that the condition of the environment itself, independent of its effects on sentient creatures, is valuable. Even if the environment has independent value of this kind, its value is small when compared to the welfare of sentient creatures: see R. Crisp, 'Values, Reasons and the Environment', in R. Attfield and A. Belsey (eds.), *Philosophy and the Natural Environment* (Cambridge: Cambridge University Press, 1994), pp. 86–7.

[25] See T. Hurka, 'The Justification of National Partiality', in R. McKim and J. McMahan (eds.), *The Morality of Nationalism* (New York: Oxford University Press, 1997), p. 148. Hurka identifies a form of collectivism about value which would allow promoting an irreducibly collective good but not often at the expense of benefits to individuals.

3.   Sources of non-instrumental value

It is clear that community in the moralized sense has non-instrumental value. It necessarily involves relationships of justice (or non-exploitation) and mutual concern, and these features are properly valued for their own sake. But what about community in the ordinary sense? Does it also possess non-instrumental value? One possibility here is that community has non-instrumental value in virtue of the cooperative activity it necessarily involves: community requires, to some degree, a shared way of life, and this is partially constituted by cooperative activity.

Cooperative activity does seem to be valuable for its own sake. The coordination and responsiveness to what others do which are required when people genuinely act together (see Chapter 1, section 2) seem to make cooperation non-instrumentally valuable. If we compare an action performed by a single individual with the very same action performed by a group of individuals acting together, then (other things being equal) the latter seems more valuable in virtue of the cooperation it involves.[26] But it is difficult to sustain the view that cooperative activity is *always* valuable for its own sake.

Suppose that two people cooperate together in order to count the number of blades of grass in a field (perhaps one divides the field into manageable squares whilst the other does the demanding job of counting). It is hard to see why we should regard the cooperation involved as non-instrumentally valuable; cooperation seems to possess such value only when the parties aim at some good. In the case described, the end of the activity is harmless enough (though lacking in value) but there are other cases in which it is morally objectionable. It would seem that it is worse, morally speaking, when a group of individuals cooperate in pursuit of morally objectionable ends than when each individual pursues the same ends on his own, and indeed that it is the cooperation which makes it worse.[27] When (as is alleged) Ian Brady and Myra Hindley acted in concert to trap and kill their victims, the fact that they worked together seems to make what was done even worse. These are, of course, intuitions, and the trouble with intuitions is that they are not always shared, so I do not want to rest anything of great weight on them. But it is hard to see

---

[26] Sometimes an individual acting separately may display independence and self-reliance, which may mean that what he does has greater value than when he cooperates with others as part of a team. But then the *ceteris paribus* clause applies: other things are not equal.

[27] Compare Joseph Raz's discussion of the value of autonomy when it is exercised in pursuit of morally bad ends. He asks whether autonomy in these cases has any value *qua* autonomy and responds that 'our intuitions rebel against such a view. The wrongdoing casts a darker shadow on its perpetrator if it is autonomously done by him. A murderer who was led to his deed by the foreseen inner logic of his autonomously chosen career is morally worse than one who murders because he momentarily succumbs to the prospect of an easy gain' (Raz, *The Morality of Freedom*, p. 380).

how else to argue on this matter except by appeal to intuitions, and then to test them for coherence. Is it coherent, then, to maintain that cooperation has non-instrumental value but only when the activity it facilitates aims at some good, and that community can have non-instrumental value in virtue of such cooperation?

Contrary to appearances perhaps, this idea is coherent. Underlying it would be the view that it is a condition of cooperation being valuable that it should be directed towards some good. On this view cooperation appears to be extrinsically valuable, for it is valuable only on certain conditions.[28] But we should not suppose that just because something is extrinsically valuable, it can only be instrumentally valuable. That would be to confuse non-instrumental value with intrinsic value, something warned against in section 1 of this chapter. It is perfectly coherent to maintain that cooperation has non-instrumental value but only when it is directed at good or unobjectionable ends. And I have claimed that such a position is intuitively plausible.

The fruits of cooperative activities – the various goods which are realized as a result of the coordination of tasks and responsiveness to what others do – may also possess non-instrumental value. Since these products are part of the very fabric of the ways of life which are partially constitutive of communities, they provide community with a further important source of non-instrumental value.

4.   Sources of instrumental value

Many have thought that communities also have considerable value in virtue of meeting a powerful universal need or desire. This is variously specified as a need or desire to belong or feel that one belongs, or a need or desire to be recognized by others,[29] or a need or desire to identify with others or with a group.[30] (For some purposes it may be important to distinguish sharply between these different desires and needs, but in this section I shall treat them together.) Hegel's writings are one of the classic

---

[28] Here again we need to be careful, for it might be argued that cooperation has intrinsic value, even though it is valuable only under certain conditions, on the grounds that when those conditions obtain its value derives from its intrinsic properties: see note 11 above.

[29] The idea that there is a need for recognition of various kinds has been stated forcefully by Axel Honneth in his *The Struggle for Recognition: The Moral Grammar of Social Conflicts* (Cambridge: Polity, 1995).

[30] It is possible to see one or other of these needs as grounded in an even deeper one. For example, the need to belong might be thought to be grounded in a need to express one's selfhood, a need to be accepted by others as one is, or a need to feel at home: see A. Margalit, 'The Moral Psychology of Nationalism', in McKim and McMahan (eds.), *The Morality of Nationalism*, pp. 83–5. Jonathan Glover postulates a deep seated need 'to create something coherent out of ourselves and our own lives' and regards this as the root of our felt need to identify with others: see J. Glover, 'Nations, Identity, and Conflict', in McKim and McMahan (eds.) *The Morality of Nationalism*, pp. 16–19.

sources of the idea that self-conscious beings have a need to be recognized by others. In his view, a person needs recognition from others in order to satisfy their desire for self-worth, and recognition of the appropriate kind must be mutual.[31] Community therefore seems uniquely well suited to meeting this need.

The idea that there is a need or desire of some such kind is often associated with nationalism and reactionary forms of conservatism (in particular those which display a nostalgia for the hierarchical communities many of which were torn apart by industrialization), but it also figures in liberal thought, especially in the light of recent communitarian criticism, and in socialist thought. For example, Joel Feinberg writes that '[t]here does seem to be a natural human need to associate, to belong, to 'identify with', to be accepted, to acquire both memberships and status within a group'.[32] Martin Buber says that man has a need 'to feel his own house as a room in some greater, all-embracing structure in which he is at home, to feel that the other inhabitants of it with whom he lives and works are all acknowledging and confirming his individual existence'.[33] Similarly G. A. Cohen maintains that a 'person . . . needs to know who he is, and how his identity connects him with particular others'.[34]

The value that community possesses in virtue of its ability to satisfy desires or needs of these kinds would appear to be instrumental. The underlying idea seems to be that community is valuable as a means to self-respect or self-esteem, or as a means to being at ease or at home in the world, or as a means to psychological security, or as a remedy for alienation or rootlessness,[35] even if it is not consciously sought or valued as a means to any of these goods. (And even if it were the case that consciously seeking it as a means to these goods might be self-defeating.) Sometimes, though, the recognition which community by its nature provides may be non-instrumentally valuable. For example, when membership of a community depends upon some valuable achievement (rather than, say, the possession of a characteristic such as ethnicity), recognizing another person as a member may be to give due acknowledgement to them for what they have done, and as such that recognition seems valuable for its

[31] See G. W. F. Hegel, *The Phenomenology of Mind*, trans. by J. B. Baillie (London: George Allen and Unwin, 1931), especially pp. 228–40.
[32] Feinberg, *Harmless Wrongdoing*, p. 98.
[33] M. Buber, *Paths in Utopia* (Boston: Beacon Press, 1958), p. 140 (quoted in Taylor, *Community, Anarchy and Liberty*, p. 32).
[34] G. A. Cohen, *History, Labour and Freedom: Themes from Marx* (Oxford: Oxford University Press, 1988), p. 139.
[35] Here we might raise questions about whether these things are always goods or whether they are goods only in certain contexts. If, for example, a racist group enables its members to feel at home in the world is the fact that they feel at home valuable? If not, then the group cannot possess instrumental value in virtue of enabling them to feel at home.

own sake. The value possessed by communities such as these in virtue of providing recognition of this kind, and at the same time satisfying desires or needs to be recognized by others, would also appear to be non-instrumental.

But the thesis that there is a *universal* desire or need to belong, or to be recognized by others, or to identify with others or a group (i.e., a desire or need of one of these kinds that can be properly attributed to all persons at all times and places) is extremely bold, to say the least. Philosophical argument alone cannot establish its truth or falsity, although it can help to clarify what is being claimed. Care undoubtedly has to be taken in specifying the alleged need. It seems highly unlikely that, say, each person has a need to belong, or feel that he belongs, to some particular ethnic group[36] or to the group into which he was born. If there is a need to belong or feel one belongs, it can surely be met by membership of narrower social groups (for example, an extended family), transnational groups (for example, religious communities), or voluntary associations (for example, the international community of scholars),[37] or even by membership of political communities not based upon shared ethnicity.

In support of the claim that there is a universal need to belong or be recognized by others, it is tempting to appeal to the idea that throughout history people have identified with groups, and indeed that alienation has often resulted when they have been unable to do so.[38] But it is uncontroversial that the strength of these identifications varies considerably from one individual to another and is deeply affected by social, political and economic conditions. For example, these identifications seem to be much stronger in the face of various kinds of social disorientation, such as those which arise when familiar social structures disintegrate. It is not enough here to respond that even though the strength of identifications may vary, people possess an unvarying need to belong or be recognized by others, by arguing that when this need is met (as it often is in ordinary circumstances) it may have no observable effect on their motivations or behaviour. For variations in identification are also compatible with the hypothesis that a need of one or both of these kinds exists only for those in particular circumstances or with particular psychological dispositions.

---

[36] This view is often attributed to Herder: see I. Berlin, 'Benjamin Disraeli, Karl Marx and the Search for Identity' in H. Hardy (ed.), *Against the Current* (Oxford: Oxford University Press, 1980), pp. 252, 257 (quoted by J. Waldron, 'Minority Cultures and the Cosmopolitan Alternative', in Kymlicka (ed.) *The Rights of Minority Cultures*, p. 96).

[37] See Waldron, 'Minority Cultures and the Cosmopolitan Alternative', pp. 102, 99–100.

[38] This would be true by definition if alienation were defined simply as lack of identification with others. But it also seems to be true on richer accounts of alienation which hold that an alienated person is estranged from her true nature, or that an alienated person has a sense of meaninglessness.

Variations in identification should also lead us to take seriously an alternative explanation for why in general people identify with groups, viz. that people identify with groups only when and because it benefits them to do so in more specific ways, for example, by giving them access to jobs or to a secure and comfortable environment. In that way, identifying with a group, and indeed membership of a community, might simply be a means to self-protection or self-advancement. Even if this alternative explanation cannot be sustained as a general hypothesis, various hybrids are possible. For instance, it might be proposed that even though (under some circumstances) people need to belong, or feel that they belong, which group they choose to identify with will be influenced by the material or other benefits to be obtained by committing themselves to it and participating in its practices.[39]

Opposing the orthodox interpretation of Marx's analysis of nationalism, Erica Benner argues that he subscribed to some hybrid view: 'Against the one-sided view that a person's collective identities reflect a need to "be defined", Marx's argument maintains that those identities are themselves defined by successive choices'.[40] For Marx, these choices, like all choices, occur in specific historical circumstances, subject to particular constraints. She rejects the idea that Marx's conception of communist society is one in which people identify with humanity as a whole and have no commitments to particular groups, and sees in Marx the different vision of a society in which people's identifications, narrow and wide, are not distorted by ignorance or by coercive or exploitative social relations. A sophisticated hybrid view of this kind will not be refuted by a casual glance at the evidence.

How much difference to our judgement about the value of community does it make which of these various views of the causes of group identification is true? If we put aside the view that self-interest, narrowly conceived, is the main or sole explanation for why people identify with groups, the remaining views will not diverge radically in their implications for the value of community. Each can accept that communities may possess widespread instrumental value in virtue of satisfying desires or needs to belong (or to identify with others, or be recognized by others) and thereby secure goods such as psychological security, self-esteem and feelings of being at home in the world, even if they deny that such needs or desires are universal and unvarying.

---

[39] See Hardin, *One for All*, p. 48.

[40] E. Benner, *Really Existing Nationalisms: A Post-Communist View from Marx and Engels* (Oxford: Oxford University Press, 1995), p. 75.

5.   Community as a necessary condition for the achievement of other values

It might be maintained that community is valuable also because in various ways it is a necessary condition for the achievement of other important values. Consider three possible accounts here:

(i) Community is a necessary condition for the *existence* of individuals, and hence in various ways a necessary condition for the achievement of numerous (perhaps all) other values. As suggested in section 2 of this chapter, it may be that persons can acquire some of the capacities essential to their nature, such as a capacity to reason, only in interaction with others.

(ii) Communities are indispensable for the realization of one particularly important value, viz. an autonomous life, because they are essential for developing in individuals the capacities necessary for autonomy, such as the capacity for reflection.

(iii) Communities are necessary for the realization of various goods.

Some of the resources for defending (iii) might be found in writers who have argued that social forms and practices are important for the realization of a range of goods. For example, Alasdair MacIntyre argues that communities are partially constituted by 'practices', without which various 'internal' goods could not exist: the goods involved in playing chess, for instance, can be realized only through it or some related cooperative activity. Joseph Raz emphasizes the way in which a person's well-being generally depends upon successful realization of her comprehensive goals, that is, goals which significantly structure important aspects of her life. He contends that many comprehensive goals depend for their existence upon social forms.[41] So, for example, one cannot realize the comprehensive goal of being a doctor in a society with no medical practice. In a society without medical practice one might cure diseases, and one might even somehow possess the knowledge which enables one to do so, but that would not make one a doctor.[42]

However, each of (i), (ii) and (iii) as they stand overlooks the important distinction between community and other social relations. Even if social

---

[41] Raz, *The Morality of Freedom*, pp. 307–11.

[42] The idea is presumably that being a doctor requires that others respond to you in a certain way, and that they have certain expectations in relation to how you will respond to them, which could not exist in the absence of a social form, constituted in part by various social conventions. Raz also claims that being a bird watcher requires the existence of a particular social form, but this is much less persuasive, for it does not seem to be other dependent in the same way. See R. Crisp, 'Raz on Well-Being', *Oxford Journal of Legal Studies*, Vol. 17, 1997, pp. 508–12, for relevant discussion.

relations of some sort are a necessary condition of the existence of individuals, this would not show that community – a particular kind of social relation which involves identification with a group and mutual recognition – is essential for their existence. Even if social relations are necessary for the autonomous life, or for the realization of a range of other important goods, this would not show that community in particular is essential for them. Note, however, that community might nevertheless be one of several possible conditions for these things, i.e., be one of a disjunction of conditions necessary for the existence of individuals, or the autonomous life, or personal well-being. We might even say that community *provides* some of the necessary conditions for the realization or achievement of these other values, although it is not itself such a condition.

6.   Sources of disvalue

Any discussion of the value of community would be one-sided if it did not take into account the possibility that community is a source of *dis*value, as indeed some have alleged. In this section I propose to consider three potential sources of this kind: first, that communal relations inevitably suppress or deny individual difference; second, that when a person identifies with a community, she compromises her ability to stand back from that community and assess its practices and way of life; third, that the existence of different communities sets the stage for intercommunal conflict. These complaints are not unrelated. If communal relations inevitably suppress or deny difference, or if identification with a community undermines a person's ability to question its traditions and practices, this may breed intolerance towards the traditions and practices of other communities.

The first charge, that community must deny or repress the differences between people, is made by Iris Young. She argues that community requires mutual identification, or understanding the other as one understands oneself. As such it represents a desire for the fusion of subjects: 'a longing for harmony among persons, for consensus and mutual understanding'.[43] She maintains that in so far as this is possible at all, it is only likely to occur between those who share a culture, history or point of view on the world.[44] So the attempt to satisfy the desire for fusion, by including those from other cultures, or those with other histories or points of view, will inevitably involve denying or repressing their differences.

It is clear, I think, that Young's critique is directed against ideals of

---

[43] I. Young, *Justice and the Politics of Difference* (Princeton, NJ: Princeton University Press, 1990), p. 229.   [44] Young, 'The Ideal of Community', p. 311.

community in the moralized sense.[45] She in effect argues that they are incoherent: in her view it is impossible for communities to be free from exploitation and oppression in the way advocates of the ideal maintain, because they must inevitably repress or deny difference in order to provide the illusion of full mutual identification and understanding. But I do not see how this charge can be sustained. Communal relations in the moralized sense do not need to be face to face or conceived as 'un-mediated', and they do not require complete mutual identification or understanding. A person can be concerned for the well-being of another without being in a face to face relationship, and without identifying with her in the way that Young thinks the ideal of community requires. Members of a community (in either sense I have distinguished) must identify with the group and its practices, but again that falls short of requiring each member to be transparent to the others.

Young might argue that I have missed the point: community must repress difference because it reflects a desire for fusion which can only be satisfied in this way. But why must it reflect such a desire? Those who value community often do so because they want to belong, or because they want or need to be recognized by others. (In section 4 of this chapter, I considered the idea that community has value because by satisfying desires and needs of this kind it supplies individuals with various goods.) Although a person might gain a secure sense of belonging by fusing with other members of a group, such a sense might also be obtained without abandoning one's independence in the way that fusion would require. Recognition by others is not merely compatible with retaining one's independence, but appears to require it. For part of what it is to be recognized by others is to receive acknowledgement of one's own separate existence.

Let us move to the second charge against community: must identifica-tion with a community undermine the possibility of critical reflection upon its practices? The idea that it does might be developed by employing a distinction drawn by G. A. Cohen in describing the dialectic which Marx believes that labour undergoes in the transition from feudal to capitalist society, and will undergo from capitalism to communism. Co-hen's distinction, which ultimately derives from Hegel, is between *engulf-ment in a relationship* and the *freedom of detachment* which a subject experiences as a result of breaking free of an 'object' (for example, her own labour, another person, the environment) to which she is related.[46] A

---

[45] *Ibid.*, p. 320n1.

[46] See G. A. Cohen, 'The Dialectic of Labour in Marx', section 2 in his *History, Labour and Freedom*. Russell Keat explicitly considers the extension of this theoretical framework to conceptions of community in his 'Individualism and Community in Socialist Thought', in J. Mepham and D.-H. Ruben (eds.), *Issues in Marxist Philosophy*, vol. IV (Brighton: Harvester, 1981).

person has the freedom of detachment from an object if she experiences it as distinct from herself and therefore could in principle conceive of it as a constraint on her actions. Complete engulfment in a relationship, in contrast, is the absence of that experience so that a person identifies wholly with an 'object' and as a result could not regard it as a constraint. Applying this distinction, it appears that the freedom of detachment from communal relations is a necessary condition for the possession of a full capacity for critical reflection, for without it a person would be unable to reflect critically upon the community's practices or, at least, its fundamental values when they are at variance with those practices. (There does not seem to be any necessary difficulty in the idea that a person engulfed in some communal relation might reflect critically upon its practices when those practices are in any case at odds with the community's fundamental values.)

But why must full identification with a group involve *permanent* engulfment in it, even if a condition of this sort provides a person with the securest sense of belonging possible? It may be the case that a person cannot *at the same time* critically reflect upon its fundamental values and identify fully with it, but that does not exclude her from intermittently taking up a critical perspective on those values at other times. Matters here can perhaps be further clarified by distinguishing between a dispositional and occurrent sense of identification: a person identifies with a group in the dispositional sense only if she is disposed to endorse its fundamental values (for example, when asked), whereas she identifies with it in the occurrent sense only when she actually does endorse those values. A person can fully identify with a community in the dispositional sense, without always identifying with it in the occurrent sense. We can also allow that the activity of critical reflection necessarily involves some degree of alienation, as Hegel apparently thought.[47] Critical reflection may still have as its outcome full identification: as a result of critical reflection upon a group and its fundamental values a person may come to treat these values as hers and its goals as her goals. In this way she would have overcome 'the moment of alienation internal to reflection *without* abandoning reflection'.[48]

It is not clear that these proposals wholly answer the worry, however. The *securest* form of identification with a community (which is not necessarily its strongest form) seems to occur only when a person is never able to conceive of herself as distinct from it. And it is a serious question whether such a person can *ever* have the freedom of detachment necessary for the

---

[47] See M. O. Hardimon, *Hegel's Social Philosophy: The Project of Reconciliation* (Cambridge: Cambridge University Press, 1994), p. 166.   [48] *Ibid.*, p. 167.

full possession of a capacity for critical reflection. For if a person is so bound up with a community that she cannot conceive of herself as distinct from it, then it seems that it will be impossible for her to hold up its fundamental values to critical scrutiny because she will lack the distance from it that is necessary to do so. I think the correct response here is to admit that there may be particularly secure forms of identification with a community that, even if they have considerable value, are nevertheless also a source of disvalue because they compromise a person's ability to reflect critically. We should not suppose, however, that this is the standard condition of members of a community: a fully committed member may identify with it without that precluding her from reflecting upon its fundamental values.

Let us now move on to consider the third possible source of disvalue of community that I mentioned. Communities (with the possible exception of a global community) set up a distinction between insiders and outsiders. So, it might seem, there will always be some degree of separation or alienation between insiders and outsiders, and hence always a tendency for conflict between them.[49] If there is a deep-seated universal need to belong, or to identify with others, or to be recognized by others, then we apparently have a recipe for disaster on a grand scale, and an explanation for it.

In response it might be denied that it is a conceptual truth that members of different communities will be alienated from one another: alienation is not a logically necessary feature of the relationship between insiders and outsiders, and members of different communities may in principle respect and admire each other. But that does not rule out the possibility that human nature or the human condition is such that different communities will tend to devalue each other or be alienated from each other to at least some extent, or worse still, tend to be at war with one another.[50] This might be put down, in part, to the fact that communities often distinguish themselves by making comparative judgements, by believing that they score better along some dimension than other communities: our community is fairer, more decent, more honest and braver.[51] But radically different communities may tend to devalue each other for even deeper reasons.

---

[49] Roger Scruton, for example, says that the 'real price of community' is 'sanctity, intolerance, exclusion, and a sense that life's meaning depends upon obedience, and also on vigilance against the enemy' (R. Scruton, 'In Defence of the Nation', in *The Philosopher on Dover Beach* (Manchester: Carcanet, 1990), p. 310).

[50] Cf. J. Gray, *Enlightenment's Wake: Politics and Culture at the Close of the Modern Age* (London: Routledge, 1995), pp. 7–8.

[51] See Glover, 'Nations, Identity, and Conflict', pp. 22–3.

Joseph Raz, for example, argues that even though communities founded upon very different ways of life may each be worthwhile because they realize incompatible values, individuals who are part of one way of life will tend to devalue the others because commitment to their way of life will encourage a dismissive attitude towards the (genuine) values contained in the others:

> pluralists can step back from their personal commitments and appreciate in the abstract the value of other ways of life and their attendant virtues. But this acknowledgement co-exists with, and cannot replace, the feelings of rejection and dismissiveness towards what one knows is valuable.[52]

Raz may be right here, but even if there is an inevitable tension between being committed to a way of life which realizes one set of values, and admiring or respecting ways of life which realize different values, the nature of this tension will surely vary. It will be experienced differently by different individuals, and be deeply affected by social and economic conditions. Some may even think better of a way of life that is not their own and regret that, for one reason or another, it is unavailable to them. For them the supposed tension may not arise, for their admiration of this other way of life can undermine the strength of their commitment to their own. A person can also be a participant in more than one way of life, for ways of life may be nested in one another. Under such conditions, the tendency to devalue which Raz claims is inevitable may be relatively insignificant. It may be that it is acute only under adverse conditions, for example, when ways of life are geographically separated from each other, and when the way of life to which one is committed is under threat in some way.

In general, we should be wary of attributing communal conflict solely or even primarily to tendencies in human nature. Individuals may commit themselves to groups and act on behalf of those groups against others largely because they believe that this is the best means of self-advancement, or simply the best response to the specific constraints they face. Indeed in extreme circumstances an individual may believe, not irrationally, that his very survival depends upon committing himself to a group that is likely to emerge the victor in a conflict with another.[53] Under such circumstances the correct explanation of communal conflict may give no role (or only a minor role) to the idea that there is a tendency to devalue ways of life based upon different values to one's own, and appeal instead to the way in which political, social and economic conditions structure

---

[52] Joseph Raz, 'Multiculturalism: a Liberal Perspective' in his *Ethics in the Public Domain* (Oxford: Oxford University Press, 1994), p. 165.
[53] See Hardin, *One for All*, Ch. 6; Glover, 'Nations, Identity, and Conflict', pp. 21–2.

people's choices, lead them to identify with different groups, and set these groups against each other.

7.   Levels and kinds of community

So far I have discussed the value of community in general. But, as I noted in the Introduction, communities can be of different *kinds*. Kinds of communities are distinguished by the nature of the values and ways of life their individual members share, or the criteria for admission to the group. So, for example, religious communities, ethnic communities, educational communities and sporting communities are different kinds of communities.

For my purposes it is also important to distinguish three basic *levels* of community, at which these various kinds of communities may exist in the context of a state system in which there is no overarching sovereign power: communities may exist at the level of the state (i.e., comprising all, or the vast majority, of the state's members, and partially constituted by its major institutions), below the level of the state (i.e., comprising some but not all, or even the vast majority, of the state's members, shaped by its major institutions but not even partly constituted by them) or above the level of the state (i.e., comprising members from a number of different states, and shaped by the major institutions in those states). Within the last category, community at the global level would be the most encompassing, for it would embrace all of humanity. (Recall that when I refer to political community, I mean not a particular kind of community, but rather community at the level of the state, which can be of a number of different kinds. Similarly when I refer to global community, I shall mean community at the global level, i.e., a community above the level of the state which incorporates all of the world's inhabitants and which can be of a number of different kinds.) In principle there may be different kinds of communities at the same level and different levels of communities of the same kind.

There may be special reasons for valuing community of a particular kind, or community at a particular level, or community of a particular kind at a particular level. For example, it might be argued that community at the level of the state is of particular instrumental value because only if citizens are linked by communal bonds of one kind or another are they likely to be willing to make compromises or sacrifices for the common good, or accept the authority of shared institutions. Or it might be argued that cultural communities, in Will Kymlicka's sense, which support a range of practices across different spheres of activity, are especially valuable because in doing so they supply their members with a structure which gives meaning and purpose to their lives and provides them with some of the conditions necessary for personal autonomy.[54]

If special value does attach to community of one particular kind or at one particular level, then this may give reason for favouring that kind or level over others if it comes into conflict with them, in so far as it is in anyone's power to do so.[55] The way in which a cultural community supplies its members with a range of options in which they can find meaning and purpose may provide grounds for protecting it against threats posed by the existence of other kinds of communities at different levels which unintentionally undermine the conditions required for it to survive or flourish.[56]

The hardest cases, however, arise when there are special reasons to value two different levels or kinds of community which are in conflict with one another. For example, the existence of diverse cultural communities below the level of the state can make it hard to realize community at the level of the state. For liberal nationalists, this sort of conflict is especially acute, for they have argued that community at the level of the state is essential for realizing the values which liberals cherish, but that it is possible in practice only if citizens share a national identity. The existence of diverse cultural communities within a state would appear to compromise the state's ability to forge or sustain the sense of belonging together amongst its citizens which is required for them to share a national identity. If the liberal nationalist is right, should the state aim to foster a shared national identity and if so, at what cost? For example, would the values supposedly served by a shared national identity be sufficient to justify restrictions on individual liberty of the kinds which might be required by a policy of assimilation?

Against the idea of fostering community at the level of the state it might be argued that this would be likely to undermine the possibility of global community, understood as an ideal which is informed by liberal principles. If citizens identify strongly with the polity or nation to which they belong, will this not undermine the possibility of a global community of

---

[54] See Kymlicka, *Liberalism, Community and Culture*, especially ch. 8, and *Multicultural Citizenship: A Liberal Theory of Minority Rights* (Oxford: Oxford University Press, 1995), ch. 5.

[55] Of course, there may also be independent reasons – i.e., reasons independent of the value of different kinds of community at different levels – for resolving a conflict one way or another. In Chapter 7, for example, I consider various arguments in favour of the principle of non-intervention, which constitutes one way of resolving conflicts between community at the global level and at the level of the state. These arguments appeal not just to the importance of respect for political community, but also to the consequences of allowing a practice of humanitarian intervention.

[56] See Kymlicka, *Liberalism, Community and Culture*, ch. 9 and *Multicultural Citizenship*, ch. 6.

this kind? Since global community, so understood, represents an ideal in the moralized sense, and because it is more encompassing (it simply contains more just relations), it might be thought that it should be granted overriding importance.

But there are competing considerations which favour the idea that community at the level of the state should take priority over the promotion of some liberal ideal of community at the global level when the two conflict. Many have implied, for different reasons, that conflicts between political community and ideals of global community should be resolved in favour of the former, because they have defended a principle of non-intervention. The importance of respect for communal autonomy, and the difficulties and dangers of humanitarian intervention, have led them to suppose that self-defence is the only legitimate reason for intervening in the affairs of sovereign political communities.

These questions about different levels and kinds of community, and their importance in relation to one another, set the agenda for Parts 2 and 3. In Part 2, I consider the question of what kind of political community, if any, should be fostered or promoted by the state, and what limits, if any, should be placed on communities (in the ordinary sense) below the level of the state. In Part 3, I explore various aspects of the relationship between political community (in the ordinary sense) and global community, understood as an ideal in the moralized sense informed by liberal principles.

Part 2

Political community in a culturally diverse society

3   Liberal political community and illiberal minorities

What kind of community, if any, is valuable at the level of the state and what steps may the state legitimately take to promote or preserve it?[1] In answering this question, liberal theorists have developed a vision of political community which they believe could be realized without unjustifiably restricting the liberty of citizens because it would be founded upon a conception of justice that was acceptable to all. I shall lay out this ideal, before piecing together the most promising correlative account of how conflicts should be resolved when they arise between it and communities (in the ordinary sense) below the level of the state. In the two subsequent chapters, I shall take a more critical look at the liberal vision itself.

1.   Liberal political community

Some liberals appear to reject the idea that political community can be achieved, or even legitimately pursued, in a society marked by pluralism. John Rawls, for example, says that the hope of political community must be abandoned 'if by such a community we mean a political society united in affirming the same comprehensive doctrine. This possibility is excluded by the fact of reasonable pluralism together with the rejection of the oppressive use of state power to overcome it.'[2] In Rawls's view, if political community involves convergence on some particular 'comprehensive doctrine', then it cannot be sustained without oppression in any society which displays 'reasonable pluralism'. But community, as I have characterized it, does not require its members to converge on what Rawls calls a comprehensive doctrine. It requires them to share values to some significant degree, but as Rawls himself maintains, that is possible even if they do not subscribe to the same comprehensive doctrine. (According to

[1] Parts of this chapter are drawn from my 'Imposing Liberal Principles', in R. Bellamy and M. Hollis (eds.), *Pluralism and Liberal Neutrality* (London: Frank Cass, 1999).
[2] Rawls, *Political Liberalism*, p. 146, see also pp. 37, 40, 42.

Rawls, citizens may share a particular conception of justice even though they endorse different comprehensive doctrines.) In the sense I intend, Rawls does advance a conception of political community, expressed, for instance, in his view of a well-ordered democratic society as a social union of social unions.[3]

The idea at the heart of most liberal conceptions of political community, including Rawls's, is that the major institutions of society should be based upon a conception of justice which is acceptable to each citizen. This idea of public justifiability (in its many different versions) supplies liberals with an account of political legitimacy,[4] and also provides the basis for a conception of political community.[5] According to this conception, persons are members of a political community if as a result of the exercise of reason they come to endorse the conception of justice which underlies their major institutions, identify with those institutions because they endorse that conception, and acknowledge each other as members.[6] Members of such a community will also share a common purpose (and constitute a collective in the sense described in Chapter 1, section 2) to the extent that they each have a commitment to sustaining those institutions together, and the realization of this goal will necessarily require cooperation of various kinds. So understood, political community appears to possess considerable non-instrumental value: the institutions which are partially constitutive of it are transparent in a way which seems to embody a fundamental kind of respect for persons, and the cooperation involved in sustaining them is also valuable for its own sake.[7]

---

[3] See Rawls, *A Theory of Justice*, p. 527. According to Rawls, a well-ordered society is a social union because its members have shared final ends – they are committed to sustaining their just institutions – and regard these institutions as non-instrumentally valuable.

[4] See, for example, J. Waldron, 'Theoretical Foundations of Liberalism', in his *Liberal Rights: Collected Papers 1981–1991* (Cambridge: Cambridge University Press, 1993), pp. 44–6; C. Larmore, 'Political Liberalism', *Political Theory*, vol. 18, 1990, p. 349; S. Macedo, *Liberal Virtues: Citizenship, Virtue, and Community in Liberal Constitutionalism* (Oxford: Oxford University Press, 1990), p. 78; G. Gaus, *Justificatory Liberalism: An Essay on Epistemology and Political Theory* (Oxford: Oxford University Press, 1996), pp. 1–2.

[5] The link between the liberal conception of political legitimacy and the liberal conception of political community is not always made explicitly. But it is made by J. Donald Moon in his *Constructing Community: Moral Pluralism and Tragic Conflicts* (Princeton, NJ: Princeton University Press, 1993), see esp. pp. 8, 12.

[6] There are liberals who regard public justifiability as a misguided or inappropriate political ideal because they suppose that any principles of justice can be reasonably rejected: see, e.g., R. Rorty, 'The Contingency of a Liberal Community' in his *Contingency, Irony, and Solidarity* (Cambridge: Cambridge University Press, 1989). But this ideal nevertheless underlies the *dominant* liberal conception of political community.

[7] According to some versions of the dominant liberal conception of political community, the members of such a community realize irreducibly social goods (in Charles Taylor's sense explained in Chapter 2, section 2) which invest it with another kind of non-instrumental value. For example, Daniel Brudney argues that in *A Theory of Justice* Rawls supposes that members of a well-ordered society realize a good which involves 'the reciprocal recognition

But a commitment to the public justifiability of institutions does not by itself distinguish the dominant liberal conception of political community from others, for some non-liberal conceptions are also committed to that ideal. Marx, for example, envisaged communism as a transparent society that would be justifiable to all, for he thought that those living in it would no longer suffer the illusions to which capitalist society gives rise, but he appeared to think that it would have no role for individual rights. What distinguishes the dominant liberal conception from Marxian conceptions is its commitment to a liberal account of justice, i.e., one which endorses the kind of individual rights described in the Introduction, which it deems to be justifiable to all citizens.

The notion of public justifiability is vague and ambiguous, however. It can be given different interpretations depending on how the notion of 'being justifiable to all' is spelt out, and these interpretations will generate correspondingly different conceptions of political community.[8] Would a principle be justifiable to all even if people had different reasons for endorsing it? Could a principle be justifiable to all even if in practice some could never be brought to accept it because they lacked the necessary skills to appreciate the arguments in favour of it? Is a principle justifiable to all simply if it is reasonable for each to accept it, or does it require the apparently more demanding idea that it must be impossible for any of them reasonably to reject it? Can a principle be reasonably rejected by a person simply on the grounds that he will do less well under it than under some alternative principle? Does a principle need to be justifiable to every potential person, or is it enough for it to be justifiable to all the actual citizens of a polity? I shall not address all these questions, but instead focus on one particularly important contrast which emerges from different answers to some of them, and which generates what might be called contractarian and contractualist variants of the dominant liberal conception of political community.[9]

Contractarians begin from the idea of prospective future citizens as a group of rational deliberators seeking to reach agreement on principles to

... of one another as contributors to the maintenance of just institutions and as beings for whom moral personality (including a willingness to apply and to act from principles of justice) is the fundamental aspect of self' (Brudney, 'Community and Completion', pp. 403–4). As Brudney points out, however, Rawls later abandons parts of this vision in order to fulfil the ambitions of political liberalism.

[8] For an examination of the different interpretations of the notion of public justification, see F. D'Agostino, *Free Public Reason: Making It Up As We Go* (Oxford: Oxford University Press, 1996), especially pp. 30–3, and Ch. 4.

[9] The distinction between these two positions is well drawn by David Gauthier, 'Political Contractarianism', in P. Koller and K. Puhl (eds.), *Proceedings of the 19th International Wittgenstein Symposium 1996: Current Issues in Political Philosophy* (Vienna: Holder-Pichler-Tempsky, 1997), pp. 22–3.

govern their society. These deliberators are concerned to further their own conception of the good (whatever it may be). Guided solely by their conception of their own advantage, they seek rules to govern the social arrangements in which they will participate.[10] Contractualists have a different starting point. They suppose that citizens are motivated by a non-instrumental desire to be able to justify to one another the principles which are to govern their arrangements, rather than merely a desire to advance their own interests. In effect they conceive of citizens as lying in an antecedent moral relationship to one another, with a non-instrumental commitment to mutual justifiability, and to that extent genuinely concerned for each other's interests.[11]

The conceptions of political community generated by contractarianism and contractualism have similarities but also some crucial differences. According to both conceptions, the citizens in a political community endorse the conception of justice which underlies their social and political arrangements. Given their contrasting accounts of what it is for a principle to be just, however, contractarian and contractualist approaches are unlikely to converge on the same conception of justice. On the best contractualist account, mutual justifiability is seen as constitutive of just principles,[12] whereas on the best contractarian account, being to everyone's advantage is seen as constitutive of those principles. A principle may be to a person's advantage in the sense that he is better off when everyone abides by it than he would be in the absence of any agreement on principles to govern their interactions, but nevertheless it would be hard for others to justify to him the adoption of that principle if he would be much better off, and others not much worse off, under the operation of some alternative principle. So it seems likely that contractarian and contractualist accounts will diverge in relation to the issue of which principles of justice should govern major institutions.

The differences between contractarian and contractualist accounts run deep. The contractarian conception ultimately expresses a version of the ordinary notion of community[13], for it does not presuppose the existence

[10] David Gauthier and Jan Narveson are prominent contractarians. See D. Gauthier, *Morals by Agreement* (Oxford: Oxford University Press, 1986); J. Narveson, *The Libertarian Idea* (Philadelphia, PA: Temple University Press, 1988).

[11] Political contractualism derives from the work of Thomas Scanlon in moral theory: see his influential 'Contractualism and Utilitarianism' in A. Sen and B. Williams (eds.), *Utilitarianism and Beyond* (Cambridge: Cambridge University Press, 1982). Within political theory, Scanlon's approach has been most fully developed by Thomas Nagel in *Equality and Partiality*, and Brian Barry in *Justice as Impartiality*.

[12] See S. Caney, 'Impartiality and Liberal Neutrality', *Utilitas*, vol. 8, 1996, pp. 280–1.

[13] There may be doubts about whether what I am calling the contractarian conception of political community is a conception of *community* at all. At one level, it does appear to bear a sufficiently strong resemblance to the ordinary conception described in Chapter 1 to

of mutual concern between citizens, even though it requires justice (as contractarians conceive it) to obtain between them.[14] According to the contractarian conception, citizens who are part of a political community endorse the conception of justice that governs their arrangements because it embodies principles which are to their own advantage, but they need not have any non-instrumental concern for each other.[15] The contractualist conception of political community, in contrast, is a version of the moralized notion, for it embodies the further requirement of mutual concern. According to the contractualist conception, members of a political community are mutually concerned because they attach non-instrumental value to being in a position to justify to one another the principles which underlie their social arrangements.

2.   Political community in relation to communities below the level of the state

Liberal conceptions of political community, whether they be contractarian or contractualist, require some account of the conditions required for realizing or sustaining it. In the wake of communitarian criticism, many liberals have accepted that these conditions may be demanding. William Galston, for example, maintains that a number of virtues are required to sustain liberal institutions, ranging from general virtues such as courage, law-abidingness and loyalty, to more particular virtues, such as those needed to sustain liberal politics.[16] A robust account of the conditions

---

count as one. When citizens accept the evaluative principles which underlie society's major institutions, identify with these institutions as a result, participate in a form of life structured by them, and recognize each other as participants, then they seem to constitute a community in the ordinary sense. But according to the purest form of contractarianism, it is not just that the parties lack genuine mutual concern. They attribute only instrumental value to each other, and it is unclear whether this could ever be sufficient for full mutual recognition. The kind of recognition it could provide would not be sufficiently robust to meet the sort of need to be recognized by others that many communitarians have alleged to exist (see Chapter 2, section 3).

14 Some would argue that we cannot conclude from the fact that a principle is to everyone's advantage that it is a principle of justice (see Barry, *Justice as Impartiality*, pp. 39–46). So it *may* be possible to show that the contractarian conception of political community does not embody an account of justice at all.

15 Contractarians of course allow that each person may, as part of their own conception of the good, have a non-instrumental concern for their fellow citizens.

16 W. Galston, *Liberal Purposes: Goods, Virtues, and Diversity in the Liberal State* (Cambridge: Cambridge University Press, 1991), ch. 10. See also Macedo, *Liberal Virtues*, ch. 7. Rawls believes that in order for a political community to be stable and enduring individuals must have a capacity for a sense of justice, which requires them to be capable of various political virtues, which are defined simply as those virtues 'necessary for them to cooperate in maintaining a just political society' (Rawls, *Political Liberalism*, pp. xlvi-xlvii). These include 'the virtues of toleration and being ready to meet others halfway, and the virtue of reasonableness and the sense of fairness' (*Political Liberalism*, p. 157, see also pp. 163, 141).

necessary for political community does, however, create the possibility of what I call 'extrinsic conflict' with communities (in the ordinary sense) below the level of the state.

Extrinsic conflict in my sense can be of different kinds. It occurs whenever a community or its current way of life has the causal effect of undermining the existence *or* current way of life of another community, or whenever promoting or protecting a community or its current way of life has that effect.[17] As a potential example of one of these kinds of extrinsic conflict, suppose that a liberal political community cannot flourish unless citizens possess the capacity to evaluate a range of different principles in the light of their impact upon different groups within the state. This requires an ability for critical reflection that in practice may be impossible to restrict within the confines of politics, and may have a corrosive effect on those ways of life which cannot survive unless their members display a relatively uncritical commitment to traditional norms and practices. Here the very existence of the community, not merely the preservation of its current character, may be at issue. In the face of such a threat, communities below the level of the state may seek exemption from those forms of civic education which aim (at least in part) to foster the traits which endanger their very survival. They accuse liberals who would make these forms of civic education compulsory of cultural imperialism, that is, of seeking to impose their culturally specific principles and values whilst claiming falsely that these principles are universally valid.

In their defence liberals cannot in good faith claim that the erosion of these communities is *simply* a by-product, or unintended consequence, of the working of liberal institutions, as they do when certain other kinds of extrinsic conflict occur, for example, when liberal institutions unintentionally foster traits – a competitive form of individualism, perhaps – which are antithetical to the values which are constitutive of some community below the level of the state. In this kind of case liberals have been able to acknowledge, and even express genuine regret, that valuable communities can be eroded as an unintentional consequence of the operation of liberal institutions. But when liberals argue that the state should play an active role in fostering the very traits that are incompatible with the survival of some communities below the level of the state, they can hardly plead that the erosion of these communities is simply a by-product of the working of liberal institutions.

---

[17] I do not of course deny that one community may have the causal effect of undermining the current character of another community without threatening its very survival: my account of 'extrinsic conflict' presupposes a distinction between the existence of a community of a particular kind and the preservation of its current character, even though in some cases that distinction may not be sharp.

The charge against liberals of cultural imperialism arises in an even more acute form in the light of some *intrinsic* conflicts between political community and communities (in the ordinary sense) below the level of the state. Like extrinsic conflicts, what I call 'intrinsic conflicts' can be of very different kinds. Intrinsic conflict occurs whenever the very existence of a community, *or* the preservation of its current character, is by its very nature impossible in the presence of some other community, or the maintenance of its current character. One of these kinds of intrinsic conflict occurs when communities below the level of the state organize themselves according to principles which are unacceptable to some of their members and force compliance with those principles, thereby destroying (by its very nature) political community as liberals conceive it, but maintaining the character of their own communities. In the most serious cases, these communities violate what liberals regard as basic rights. Liberalism, in its most strident and tough-minded form, holds that any practice which violates such rights is intolerable: it maintains that these intrinsic conflicts between political community and communities (in the ordinary sense) below the level of the state should be resolved by forcing the latter to respect the basic rights of their members.

Liberals have often met the charge of cultural imperialism head-on by trying to show that the principles of justice they favour cannot reasonably be rejected, or at least that even if they are not universally valid they nevertheless cannot reasonably be rejected by those who start from ideas which are common currency in the public culture of Western democratic regimes. (Indeed most believe that if these principles could reasonably be rejected, then there would be no justification for imposing them.[18]) I have considerable doubts about the possibility of showing that any particular conception of justice, or even any set of liberal principles more abstractly conceived, can meet such a high standard of justification, but I shall not pursue the point here, for it threatens the dominant liberal conception of political community itself. Instead I shall explore the resources within liberalism for developing an indirect reply that might prove to be less inflammatory. In doing so, I shall construct what I take to be the best account available to liberals of how intrinsic conflict between political community and communities (in the ordinary sense) below the level of the state should be resolved. (It can in principle be extended to give an

---

[18] There are exceptions to this generalization. John Gray, for example, agrees that by forcing non-liberal communities to respect liberal principles, a state would be imposing those principles without being able to provide a justification for doing so that those communities could not reasonably reject, but argues that nevertheless 'a liberal state cannot be neutral with regard to illiberal forms of life within its jurisdiction'. See Gray, *Enlightenment's Wake*, p. 142.

account of how various extrinsic conflicts should be resolved, although I shall not do so.)

The reply I develop focuses not on the issue of whether the principles of justice which liberals favour are universally valid, but on the question of to what extent and in what way liberalism can properly be said to be seeking to *impose* its principles on others. In particular, I shall examine the scope that the dominant form of liberalism can allow for cultural groups to be involved in the process of defining the basic rights, and investigate the circumstances in which liberals of this kind can consistently support forbearance when a community is violating what they regard as the basic rights of its members.

3.   Basic rights

Liberals believe that there is a set of rights which are basic in the sense that they deserve robust protection, such as that afforded by entrenching them in a constitution. Liberals are primarily concerned with preventing these rights from being violated by the state, so constitutions are designed mainly to draw limits to the legitimate use of state power. But they have also regarded constitutions as providing a way of preventing citizens from violating each other's rights.

The dominant form of liberalism regards basic rights as justifiable to all citizens; institutions which embody and protect them pass the test of public justifiability and form the basis of political community. Unfortunately there is disagreement amongst liberals over exactly which rights are basic in the relevant sense. Some defend an extensive set which includes rights to a variety of freedoms: political liberty, freedom of conscience and religious practice; freedom to engage in consensual sexual relationships; freedom of association; freedom of speech; freedom of the person; freedom from arbitrary arrest and seizure.[19] Others, however, favour a much more limited set, for instance one that is exhausted by a right to freedom of association and a right against cruel, inhuman or degrading treatment.

This disagreement is of considerable significance for debates over the limits of toleration and for the charge of cultural imperialism; if the limits of toleration are drawn by reference to the set of basic rights, then they will appear in different places depending on the extensiveness of the set, making liberalism more or less vulnerable to the charge of cultural imperialism. The extent to which political community comes into conflict with communities (in the ordinary sense) below the level of the state will also depend upon what rights, and which particular interpretations of them,

---

[19] Most of these are included in Rawls's list of basic liberties. See Rawls, *A Theory of Justice*, p. 61.

are deemed to be justifiable to all, for political community as liberals conceive it is partly constituted by living amongst institutions that are founded upon a conception of justice that is publicly justifiable.

Chandran Kukathas, for example, defends as basic only the right of freedom of association – including the right of exit from a community which he thinks it implies[20] – and a right against cruel, inhuman or degrading treatment. He argues that provided a community respects these two rights, it should be allowed to determine its affairs in any way it chooses which is within its power. Demanding more from it is akin to cultural imperialism. So, for example, a community should be allowed to restrict freedom of worship or discriminate against women. Allowing communities to be self-governing within the limits set by a right to freedom of association and a right against cruel or inhuman treatment will permit them to behave unjustly towards their members, although a community will not be entitled to expect the wider society to enforce these injustices when it is not in the community's power to do so itself.[21]

Although Kukathas's form of liberalism appears to be less susceptible to the charge of cultural imperialism, it is unstable. Why should the right of free association take priority over the prevention of various injustices which communities may inflict upon their members? It can not be that preventing these other injustices would involve imposing liberal principles upon communities whereas merely insisting on a right of free association does not, for *both* do. Illiberal communities may reject the idea that there should be freedom of association (and the freedom of exit which Kukathas thinks is implied by it), just as they reject the idea that, say, there should be freedom of worship. Nor can it be that injustice should be permitted if people voluntarily embrace it, for Kukathas thinks

[20] See C. Kukathas, 'Are There Any Cultural Rights?', *Political Theory*, vol. 20, 1992, pp. 117, 128. It is not clear that Kukathas is right in thinking that freedom of association necessarily implies freedom of exit.

[21] Kukathas, 'Are There Any Cultural Rights?', pp. 132–3. Kukathas does sometimes suggest that remaining within a community which restricts, say, freedom of worship or freedom of speech when one is free to leave amounts to *waiving* one's right to those freedoms. For example, he suggests that a member of a Muslim community has 'to choose between being part of that community and retaining his right of free speech' (Kukathas, 'Are There Any Cultural Rights?,' p. 127). If members of communities which allow freedom of exit waive their right to freedom of speech, then no injustice would be done when some of them are prevented from saying things that are frowned upon within that community. In his reply to Kymlicka, however, Kukathas reaffirms the idea that communities which restrict those freedoms are committing injustice. See C. Kukathas, 'Cultural Rights Again: A Rejoinder to Kymlicka', *Political Theory*, vol. 20, 1992, p. 678. For a view with some important similarities to Kukathas's, see J. Narveson, 'Collective Rights?', *Canadian Journal of Law and Jurisprudence*, vol. 4, 1991, pp. 342–3. Kukathas's argument is really just a refinement of an old one: the idea that provided individuals consent to the arrangements under which they live, then these arrangements are legitimate.

that some injustices are intolerable even if they are voluntarily embraced, i.e., cruel and inhuman treatment.

Kukathas's justification for giving priority to freedom of exit seems to be based on the idea that in assessing the political arrangements of a society we should be concerned with the flourishing of its individual members, but should take seriously those individuals' own judgements about whether their lives are going well. Consequently 'what matters most when assessing whether a way of life is legitimate is whether the individuals taking part in it are prepared to acquiesce in it'.[22] But that is a questionable inference. Kukathas allows that people may possess freedom of exit from a community even if the costs and risks of leaving are high.[23] Under such circumstances the fact that people are prepared to acquiesce in a way of life will not be a good measure of its conduciveness to their flourishing, even by their own standards.

Those who think that a right of exit is the only basic right have to conceive that right as a demanding one if they are to defend it in the way that Kukathas does. Otherwise it will simply be invalid to conclude that an arrangement is conducive to the flourishing of the individuals living in it from the fact that they do not leave despite possessing the freedom to do so. Suppose that a person could be said to possess freedom of exit from a community even when they have inadequate information about other communities, or even when they have insufficient ability to assess the alternatives when deciding whether to stay or leave,[24] or even when it would be grossly unreasonable for them to take the risk of leaving. We could not then justifiably conclude from their failure to 'take advantage' of their freedom that the arrangements under which they currently live are conducive to their flourishing.

Once freedom of exit is conceived in robust terms, however, it may be that in practice it is sometimes impossible to secure; in some cases the risks and costs of leaving a community will always be so high that we cannot say that its members are free to leave. This is most likely to be the case when people are born into a community (rather than join it voluntarily) and then grow up acquiring a distinctive culture and outlook on the world.[25] In such cases the best way to promote the flourishing of all of its

[22] Kukathas, 'Are There Any Cultural Rights?', p. 124.
[23] Kukathas does not regard the mere possibility of leaving a community as sufficient for genuine freedom of exit from it (see *ibid.*, p. 134), but nevertheless thinks that this freedom can exist even when the costs of exit are high (see Kukathas, 'Cultural Rights Again', p. 677).
[24] See W. Kymlicka, 'The Rights of Minority Cultures: Reply to Kukathas', *Political Theory*, vol. 20, 1992, p. 143.
[25] See L. Green, 'Internal Minorities and their Rights', in W. Kymlicka (ed.), *The Rights of Minority Cultures* (Oxford: Oxford University Press, 1995), pp. 266–7.

individual members, as they conceive it, may be to ensure that dissenters from its traditions at least possess various other freedoms such as freedom of expression and freedom of religion.

It may also be the case that the best way in practice of protecting a robust right of exit *is* to protect a variety of other rights. So even if a right of exit were foundational to liberalism because all other genuine rights could be derived from it, it would not follow that it was the only basic right *in the relevant sense*. For a right is basic in the relevant sense if it can be shown that it deserves robust protection. If it is possible to show that some freedom deserves such protection because in a variety of circumstances it offers the best means of ensuring a basic right of exit, then it will follow that there is a basic right to that freedom. It is not implausible to suppose that a case of this kind can be made for a range of freedoms. If a right of exit were the only right which was given robust protection, there would be grave problems in determining whether a person really enjoyed that right. When other freedoms are protected, such as freedom of expression, freedom of religious worship and freedom of sexual relationships, we can be more confident that a person also possesses genuine freedom of exit; they are better able to make an adequate choice, i.e., one which is better informed about possible ways of life in which they might flourish outside the community and about the real risks of leaving it.

These reasons do not provide a conclusive argument against liberals who think that the set of basic rights is pretty much restricted to a right of exit. I suspect that this issue cannot be treated in a wholly satisfactory manner without delving more deeply into the question of how these rights are to be justified. Since that would take me too far afield, I am going to assume that my arguments provide sufficient support for the view that most of the rights in the extensive set I listed at the beginning of this section deserve constitutional protection, or something similar, and hence are basic in that sense. (When I refer to 'liberal principles' it is principles which protect these basic rights, on some reasonable interpretation of what these rights involve, which I have in mind.) This does have the merit of offering the largest target to those who accuse liberalism of cultural imperialism.

4. Varieties of constitutionalism

In drawing the limits of toleration in practice, and resolving intrinsic conflict between political community and communities below the level of the state, liberals think that an important role is played by constitutional structures. Constitutions can serve a number of different purposes, however. Liberals have focused upon the important role they can play in controlling the abuse of power by providing mechanisms to ensure good government and protecting individual rights. But in the context of a culturally plural society, constitutions should also provide a framework which enables diverse social groups to live together.[26] This creates potentially important practical difficulties for liberalism. In a society where some groups are committed to practices which violate what liberals take to be basic rights, is it possible to produce a constitutional settlement which protects these rights but will also be regarded as acceptable by those groups? Indeed this raises more than just practical difficulties for liberalism. It provides a focus for the charge of cultural imperialism, for it will be maintained that in setting up constitutions to protect individual rights, liberals are simply imposing their ideals on groups who do not share them.[27] In this section, I shall explore some possible ways of responding to this form of the charge.

The idea that in order to design a just constitution, we need first to identify a set of rights which deserve robust protection, is challenged by those who believe that a just constitution is simply a freely negotiated settlement between different cultural groups and their members. James Tully, for example, argues that any constitution which emerges from a process of just mediation and negotiation, in accordance with the conventions of mutual recognition, consent and cultural continuity, is itself just.[28] The idea that a just constitution is simply a freely negotiated settlement between different groups and their members suggests a distinction between a procedural conception of a just constitution, which defines a just constitution as the outcome of a specified procedure – a procedure that is actual not merely hypothetical – and a non-procedural conception, which defines a just constitution as one which protects certain rights which can be given a justification which is independent of the outcome of any actual procedure.

Liberalism in its dominant form seems to be committed to a non-procedural conception of a just constitution, as does the dominant liberal conception of political community. And one might think that the only way of avoiding the charge of cultural imperialism is to move to a purely procedural conception; unless a just constitution is simply a freely negotiated settlement between different groups, it will involve imposing ideals

---

[26] See J. Tully, *Strange Multiplicity: Constitutionalism in an Age of Diversity* (Cambridge: Cambridge University Press, 1995); R. Goodin, 'Designing Constitutions: the Political Constitution of a Mixed Commonwealth', *Political Studies*, vol. 44, 1996, p. 635.

[27] See, for example, Kukathas, 'Are There Any Cultural Rights?', esp. pp. 120–4; S. Mendus, *Toleration and the Limits of Liberalism* (Basingstoke: Macmillan, 1989), pp. 103–8; B. Parekh, 'Decolonizing Liberalism', in A. Shtromas (ed.), *The End of 'Isms'? Reflections on the Fate of Ideological Politics after Communism's Collapse* (Oxford: Blackwell, 1994).   [28] See Tully, *Strange Multiplicity*, esp. pp. 30, 209.

on those who do not share them. I think this appearance is misleading, however. It is not clear that pure procedural conceptions of this kind are coherent. But impure procedural conceptions may be just as vulnerable to the charge of cultural imperialism, and some non-procedural conceptions may be less vulnerable to it than they appear.

First, any stable conception of a just constitution will be committed to the idea that there are, in effect, various rights which can be given a justification that is independent of the outcome of actual procedures. Any purely procedural conception will be unstable, for it will be unable to acknowledge the existence of various constraints, respect for which is a condition for the effective operation of the procedures, or for the realization of the values which the procedures are supposed to embody. When, for example, the procedure is supposed to facilitate a freely negotiated settlement, these constraints may include a right of freedom of expression as well as individual and collective rights of participation, representation guarantees, rights to veto and the like. (Some defenders of the ideal of deliberative democracy will go even further. Joshua Cohen, for example, thinks that the entire set of basic liberties, not just freedom of expression, can be justified as preconditions for the effective realization of that ideal.[29]) Since impure procedural conceptions of this kind endorse a set of rights (or something similar) which are independent of the outcome of procedures, they are potentially vulnerable to the charge of cultural imperialism, for not every cultural group is guaranteed to share a commitment to that set.

Consider in this light Tully's conception of a just constitution as that which emerges from a process of just mediation and negotiation conducted in accordance with the conventions of mutual recognition, consent; and cultural continuity. When he draws out the implications of this conception, it becomes clear that the crucial convention is that of consent: not only communities, but dissident individuals within them, must consent to the arrangements under which they live.[30] But in order to be in a position to refuse consent, individuals must be able to speak out against any proposed constitutional settlement, so they must at least possess freedom of expression. If consent is to stand a chance of being genuine, they must also possess freedom of exit from the communities to which they belong. Tully therefore seems committed to the idea that a just

[29] See J. Cohen, 'Deliberation and Democratic Legitimacy', in A. Hamlin and P. Pettit (eds.), *The Good Polity: Normative Analysis of the State* (Oxford: Blackwell, 1989), pp. 28–30, and note 22.

[30] See Tully, *Strange Multiplicity*, pp. 165–82. The convention of cultural continuity seems to become redundant since the convention of consent allows cultures to choose to abandon their traditional ways; it is consent to any settlement that is fundamental to his account, not cultural continuity.

constitution must protect at least freedom of expression and freedom of exit from each community, otherwise any settlement which is reached could not be said to be consensual for their individual members. Since it is likely that some communities will deny that there are such rights, imposing them will invite the charge of cultural imperialism from those minded to make it.

Second, we should not suppose that non-procedural conceptions have no important role for dialogue. (If that were so, it would be harder for them to avoid the charge that they favour simply imposing ideals on those who reject them and amount to forms of cultural imperialism.[31]) They can maintain that dialogue between members of different groups is crucial for understanding each other's practices, and therefore is a precondition of any adequate view of how these practices affect the rights of their participants. As we shall see in the final section of this chapter, practices which are sometimes thought to violate what liberals regard as basic rights, for example arranged marriages, may not do so. The outcome of such a dialogue is likely to be some mutual adjustment, perhaps with the result that the specifications of the rights become refined, and practices in both the dominant community and minority communities are modified in the light of these refinements.

Liberal defenders of non-procedural conceptions (let me refer to them from now on simply as 'non-proceduralists') can also give a more fundamental role to political dialogue. They can maintain that even though the justification of a set of basic rights might in principle proceed independently of any actual political process, in practice, when there is disagreement over which set of rights receives the best justification, political dialogue can play an important role in providing the legitimate *authority* to select one disputed set over another.[32] The fact that some set of rights emerges from a dialogue to which all are able to contribute can be seen as at least part of a sufficient condition for the state's possessing the legitimate authority to impose it.[33] Non-proceduralists need to distinguish

---

[31] See *ibid.*, pp. 183, 191–2.

[32] See J. Waldron, 'A Right-Based Critique of Constitutional Rights', *Oxford Journal of Legal Studies*, vol. 13, 1993, esp. pp. 31–4; R. Bellamy, 'The Constitution of Europe: Rights or Democracy?', in R. Bellamy, V. Bufacchi and D. Castiglione (eds.), *Democracy and Constitutional Culture in the Union of Europe* (London: Lothian Foundation Press, 1995), especially p. 161.

[33] I leave the notion of an inclusive political dialogue deliberately vague, but it is intended to resonate with ideals of deliberative democracy. See Cohen, 'Deliberation and Democratic Legitimacy'; A. Gutmann and D. Thompson, *Democracy and Disagreement* (Cambridge, MA: Harvard University Press, 1996). In *Republicanism: A Theory of Freedom and Government* (Oxford: Oxford University Press, 1997), Philip Pettit defends a model of deliberative democracy which is intended to be both inclusive and responsive: see pp. 185–205.

between the question of which set of rights receives the best independent justification (if there is any particular set that does) and the question of which set of rights should be adopted in the face of disagreement over which receives the best justification. Even if the set of rights yielded by an inclusive dialogue is not the set of rights which receives the best independent justification, that dialogue might play an important role in providing the legitimate authority to adopt it. (Some non-proceduralists will allow that there may be a plurality of sets of rights, none of which can properly be said to receive the best independent justification. In that case an inclusive dialogue can be seen by them as providing the authority to adopt one particular set in preference to the others, despite there being no independent justification for doing so. But this kind of non-proceduralism is hard to reconcile with the dominant liberal conception of political community, for the latter requires convergence on a particular conception of justice through the exercise of reason.)

Some non-proceduralists will insist that the fact a set of rights emerges from an inclusive political dialogue is not, on its own, sufficient to provide the state with the legitimate authority to impose that set of rights. They may argue that when the set of rights which emerges from a political process permits or requires serious injustice, then the state has no legitimate authority to impose it.[34] Suppose, for example, that an inclusive political dialogue endorses the idea that the family of a woman who sleeps with a man before marriage is entitled to kill her in order to salvage its honour. The non-proceduralist will maintain that this outcome is seriously unjust when judged by independent standards, and may also conclude that the state has no legitimate authority to enforce it. (This would not involve denying the obvious point that these 'independent standards' are precisely what is in dispute in such cases, though it would require acknowledging that the state's legitimate authority to impose a set of rights may itself be a matter of dispute.) Of course the non-proceduralist who takes this line would be vulnerable again to the charge of cultural imperialism. They will either have to concede the charge but shrug it off as inconsequential, or meet it head-on by arguing that no one can reasonably reject the relevant independent standards.

But taken together, the points I have made about the importance of dialogue and the political process show that non-proceduralism (which I am regarding as the dominant form of liberalism, and as presupposed by the dominant liberal conception of political community) can and should allow that there is a role for constitutional politics, i.e., for the citizen body to devise, interpret and amend the constitution, as opposed to a role

---

[34] See Gutmann and Thompson, *Democracy and Disagreement*, p. 30.

solely for constitutional interpretation by judges.[35] Liberal constitutionalism is not without some resources to rebut the charge that it is a form of cultural imperialism, simply in favour of imposing its principles. It is able to emphasize the important role which an inclusive political dialogue can play in authorizing the adoption of a set of basic rights, even when that set of rights is not the best (and even when the dialogue does not lead to a full consensus on it).

5. The primacy of justice and its implications

The arguments of the previous section show that non-proceduralists need to keep two questions apart: first, the question of what account of basic rights is correct or best, judged by independent standards; second, the question of what account of basic rights should, in the end, be adopted by a state. They should not simply assume that the answer to the second question is given by the answer to the first, for an adequate answer to the second question must take into account the political process.

There is also a further distinction that cuts across the first that proceduralists need to draw: between the question of what account of the basic rights is the best when judged by independent standards, and the question of whether it should be imposed by the state.[36] Sometimes the consequences of imposing that account would be so dire that there is strong reason to show forbearance. This possibility might seem to be excluded by the idea that justice has primacy; since violations of basic rights are seriously unjust, and justice is the most important political value or consideration, they should never be permitted. But any plausible formulation of the primacy of justice must allow that there are occasions on which injustice should be permitted because eradicating it would make matters worse.

---

[35] Admittedly this goes against the dominant liberal position on these matters: see D. Miller, 'Citizenship and Pluralism', *Political Studies*, vol. 43, 1995, p. 449. But as Waldron shows, there is nothing anti-liberal in objecting to the idea that the role of interpreting and (in effect) amending the constitution should be restricted to judges: see Waldron, 'A Right-Based Critique of Constitutional Rights'.

[36] Kymlicka draws a related distinction between the correct liberal theory of toleration and its limits and the issue of whether it should be imposed on those who do not accept it. See W. Kymlicka, 'Two Models of Pluralism and Tolerance', *Analyse und Kritik*, vol. 13, 1992, pp. 51–2; *Multicultural Citizenship*, p. 164. I think the distinction is better framed in terms of a contrast between the best account of the basic rights and when they should be imposed. After all, the correct liberal theory of toleration should surely include an account of the conditions under which basic rights may be legitimately imposed, unless it is argued that in refraining from imposing basic rights the state is displaying mere forbearance rather than toleration, and hence an account of the conditions under which the state should refrain from imposing basic rights does not, strictly speaking, fall under the theory of toleration.

Consider, for example, John Rawls's relatively careful statement of the primacy of justice at the beginning of *A Theory of Justice*:

Justice is the first virtue of social institutions, as truth is of systems of thought. A theory however elegant and economical must be rejected or revised if it is untrue; likewise laws and institutions no matter how efficient and well-arranged must be reformed or abolished if they are unjust . . . The only thing that permits us to acquiesce in an erroneous theory is the lack of a better one; analogously, an injustice is tolerable only when it is necessary to avoid an even greater injustice.[37]

Implied by these claims is the idea that unjust laws and institutions should be reformed or abolished unless to do so would lead to even greater injustice. This suggests that Rawls would allow minorities to violate the basic rights of their members when, but only when, greater injustice would result (or be extremely likely to result) from forcing them to respect those rights.

Under what circumstances might more injustice result from the enforcement of basic rights? According to the account of justice that Rawls goes on to develop, greater injustice would result only if greater violations of basic rights would occur. So Rawls would deny that increased welfare in the group or in society as a whole, or even benefits to the worst off in either, are sufficient on their own to warrant allowing rights violations to occur.

The main type of case that Rawls seems to have in mind is when grave public disorder would result from the enforcement of basic rights. But it is not obvious that this is the only circumstance in which greater injustice might result from enforcement. There are also cases where the enforcement of basic rights would be likely to lead to the disintegration of a community. In some of these cases, it is at least possible to develop an argument for forbearance, on the grounds that members of the community which disintegrated would suffer grave disadvantages through no fault of their own, and that this would constitute an injustice which could be of sufficient magnitude to outweigh the violations of basic rights which are occurring in it. Indeed this style of argument figures as part of Will Kymlicka's case for granting cultural communities group-differentiated rights in some circumstances, to protect them from threats posed by the wider society.[38] These cases may be much less common than Kymlicka supposes, however. It is not always the case that a person's flourishing is dependent upon a single cultural structure which gives meaning to their lives.[39] The disintegration of a particular culture may not always have

---

[37] Rawls, *A Theory of Justice*, pp. 3–4. Rawls concedes that this view of the priority of justice may be too strong.   [38] See Kymlicka, *Liberalism, Community and Culture*, chs. 8–9.
[39] See Waldron, 'Minority Cultures and the Cosmopolitan Alternative'.

disastrous effects on the well-being of those who grew up in it, for they may be inhabitants of more than one culture (signified, for example, by the use of a hyphen to describe their identity) or be able to find meaning outside of it.

Rawls contends that an injustice should be permitted only if greater injustice would result from trying to eradicate it, but he acknowledges that his claims about the primacy of justice may over-state the case. I think they do. Greater forbearance should sometimes be shown to rights violations when the costs of forcibly eradicating them in terms of misery and suffering, or the alienation of a minority group, would be great, and other measures short of coercion (for example, the use of taxation, subsidy, incentives, dialogue or education), could reasonably be expected to be successful in ending these violations in the longer term. It is implausible to suppose that justice is always so important that it should be achieved now, even if it could be achieved at much less cost to other values at some later date. So minorities should sometimes be permitted to violate the rights of their members when preventing them from doing so would cause great misery and suffering or alienate them irrevocably from the wider society, and other measures stood a good chance of changing their practices over a longer period of time. The case for pursuing non-coercive measures is strongest in two sets of circumstances. First, when the group concerned allows its members freedom of exit, even if only in a formal sense. Second, when a significant proportion of the moral cost of preventing a minority group from violating the rights of its members would be borne by those who are the victims rather than the perpetrators of those rights violations.

The proposals I have described leave relatively open the question of when the costs of forcing others to respect basic rights would justify using non-coercive measures, and leave open the question of under what circumstances greater injustice would be created by forcibly preventing a rights violation from occurring than by allowing it to happen. These matters are best deliberated about in particular contexts.

What I have argued so far may seem commonsense. But there are, in principle at least, positions on the prevention of rights violations which stand opposed to it. The tough-minded liberal who believes that the state should never permit practices which violate (what he regards as) basic rights is largely a fictional character, but he holds a position for which there is conceptual space – that the prevention of rights violations or injustices is an absolute goal in the sense that the state should never *allow* an injustice or rights violation to occur if they can prevent it, even if by preventing it other injustices or rights violations would occur which could not be prevented.⁴⁰ In other words, when there is an intrinsic conflict between political community and communities below the level of the state, this should always be resolved by forcing the latter to respect the basic rights of their members. This tough-minded approach is hard to sustain, however. It may be reasonable to suppose that the state should never commit an injustice in order to prevent an injustice, but it is hard to see why the state should always be required to prevent an injustice whatever costs in terms of justice would result from doing so. There is not, for instance, a difference of act and omission here which could count in the right way. Nor would it be reasonable to maintain that we can *never* know (or have good reason to think) that allowing violations of basic rights will create less injustice overall. These judgements are difficult but not always impossible to make. Liberalism should show greater forbearance than the uncompromising approach advocated by the tough-minded liberal, and for that reason is less vulnerable to the charge of cultural imperialism.

Convictions about the primacy of justice should not, however, lead us to discard the conclusion reached in the previous section, concerning the state's authority to impose one set of rights rather than another in the face of disagreement about which set is the best. The non-proceduralist can allow that it is sometimes justified to enforce a set of rights which there is good reason to think is not the best because it emerges from some political process which provides, at least in part, the authority to impose it. So too, in judging whether enforcing basic rights would lead to greater injustice, or an unacceptable sacrifice of other values, the non-proceduralist can allow that we should employ the set of rights which emerges from such a process even if it is not the best.

6.   The authority of the state and national minorities

Will Kymlicka maintains that there are other reasons why the state should sometimes show forbearance when rights are being violated. He argues that Rawls and other liberals have ignored an important distinction between national minorities and ethnic groups, and that national minorities should be given greater licence.

Kymlicka defines a nation as 'a historical community, more or less institutionally complete, occupying a given territory or homeland, sharing

---

⁴⁰ Kymlicka remains agnostic on the question of whether we should treat rights violations as side constraints in *Liberalism, Community, and Culture*, pp. 198–9. The position that Kymlicka develops in *Multicultural Citizenship*, ch. 8, is inconsistent with treating rights violations as side-constraints, however.

a distinct language and culture'.[41] Ethnic groups, in contrast, are formed by relatively recent immigrants who, although they come from nations, participate in the public institutions of the society they have joined, and do not occupy a homeland. Kymlicka argues that just as one state should not in general attempt to impose liberal principles on another, so too a state should not in general impose liberal principles on national minorities.[42] Even if national minorities unambiguously violate liberal principles, they should be allowed to do so, provided that this does not take the form of 'gross and systematic violation of human rights'.[43] With ethnic groups, however, there is a strong case for imposing liberal principles, unless they were originally granted exemptions from the usual arrangements regarding integration, since in general they voluntarily emigrated to countries which they knew were governed by liberal principles.[44]

In effect, Kymlicka thinks that when there are intrinsic conflicts between political community and a community below the level of the state, how these conflicts should be resolved will depend on the nature of the latter, in particular whether in his terms it is a nation or an ethnic group. Broadly speaking, if it is an ethnic group, the conflict should be resolved in favour of the wider political community, whereas if it is a nation, the conflict should instead be resolved in its favour. If Kymlicka were right, liberalism would have reason for showing forbearance towards the illiberal practices of national minorities, and in that way could provide at least a partial response to those who accuse it of cultural imperialism. Some, however, have thought that his position demands greater respect for state sovereignty than can be justified.[45] Are there really principled reasons for not intervening to prevent states from visiting injustices on their members, or merely 'pragmatic' or other moral reasons for non-intervention, which relate to the difficulties of intervening successfully and to the risk that intervention may make matters worse?[46]

The issue here seems to be essentially about who has the legitimate authority to impose liberal principles on a group of people. Kymlicka appears to think that one state does not (in general) possess the legitimate authority to impose those principles on another and, by analogy, that states do not possess the legitimate authority to impose them on national minorities within their borders. This argument is hard to evaluate in the absence of a developed theory of the state's authority. Consider, however,

[41] Kymlicka, *Multicultural Citizenship*, p. 11.   [42] *Ibid.*, pp. 165–7.
[43] *Ibid.*, p. 169.   [44] *Ibid.*, p. 170.
[45] See B. Barry, 'Review of W. Kymlicka, *Multicultural Citizenship*', *Ethics*, vol. 107, 1996, pp. 154–5; 'Statism and Nationalism: A Cosmopolitan Critique', In I. Shapiro and L. Brilmayer (eds.), *NOMOS*, vol. 41, *Global Justice* (New York: New York University Press, 1999).   [46] These questions will be addressed in more depth in Chapter 7.

the following, which stands in need of considerable refinement, but which might seem to be along the right lines: the state possesses legitimate authority over someone, in relation to some sphere of behaviour, if and only if it enables her to achieve her own ends better than she would otherwise be able to do, for example by facilitating mutually beneficial cooperation.[47] A theory of this kind could allow that the state may lack legitimate authority over some of its citizens, in some sphere, when it would be possible in practice to establish an alternative authority which would be more beneficial to them, by their own lights, in that sphere.[48] (This will rarely be possible, however, for in most circumstances members of a polity would disagree over what authority would serve them better, and so would not be able to achieve the coordination necessary to establish a different one.) The implications of such a theory for the question of whether the state has the legitimate authority to impose liberal principles on a national minority are not entirely clear, but they do not seem to support Kymlicka's position.

Suppose we take the boundaries of the state as fixed. The theory described seems to imply that, unless it is possible for members of a national minority to establish an alternative or reformed authority within these boundaries which would be more beneficial to them, the state has the legitimate authority to impose liberal principles on them. In some cases it may be possible for a national minority to secure the cooperation of other citizens necessary to divide the powers of the existing authority in order to create a federal structure which allowed them to live by non-liberal principles. But in many cases that will not be a genuine possibility, and then the state will possess the legitimate authority to impose liberal principles on them. In other words, the theory provides no *principled* reason to allow national minorities to live by non-liberal principles. (It can of course accept that secession is justified in some circumstances. But that will not provide support for Kymlicka's position, for he needs a

---

[47] An account of roughly this kind can be found in a number of writers. See especially C. McMahon, *Authority and Democracy: A General Theory of Government and Management* (Princeton, NJ: Princeton University Press, 1994), pp. 44–45, 102–23. McMahon's analysis of legitimate authority draws heavily upon Joseph Raz's work. Raz defends the idea that 'the main argument for the legitimacy of any authority is that in subjecting himself to it a person is more likely to act successfully for the reasons which apply to him than if he does not subject himself to its authority' (see Raz, *The Morality of Freedom*, p. 71). Raz's account allows that the state's legitimate authority may derive in part from enabling an individual to comply with moral obligations he is under even when such compliance does not benefit him (see Chapter 7, section 5, for an important consequence of this idea). For a critique of this general approach to legitimate authority, see L. Green, *The Authority of the State* (Oxford: Oxford University Press, 1990), ch. 4.

[48] McMahon, *Authority and Democracy*, pp. 128–9, 151.

theory of legitimate authority which implies that the state cannot legitimately impose liberal principles on those *within* its jurisdiction.)

The fact that the theory of authority I have described produces this result might make some suspicious of it, and encourage them to look for a more communitarian account. An account of this kind might hold that the state can only possess legitimate authority over those for whom it is a vehicle of self-determination, in particular those whose identity it expresses and protects. But it is unclear whether such an account could in principle place national minorities in a significantly different position to what Kymlicka calls ethnic groups. Either the state is a vehicle for the self-determination of all its citizens or for just some of them. If the latter, then the excluded group may in principle be a national minority or an ethnic group. In response, however, it might be argued that in practice national minorities are differently situated to the dominant community, and in a way that makes a difference, from a communitarian perspective, to the state's authority over them.

According to Kymlicka's account, a national minority, unlike an ethnic group, possesses what he calls a 'societal culture', i.e., 'a culture which provides its members with meaningful ways of life across the full range of human activities, including social, educational, religious, recreational and economic life, encompassing both public and private spheres'.[49] If the state is a vehicle for the self-determination of the dominant community within its borders, then it may not be so for national minorities living there. Ethnic groups, in contrast, do not have their own public institutions and members of them can only participate in the public institutions of the society they have joined. The state therefore can become a vehicle for their self-determination simply by being a vehicle for the self-determination of the dominant community. But this reply seems to ignore the way in which ethnic groups may to some extent create their own societal cultures even if initially they simply participated in the public institutions of the dominant community.[50]

Kymlicka might argue instead that ethnic groups have consented to the imposition of liberal principles by emigrating to a state which is governed

---

[49] Kymlicka, *Multicultural Citizenship*, p. 76.

[50] As Spinner points out, however, the cultural structures immigrants succeed in creating are likely to be significantly different from those they left behind, and much less secure. Indeed he suggests that in the absence of serious discrimination or prejudice, these structures are likely to wither away relatively quickly. See J. Spinner, *The Boundaries of Citizenship: Race, Ethnicity and Nationality in the Liberal State* (Baltimore: Johns Hopkins University Press, 1994), pp. 65–6, 173–6. There may, however, be reasons other than prejudice which help sustain the cultural structures immigrants create: for example, immigrants may have a desire to show the relatives they have left behind that they have preserved their traditions.

by these principles, and this is part of what gives the state the legitimate authority to impose them. But this draws attention to the questionable significance of the distinction that Kymlicka draws between ethnic minorities and national minorities in terms of the voluntariness or otherwise of their membership of the state. Even if the original members of ethnic groups did to some degree choose to leave their countries of origin, their current members will often be the children or grandchildren of those original immigrants and hence non-voluntary members of the polity.[51] Therefore, even if their ancestors did not secure exemptions at the point of entry from the usual requirements of integration, their position does not seem to be relevantly different in this respect from national minorities.[52]

So a communitarian account might be able to justify the idea that the state lacks the authority to impose liberal principles on national minorities but only at the expense of making it hard to see how the state can possess the authority to impose liberal principles on established ethnic groups. This is at odds with Kymlicka's position, but it may be a price that some would be willing to pay. They would need good reason, however, to endorse the communitarian constraint on legitimate authority (viz. that a state can only possess legitimate authority over those for whom it is a vehicle for self-determination) in preference to other possible accounts of how that authority is attained. It is hard to see how they could justify that constraint in preference to some alternative theory, such as the one I described, which grounds the state's legitimate authority largely on its ability to secure mutually beneficial cooperation among its citizens.

The position I have been defending need not deny the importance of communal self-determination. It can accept that communal self-determination has considerable value, at least for those communities which possess what Kymlicka calls a societal culture, for self-determination may in various ways enhance the well-being of their members by providing them with a means to express their collective identity and protect their practices.[53] The value of communal self-determination may in some cases justify allowing national minorities to secede. In other cases, it may justify

---

[51] See my review of *Multicultural Citizenship*, in *The Philosophical Quarterly*, vol. 47, 1997, pp. 250–3.

[52] Kymlicka does to some extent acknowledge the complexities here, but in my view does not properly incorporate them into his theory: see *Multicultural Citizenship*, p. 170.

[53] I do not deny that communal self-determination may have some value which cannot be reduced to the value that it has for individual members of the community. But as I suggested in Chapter 2, even if it does possess that value, it is implausible to suppose that this is its most important source of value.

some degree of forbearance when it comes to the imposition of basic rights. Let me explain.

Liberal principles, and the basic rights which they express, can surely be given different reasonable interpretations. Let us say that an interpretation of a principle *cannot* be reasonably rejected if it is the case that anyone who accepts the principle is necessarily committed to that interpretation in virtue of the beliefs they actually hold, and those beliefs and norms of inference they must accept on pain of absurdity or unintelligibility.[54] So an interpretation of a principle can be reasonably rejected if it is possible for someone to accept the principle but not be committed to that interpretation, even when we take into account those beliefs and norms she must accept on pain of absurdity or unintelligibility. What counts as a reasonable interpretation can, of course, also be a matter of reasonable dispute. When there is a range of interpretations of a principle that are reasonable, it does not follow that they are equally good, for there may still be a best interpretation which the balance of reasons supports. Given the importance of communal self-determination, liberals should allow minorities to govern themselves according to the interpretations (from amongst those which are reasonable) which they prefer. This would provide liberals with a further response, albeit partial, to the charge of cultural imperialism. In practice, judgements about which interpretations of a right are reasonable are best left to an inclusive political process. Here again there is a role for the form of constitutional politics I described earlier in which the citizen body, or their representatives, interpret the rights protected by the constitution and draw limits to what will count as a reasonable interpretation of them.

What about cases of intra-communal conflict? When different members of a cultural community come into conflict over their basic rights in particular situations, or over whether they have any, how should this conflict be resolved? In practice the authority to adopt one interpretation of the basic rights, like the authority to adopt one set rather than another, may derive in part from its being the outcome of an inclusive political dialogue. The citizen body (or their representatives) can be conceived by non-proceduralists as an umpire whose decisions bind even when it fails to select what, judged by independent standards, is the best interpretation.[55]

In the next section I shall illustrate how these last proposals might have practical significance by looking at a number of cases which have been a matter of public concern in liberal democracies such as Britain.

[54] This formulation is influenced by Gaus, *Justificatory Liberalism*, ch. 3.
[55] See *ibid.*, pp. 188–9.

7.   Some cases: clitoridectomy, circumcision, and arranged marriages[56]

Some practices are condemned by liberal principles whatever reasonable interpretation is given to these principles. The practice of so-called 'female circumcision' below the age of consent is generally thought to fall into this category, although it is not entirely obvious on what grounds.[57] One approach would be to see it as a violation of a right to personal freedom (on any reasonable interpretation of that right). If there is a right to personal freedom, then it seems that it must minimally imply that there are some things which should not be done to a person without her consent, and this will mean that they should not be done to children who are below the age of consent since they can not consent. Falling into this category will be various actions which carry with them a high risk of disabling injury and which are not required for good medical reasons[58] and clitoridectomy would seem to be of this kind.

There are two problems with such an argument, however. First, even though it is true that the practice of clitoridectomy as it is conducted in most parts of the world carries with it a very high risk of disabling injury because of the conditions under which it is done, it could in principle be carried out (under anaesthetic) by medically qualified individuals in hygienic conditions, without the same kind of effects. Second, there are more or less radical forms of clitoridectomy: even if the radical forms are always likely to have seriously adverse effects on girls' and women's health, it is not clear that the more 'moderate' forms, in which only the hood of the clitoris is removed, need have such effects.

Liberals who think that there is no reasonable interpretation of liberal principles which would permit any form of clitoridectomy have a number of potential lines of argument available to them. They might argue that clitoridectomy, even in its 'moderate' form, is part of a pattern of social relations which subordinates women and thereby violates their rights on any reasonable interpretation. But this response is going to be hard to make out in the required form, for it will have to rest on some

---

[56] The choice of cases is indebted to Sebastian Poulter's, *English Law and Ethnic Minority Customs* (London: Butterworths, 1986), which provides an invaluable discussion of the way in which English law has attempted to accommodate cultural diversity. Bhikhu Parekh discusses the same cases and reaches similar conclusions but using a different approach: see B. Parekh, 'Minority Practices and Principles of Toleration', *International Migration Review*, vol. 30, 1996, pp. 266–83.

[57] For some questions about the role of discussions of clitoridectomy in the literature on multiculturalism, see Y. Tamir, 'Hands off Clitoridectomy: What Our Revulsion Reveals About Ourselves', *Boston Review*, vol. 21, Summer 1996.

[58] Here liberals require some notion of injury, narrowly conceived, which is independent of any particular conception of the good and common to different cultural communities.

empirical account of the structure of women's subordination in cultures where this practice occurs, and the role of clitoridectomy in them, which may be open to reasonable rejection. Liberals who want to outlaw circumcision need some account which shows that clitoridectomy (below the age of consent, at least[59]) violates the rights of girls even when considered in isolation.

In my view the best approach here is one which holds that the right to personal freedom, on any reasonable interpretation, requires that a child not be subject to treatment which would deprive her of the possibility of pursuing what she might reasonably come to regard as an important good. Clitoridectomy might be held to violate this right since it denies girls the possibility of kinds of sexual experience they might come to value. Even if it were the case that the 'moderate' form, in which only the hood of the clitoris is removed, need not have this effect, it might nevertheless be argued that a ban on all forms of clitoridectomy is required to prevent the more radical forms from taking place.[60]

The fact that the best arguments support the idea that protecting the girl's right to freedom of the person, on any reasonable interpretation, requires a ban on clitoridectomy below the age of consent does not by itself show that it should be banned in practice. We need to bear in mind the distinction, required by the non-proceduralist, between the question of what (if any) is the best account of the basic rights, and the question of when that account should be adopted by a state. Could an inclusive political dialogue provide the state with the authority to adopt a different solution which permits some forms of clitoridectomy below the age of consent? The decisions which emerge from a process of political dialogue can be so unjust in the light of independent arguments that they may lack the authority which they would otherwise have possessed. The authority of a decision does not seem to depend solely on the process from which it emerged (see section 4 of this chapter). Arguably clitoridectomy is so unjust that no state has the authority to permit it, even if such a policy were to emerge from an inclusive political dialogue.

Some versions of the right to personal freedom will rule out any violation of a person's bodily integrity without their consent, unless it is required for good medical reasons, and hence will rule out not only clitoridectomy but also the circumcision of boys. Other reasonable interpretations are available of the right to personal freedom, however, which permit circumcision of boys and even ritual scarification to be performed on a child, provided that there is no significant danger to the health of the

---

[59] Liberal principles can be given a reasonable interpretation which permits consensual clitoridectomy, however: cf. Poulter, *English Law and Ethnic Minority Customs*, p. 291.
[60] *Ibid.*, p. 159

child, and it would not deprive the child of the possibility of pursuing what he or she might reasonably come to regard as an important good. On the principles I have outlined, cultural communities should be allowed to interpret the right to personal freedom in such a way that it permits these practices (where what counts for practical purposes as a reasonable interpretation is to be determined by the citizen body or its representatives). But if the wishes of parents as the custodians of their children come into conflict with those of the cultural community to which they belong, then the best interpretation of the right to personal freedom should prevail, again, as judged by the citizen body or its representatives.

Consider now the practice of arranged marriage. Is this a violation of the basic rights of those who participate in it? Liberal principles are unambiguously opposed to coerced marriages. But arranged marriages often differ only in degree from marriages which are decided by prospective spouses and it would be a mistake simply to suppose that they are coerced. In some forms of arranged marriage the parties concerned have a veto over the proposed arrangements, and then clearly no coercion need be involved.[61] Liberal principles do not unambiguously stand opposed to arranged marriages of this kind – these marriages may not give individuals maximum autonomy or maximum choice over life partners, and perhaps might not even involve the giving of 'full and free consent' in some sense, but they are not coerced. When one or both of the parties is not consulted about the match, and they have no veto, then there is a danger of coercion. But that danger is not by itself sufficient to justify the conclusion that all arranged marriages should be outlawed, so long as in practice it is possible to provide some degree of protection for those who run the risk of being coerced. For then there are still reasonable interpretations of liberal principles which permit the practice.

There is scope for reasonable disagreement over what counts as being coerced into an arranged marriage, which makes room for some such disagreement about what kind of protection should be provided against the risk of coercion in them. Credible threats of death are clearly cases of coercion, as sometimes is the threat that one will be turned out of one's home, but what about the threat of ostracism, or the accusation that one will betray one's community by refusing to marry the partner who has been chosen? Here there does seem to be room for reasonable disagreement over the kind of pressure which would count as duress. Even if an accusation of disloyalty would clearly be too weak to count, the threat of ostracism is harder to evaluate.

In some cases when the threat of ostracism is made, a person may be

---

[61] *Ibid.*, pp. 23–4.

faced with a stark choice between complying with the wishes of her parents or being excluded from the practices which give her life meaning, including perhaps forsaking the opportunity to practise her religion. These are plausibly represented as cases of coercion, and indeed there may be no reasonable interpretation of the right to personal freedom which would permit a marriage entered under such circumstances to bind the parties to it. In other cases, however, the costs of being ostracized might be much less severe, such that on some reasonable understanding of 'duress' the threat of ostracism would not count as such. According to the principle I have outlined, if members of a cultural community come into conflict over what rights they have, and whether they are sufficient to show that their marriage was coerced and should be declared void, then the interpretation which the citizen body, or its representatives, judges to be best should prevail. If that interpretation rules out as coerced a marriage in which one or both of the partners have been threatened with ostracism unless they comply, then if one of the parties seeks to have the marriage declared void on such grounds, their wishes should be granted, and those who made the threats should be liable to prosecution.[62]

8.   Conclusion

According to the dominant liberal conception of political community, citizens form such a community if through the exercise of reason they endorse the conception of justice which underlies their major institutions, identify with those institutions as a result, and acknowledge each other as members. (The dominant liberal conception is also non-procedural, in the sense that it assumes there are standards, independent of any actual political process, to be used in determining which conception of justice is the best.)

Political community can come into conflict with the existence, or maintenance of the current way of life, of communities (in the ordinary sense) below the level of the state in a variety of ways. I have tried to provide non-proceduralists with the best available account of how intrinsic conflicts of this kind should be resolved, in light of the charge that they are guilty of cultural imperialism. In response to that charge non-proceduralists can point to the role which they can give to a form of constitutional politics in which all are entitled to engage, and which can provide the authority to adopt one set of rights rather than another in the face of

---

[62] In the case of *Hirani* vs. *Hirani* in England, the Court of Appeal ruled that a nineteen-year-old Hindu girl was subject to duress when she married because she had been threatened with eviction from the family home if she refused to proceed with the wedding: see Poulter, *English Law and Ethnic Minority Customs*, pp. 29–30.

disagreement about which is best. They can point to the way in which they can justify refraining from imposing their principles where that would create greater injustice, or when the costs of doing so would be great. And they can also point to the scope which they can allow for communities to govern themselves in accordance with those interpretations of liberal principles which best suit their practices. When political community, as non-proceduralists conceive it, comes into intrinsic conflict with communities below the level of the state, they are not always committed to resolving that conflict by forcing those communities to respect the basic rights of their members.

So far I have taken for granted the dominant liberal conception of political community. In Chapter 4 I move on to consider a direct challenge to it, at least in its moralized version.

4   Republican political community

The dominant liberal conception of political community can be probed in a variety of ways.[1] In this chapter I shall focus on what I call the republican challenge, which maintains it is insufficiently demanding. Republicans, in my sense, argue for an ideal of political community which requires the citizens of a polity to be united in some substantial way by the good of citizenship.[2] To fulfil this republican ideal of political community, it would not be enough for the members of a polity to recognize each other as fellow citizens and identify with their common institutions as a result of endorsing the same principles of justice. For in its most powerful version, the republican challenge maintains that a fully-fledged ideal of political community requires citizens to acknowledge and act upon special obligations to one another that are independent of justice (at least as liberalism, in its dominant form, conceives of justice). I shall examine the nature of this republican challenge and some potential liberal responses to it. I do not assume that republicanism, as I construe it, is inconsistent with liberalism in my broad sense (see Introduction). Indeed it is part of the purpose of this chapter to argue that it is not.

1.   The good of citizenship

Republicans suppose that members of a fully-fledged political community must be united in some substantial way by the good of citizenship. But what is citizenship and in what does the good of citizenship consist?

In answering this question, it is important to keep in mind two distinctions. First, there is the three-fold distinction, introduced in Chapter 2, between having instrumental value, non-instrumental value, and being a

---

[1] The bulk of this chapter is based on my 'Special Obligations to Compatriots', *Ethics*, vol. 107, 1997.

[2] This should be understood as a stipulation. The way I employ 'republicanism' bears some resemblance to conventional usage, but is not entirely coextensive with it. On my account, the republican conception of political community differs from the dominant liberal conception in terms of the role it gives to the good of citizenship rather than, say, in terms of its understanding of freedom.

necessary condition of realizing something of value. If citizenship is a good, is it that because it is instrumentally valuable, non-instrumentally valuable or a necessary condition of realizing something of value, or some combination of the three? Second, the good of citizenship needs to be distinguished from the ideal of being a good citizen. Any adequate account of citizenship must distinguish between the status, rights, opportunities, obligations or responsibilities which define what it is to be a citizen, and which make citizenship valuable, and being a good citizen, which may, for example, be described in terms of fulfilling the responsibilities and obligations of citizenship.[3] (Later in the chapter I shall argue that the fulfilment of the special obligations which are part of the nature of citizenship also contribute to the good of citizenship. But that link cannot simply be assumed.)

Most political theorists regard citizenship as a necessary condition of realizing various things of value. Citizenship appears to be a necessary condition of secure individual liberty because it provides various protections against interference. On some accounts which construe liberty in a positive rather than negative fashion, citizenship is a crucial condition of individual liberty in another way because it provides various welfare rights which are enabling.[4] But republicans, in my sense, would not be satisfied with any account of citizenship which supposed that its value was *exhausted* by the general way in which it secures liberty. They would want to insist that a considerable part of the value of citizenship lies in the entitlements and opportunities it provides for political participation. (This need not involve claiming that citizenship is non-instrumentally valuable, but it at least points towards a further way in which it might be thought to provide a necessary condition for something valuable.)

If citizenship is valuable in part because it secures a necessary condition for political participation, we are owed some account of why political participation is itself valuable. Here as well there is a range of possibilities. On some accounts, political participation will be regarded merely as a means to some further good, for example, the protection of free institu-

---

[3] This distinction is often overlooked. For example, David Miller appears to ignore it in his 'Citizenship and Pluralism': see, for example, pp. 437, 443–4, 448. Richard Dagger also seems to ignore it when he moves effortlessly from the idea that true citizenship 'entails a duty to work with one's fellow citizens to promote the public good' to the idea that true citizens 'will take an active part in public life': see his *Civic Virtues: Rights, Citizenship, and Republican Liberalism* (Oxford: Oxford University Press, 1997), pp. 99–100.

[4] The classic account here is T. H. Marshall, 'Citizenship and Social Class', in his *Class, Citizenship and Social Development* (New York, 1964). For a recent development of this kind of approach, see R. Plant, 'Citizenship and Rights', in R. Plant and N. Barry, *Citizenship and Rights in Thatcher's Britain: Two Views* (London: IEA Health and Welfare Unit, 1990).

tions, or perhaps the avoidance of alienation.[5] On other accounts, political participation will be regarded as non-instrumentally valuable, on the grounds that it provides an important kind of fulfilment.[6] In other words, it will be seen as an ingredient of human flourishing. Those who take this view may differ over exactly how important it is as an ingredient. Some may say that it is an essential ingredient of the good life, i.e., that a person cannot flourish unless they are to some extent politically active. Others may maintain that it is merely a possible ingredient of the good life, for example, they might hold that other things being equal a person's life goes better if they are politically active because of the direct contribution of that activity to well-being, but allow that a person may flourish even if they are not committed to political participation.

Of the positions so far described, only the idea that political activity is an essential ingredient of the good life is potentially at odds with the dominant liberal conception of political community. Citizens might reasonably deny that political activity is an *essential* ingredient in the good life for *everyone*, and therefore such a view cannot meet the requirements of public justifiability. Those who defend the dominant liberal conception will argue that if political community requires the members of a polity to converge on the idea that political activity is an essential ingredient of the good life, then it cannot in practice be sustained without the oppressive use of state power. Indeed this is Rawls's response to essentially the position under consideration, which he calls civic humanism. (Civic humanism, as he defines it, involves the view that 'man is a social, even a political, animal whose essential nature is most fully realized in a democratic society in which there is vigorous participation in political life' and maintains that participation in democratic politics is 'the privileged locus of the good life'.[7])

The republican challenge can be construed differently, however, and in a way that is not so obviously vulnerable to this liberal response. Indeed it is best conceived as a challenge to the moralized version of the dominant liberal conception of political community. It focuses not on the nature of citizenship and why it is a good, but rather on what it is to be a good citizen, and conceives a good citizen as someone who fulfils the responsibilities and obligations of citizenship. It is a challenge which maintains that in order for citizens to constitute a community in the moralized sense

---

[5] David Miller, for example, suggests that it is important for the laws and policies of a state not to appear simply as alien impositions but rather as the outcome of a reasonable agreement to which one has been party: see Miller, 'Citizenship and Pluralism', p. 448.
[6] Note that to deny citizenship non-instrumental value need not be to regard it as unimportant, for citizenship may still possess massive instrumental value or be enormously important because it provides a necessary condition of something with considerable instrumental or non-instrumental value.   [7] Rawls, *Political Liberalism*, pp. 205–6.

they must acknowledge and act upon special moral obligations to one another, for only then can they be said to be genuinely mutually concerned. Mutual concern between citizens is thus conceived as a form of *special* concern.

Fellow citizens have generally been regarded as bound by a variety of special obligations, prominent amongst these are an obligation to give priority to each other's needs and an obligation to participate fully in public life.[8] The idea that we have a special obligation to attend to the welfare of our fellow citizens[9] might be regarded as a natural extension of the traditional saying 'charity begins at home', with the proviso that charity is usually taken to refer to actions that are beyond the call of duty rather than those which are obligatory.[10] So understood it would minimally imply that the needs of fellow citizens should take priority over the needs of outsiders, other things being equal.

The idea that we have a special obligation to our fellow citizens to participate in public life has been thought to include or entail various specific obligations such as an obligation to vote, to take one's turn at jury service, and to keep a watchful eye on government and speak out when it acts unjustly. Bhikhu Parekh, for example, maintains that citizens have obligations to each other

to take an active interest and to participate in the conduct of public affairs, to keep a critical eye on the activities of the government, to speak up against the injustices of their society, to stand up for those too demoralized, confused and powerless to fight for themselves, and in general to help create a rich and lively community.[11]

The idea that we have special obligations of this kind is endorsed not just

---

8   Many political theorists also suppose that we have an obligation to obey the law which can be understood as a special obligation to fellow citizens rather than as a special obligation to the state. This idea has a long pedigree. It is to be found in social contract theories such as Thomas Hobbes's as well as in theories which attempt to ground an obligation to obey the law on a principle of 'fair play': that since one has enjoyed the benefits of others obeying the law, one should accept the burdens of one's own compliance with it. The fair play argument seems first to have been invoked by Socrates in the *Crito*, when he explained why he should receive the punishment handed to him rather than escape from Athens. John Rawls explicitly proposed the argument in his 'Legal Obligation and the Duty of Fair Play', in S. Hook (ed.), *Law and Philosophy* (New York: New York University Press, 1964). I shall not discuss this idea here because of the particular problems it raises, although some of what I say is relevant to it.

9   Diemut Bubeck has developed an interesting feminist version of this idea, arguing that citizens have a special obligation to engage in the *activity* of care: see D. Bubeck, 'A Feminist Approach to Citizenship', EUI Working Paper EUF No. 95/1, especially pp. 31–7.

10 But the meaning of the saying that charity begins at home is not transparent: it might mean that there is no obligation to provide charity, but if you do provide it, then you ought to start at home.

11 B. Parekh, 'A Misconceived Discourse on Political Obligation', *Political Studies*, vol. 41, 1993, p. 243.

by those who see themselves as heirs of the classical republican tradition,[12] but also by their communitarian allies who think that we should emphasize the obligations or duties of citizens rather than just their rights.[13]

The republican challenge to the liberal conception of political community, namely that political community consists, in part, of citizens acting upon their special obligations to one another, might seem misplaced. If citizens do possess special moral obligations towards one another, then will not these moral obligations simply be derivable from principles of justice? If so, they would be included within any adequate account of the liberal conception of political community. For according to that conception, citizens are members of a political community only if they identify with their major institutions as a result of endorsing the principles of justice which underlie them. And if they endorse these principles, will they not be disposed to comply with any special obligations which they acknowledge can be derived from them?

In the remainder of the chapter I want to suggest that justice cannot account for the various special obligations which bind citizens, and that the republican conception of political community really is distinct from the dominant liberal conception. These special obligations cannot be derived from general principles of justice, but are justified instead by the good of citizenship. This is not to deny that justice may require the redistribution of resources between citizens; if, say, a contractualist account is along the right lines, the set of principles that no one can reasonably reject is likely to require significant redistribution.[14] But even if justice does have redistributive implications, that would not subvert the idea that there are special obligations between citizens that hold independently of justice, and the fulfilment of which give content to what it is for citizens to be mutually concerned.

[12] See, for example, Q. Skinner, 'The Idea of Negative Liberty: Philosophical and Historical Perspectives' in R. Rorty, J. B. Schneewind and Q. Skinner (eds.), *Philosophy in History* (Cambridge: Cambridge University Press, 1984); M. Viroli, *For Love of Country: An Essay on Patriotism and Nationalism* (Oxford: Oxford University Press, 1995), p. 9; R. Bellamy, 'Citizenship and Rights', in R. Bellamy (ed.), *Theories and Concepts of Politics: An Introduction* (Manchester: Manchester University Press, 1993), p. 63; Dagger, *Civic Virtues*, especially pp. 98–100. Civic republicans often prefer to talk about the virtues of citizens rather than the obligations or duties of citizenship, but it is clear that they regard the fulfilment of such obligations as partially constitutive of what it is to be a good citizen. Cf. Macedo, *Liberal Virtues*, esp. pp. 272–4.

[13] See, for example, Etzioni, *The Spirit of Community*. David Selbourne argues that citizens have an obligation to sustain the civic bond, which includes an obligation to inform themselves about the nature of the civic order to which they belong, and an obligation to participate in local civic affairs. See Selbourne, *The Principle of Duty*, especially pp. 156, 230–1.

[14] See Nagel, *Equality and Partiality*, esp. ch. 7.

2. Deriving special obligations to fellow citizens from principles of justice

The strategy of deriving special obligations to fellow citizens from general principles of justice faces what might be described as a phenomenological objection – we have more confidence in the existence of these special obligations (even when we disagree about their content) than we do in any complex story about how they are entailed by general principles, and hence no such story could provide the real justification for them.[15] Although this argument has some force, it is at best a *prima facie* objection to the strategy. It cannot be a conclusive objection since it might be maintained that our confidence in these special obligations is unwarranted unless they can be shown to be derivable from general principles. Indeed it might be argued that the very coherence of morality relies upon the possibility of some such derivation.[16] And an ingenious consequentialist might even be able to show that benefits flow from the (supposedly false) belief that these obligations are not derivable in this way.

I propose to consider four candidates for providing a defence of the relevant special obligations: two rights-based approaches (one developed by Alan Gewirth, the other by Richard Dagger), a duty-based approach favoured by Jeremy Waldron, and a broadly consequentialist approach which has been defended by Robert Goodin. I shall argue that each fails to explain why these obligations are owed to fellow citizens rather than to the residents in a given territory. The authors I consider may not be particularly disturbed by this failure, and might treat my remarks as an argument for the idea that the special obligations they defend are really owed to the residents in a given territory rather than to fellow citizens, or as an argument for the idea that citizenship should be automatically extended to residents. In this light, let me say that my primary purpose is not to undermine the arguments of Gewirth, Dagger, Waldron and Goodin, but rather to show that *if* we think citizenship as opposed to residency is of moral significance, then we cannot explain its significance by focusing on contingent features of the relationship between citizens, or the state and its citizens, in the way that justice-based approaches do.

Even if common sense morality attaches moral significance to the distinction between mere residents and fellow citizens, it is not obvious that we should do so. Later in the chapter I shall give some reasons for thinking that this distinction should be regarded as morally important. But let me begin by trying to remove some initial barriers which stand in

[15] Cf. J. Horton, *Political Obligation* (Basingstoke: Macmillan, 1993), p. 156.
[16] See A. Gewirth, 'Ethical Universalism and Particularism', *Journal of Philosophy*, vol. 85, 1988, pp. 284–5.

the way of taking that idea seriously. First, someone who believes that the distinction between mere residents and citizens is of non-instrumental moral significance is not committed to any particular account of when the status of citizenship should be conferred, or indeed to any particular account of the morality of immigration controls. For example, it would be perfectly consistent to argue that citizenship should be granted to any long-term resident who wants it.[17] As I hope will become clear later in this chapter, such a policy would not deprive citizenship of its moral importance. Second, mere residency – or at least, mere long-term residency – might generate its own special obligations, even if it does not generate the range that citizenship does. (Indeed some of the accounts I consider might justify the idea that residents are bound by some special obligations.)

Let me begin by considering Gewirth's argument. It is based upon what he calls 'the general principle of human rights', which states that all persons have equal rights to freedom and to well-being.[18] Gewirth has attempted a detailed defence of this principle elsewhere,[19] but the guiding idea behind it is that we have equal rights to freedom and well-being because freedom and well-being are necessary conditions of agency or the achievement of purposes. His general approach to grounding special obligations is to say that the principle of human rights justifies social rules and institutions if they express or protect people's equal freedom and well-being.[20] In this way Gewirth overcomes what might be thought a general difficulty with a Kantian approach to justifying special obligations to fellow citizens: that it is committed to a voluntarist account of special obligations according to which these obligations can arise only from promises or contracts, and there has been no such contract between citizens or between citizens and the state.

Gewirth argues that the general principle of human rights permits the emergence of states with jurisdiction over particular territories (though the actions of these states are still constrained morally by the general principle of human rights). That principle also justifies each state providing its citizens with a benefit that it does not provide for others, viz. equal protection of their basic well-being through the impartial enforcement of the criminal law, where basic well-being consists in having the necessary conditions of agency, such as life and mental equilibrium.[21] The fact that

---

[17] Michael Walzer argues that political justice requires that long-term 'guest' workers be given the opportunity to become citizens: 'the processes of self-determination through which a democratic state shapes its internal life, must be open, and equally open, to all those men and women who live within its territory, work in the local economy, and are subject to local law' (Walzer, *Spheres of Justice*, p. 60).

[18] See Gewirth, 'Ethical Universalism and Particularism', p. 291.

[19] See A. Gewirth, *Reason and Morality* (Chicago: University of Chicago Press, 1978), esp. chs. 2–3.   [20] Gewirth, 'Ethical Universalism and Particularism', p. 292

[21] *Ibid.*, p. 299.

states provide their citizens with special protection justifies the particular concern the citizens of a state display for it, and indeed for their fellow citizens who are indirectly responsible for supplying the means for this protection through taxation.[22] At this stage of the argument it seems that Gewirth has shown only that it is morally permissible for state officials to show special concern for citizens and that it is morally permissible for citizens to have special concern for their states and for their fellow citizens. He has not established that there are corresponding special *obligations*.[23] Gewirth, however, might plausibly close this gap in his argument by maintaining that these special obligations arise because they specify what is required in order to secure equal basic well-being once a state system is in place.

From a Kantian perspective, this argument can provide a plausible case for saying that states have special obligations to those resident in their territories to enforce the criminal law impartially, and that residents have special obligations to one another to provide the means for the state to do so. But it can't explain why a state has special obligations to its *citizens* as opposed to all and only those resident in the territory over which it has legal jurisdiction. Impartial enforcement of the criminal law seems to be just as necessary to secure the basic well-being of residents who are not citizens, and does not in any distinctive way promote or protect the basic well-being of citizens who are resident in other states.[24] For the same reason Gewirth's approach cannot show why citizens have special obligations to one another rather than to all and only those resident in the state's territory since in most cases 'resident aliens' will contribute to providing the means necessary for enforcing the criminal law whereas citizens currently living abroad may not. In short Gewirth's account does not have the resources to explain what is special about our fellow citizens.

Richard Dagger develops an account of the special obligations fellow citizens possess towards each other which is also Kantian in some respects since it has as its cornerstone the right of autonomy.[25] His idea is that fellow citizens have special obligations towards one another which derive

---

[22] *Ibid.*, pp. 298–302.
[23] In the first part of his paper Gewirth says that his argument 'will uphold, for the most part, the . . . thesis that ethical universalism, in the form of a principle of human rights, can show that certain kinds of ethical particularism are morally required or mandatory' (Gewirth, 'Ethical Universalism and Particularism', p. 289). But in the body of the article he does not make any explicit case for saying that the forms of ethical particularism he discusses are morally *required*.
[24] Gewirth could argue that states usually provide various protections to citizens living abroad through diplomacy. But these protections by their nature are much more limited than those mere residents receive through the impartial enforcement of the criminal law.
[25] See R. Dagger, 'Rights, Boundaries, and the Bond of Community: A Qualified Defense of Moral Parochialism', *American Political Science Review*, vol. 79, 1985. See also his *Civic Virtues*, especially ch. 4.

from a principle of fair play; they participate together as equals in a cooperative enterprise for mutual advantage, so they are obligated to take their fair share of the burdens of that cooperation as well as its fruits. When fellow citizens fail to take their fair share of the burdens, they violate the rights of other citizens to autonomy because, in Kant's terms, they thereby treat them simply as a means to their own ends.

Let us suppose that Dagger (like Rawls) is right to treat polities as cooperative enterprises for mutual advantage, and to suppose that because they are enterprises of this kind a principle of fair play is applicable to them. Dagger seems to think that on this basis we can justify a range of special obligations, from an obligation (other things being equal) to obey the law to an obligation (other things being equal) to give priority to the claims of needy fellow citizens.

But consider Dagger's claim that the principle of fair play can justify the existence of a special obligation to give priority to the claims of needy fellow citizens. The idea here is presumably that because each citizen enjoys the benefits of cooperation with others (including, when there is a welfare state, the security of knowing that she will be taken care of if she is sick or unemployed), fair play requires that she accept the burdens imposed when others are unable to contribute fully to the cooperative enterprise. However, in many polities the benefits of cooperative activity (including welfare benefits) are created and enjoyed by residents who are not fellow citizens, so by parity of reasoning citizens should have special obligations to them, and residents should have special obligations to other residents, fellow citizens or not. Furthermore, the citizens of a state currently living abroad may not in any distinctive way contribute to the cooperative enterprise of the state to which they belong, so it is unclear why special obligations are owed to them. For these reasons it is hard to see how a principle of fair play could establish an obligation amongst fellow citizens to give priority to each other's needs as opposed to the needs of all residents (and generally only those of residents), except perhaps in a polity in which welfare benefits are provided only to citizens and the taxes which finance them come only from citizens. As regards the supposed obligation to participate in public life, it is true that in so far as non-citizens are disallowed from voting, holding public office, or jury service, etc., they cannot be under any obligation to participate in public life in these ways, nor violate any principle of fair play when they do not, but they still enjoy the benefits of the participation of others. At best Dagger's account has the resources to establish the existence of a range of special obligations to those engaged in the same cooperative enterprise, rather than special obligations to fellow citizens as such.

Dagger's argument also faces another difficulty. It is far from clear that the principle of fair play can justify the idea that citizens have special obligations to give priority even to the claims of every needy fellow citizen. As Robert Goodin has pointed out in a similar context, some needy citizens, for example, those who are severely disabled, may never produce much in the way of benefits to others (other than perhaps the benefits that are intrinsic to the activity of caring for them): a principle of fair play based on a notion of reciprocity will do nothing to justify the idea that the able-bodied have special obligations *to them*.[26] Goodin makes this point in rejecting what he calls the mutual benefit model of justifying special obligations to citizens. As an alternative he presents what is perhaps the most well-worked out consequentialist defence of those obligations, which he calls 'the assigned responsibility model'. He maintains, on broadly consequentialist grounds, that we have a general obligation to protect the vulnerable, and argues that our special obligations derive largely from this general obligation: 'special obligations are . . . merely devices whereby the moral community's general duties get assigned to particular agents'.[27] Our general moral obligations are most effectively fulfilled by assigning particular people with special responsibilities and the means to discharge them. States acting through their officials are assigned special responsibilities for protecting and promoting the interests of their own citizens because this is the most effective way of ensuring that everyone's interests are protected and promoted.

Goodin's general approach is illuminating, and no doubt can underpin some special obligations, but it also seems inadequate to explain why *fellow citizens* are a relevant group when it comes to justifying these obligations.[28] It is unclear why the assigned responsibility model should distinguish between citizens and long-term residents.[29] Making a distinction between citizens and mere residents does not seem to serve any useful role in determining the most effective way of discharging our general moral duties. Why is not the most effective way of discharging general moral obligations to assign states and their officials special responsibility for those living within their territories over a sustained period, irrespective of whether they are citizens? In some cases the beneficiaries of special obligations to fellow citizens might be all residents (for example, all residents are likely to benefit from citizens recognizing a special obligation to each other to keep a watchful eye on government), but that

---

[26] Goodin, 'What Is So Special about Our Fellow Countrymen?', pp. 676–8.
[27] Ibid., p. 678.
[28] Goodin's account should also be of interest to non-consequentialists of various stripes, for (as he argues) it is compatible with standard forms of non-consequentialism: see R. Goodin, *Protecting the Vulnerable: A Reanalysis of Our Social Responsibilities* (Chicago: University of Chicago Press, 1985), pp. 115ff.
[29] By 'long-term resident', I just mean to exclude tourists.

does not seem to be the case with, for instance, the special obligation to give priority to the needs of fellow citizens.

Goodin might appeal to the powerful sentiments that often bind together fellow citizens and argue that it is these which make the special obligations a particularly effective way of discharging general obligations;[30] for example, people will be motivated to pay their taxes, and support redistributive policies, if they see their fellow citizens as beneficiaries. But, it will be argued, these sentiments tend to exist amongst those who share a national identity rather than amongst those who are simply citizens of the same state, and a number of states today which are multiethnic or multinational lack an overarching national identity. So Goodin cannot unproblematically appeal to the prior existence of strong bonds *between citizens* to justify the idea that the most effective way of discharging general duties is to have a state system in which states recognize special obligations to their citizens and citizens recognize special obligations to each other.

Goodin might argue that in so far as the most effective way of discharging general obligations really is for each state simply to take responsibility for those living in its territory, then the state system should be reformed in accordance with this way of assigning responsibilities.[31] But then his theory will not provide a foundation for the idea that states have special obligations to fellow citizens as opposed to special obligations to those living in the same territory, subject to the jurisdiction of the same state.

Goodin might argue instead that states should continue to be assigned special responsibility for just their citizens, but that all those resident long term within a territory should be given citizenship, and hence that special obligations to fellow citizens should be owed to all long-term residents. But again this would in effect be to concede the force of the objection: it is residency not citizenship which is on his account the most important factor in determining special obligations. Such a proposal would also disallow people the choice of residing temporarily but long term in another state without relinquishing their existing citizenship or acquiring dual citizenship, and hence without incurring whatever political or legal obligations and responsibilities that would involve. This might even have detrimental effects since residents who do not wish to be citizens, but who are forced to become citizens if they want to remain in the territory, may as a consequence lack loyalty to the state or fellow citizens. So there are independent reasons for thinking that the distinction states currently make between mere residents and citizens has some point from a consequentialist perspective, even though states may exploit residents who are

---

[30] See D. Miller, *On Nationality* (Oxford: Oxford University Press, 1995), p. 63.
[31] Cf. Goodin, 'What Is So Special about Our Fellow Countrymen?', p. 685.

not citizens and do not always provide them with the opportunity of becoming citizens. And it is plausible to suppose that the most effective way of discharging our general obligation to protect the vulnerable is to assign states with ultimate responsibility for residents rather than specifically for citizens.

Consider finally the idea that we might derive special obligations to fellow citizens from a natural duty to support just institutions. At first sight that approach might seem to make it hard to explain why this obligation applies only to those who live under a particular set of just institutions as opposed to anyone who is in a position to support or undermine them. For instance, it does not explain 'why Britons have a special duty to support the institutions of Britain'.[32] Jeremy Waldron, however, has attempted to answer this objection by making a distinction between those who are insiders in relation to a principle and the institution which administers it, and those who are outsiders in relation to them. A person is an insider in relation to a principle 'if it is part of the point and justification of the principle to deal with his conduct, claims, and interests along with those of any other persons it deals with',[33] and an insider in relation to an institution 'if and only if it is part of the point of that institution to do justice to some claim of his among all the claims with which it deals'.[34] An insider has special obligations, not incurred by outsiders, which derive from the natural duty to support just institutions: they are morally required to accept the implementation of the principles whose point is to regulate *their* conduct. A Briton must accept the implementation of principles by British institutions, so long as those institutions and principles are tolerably just. Outsiders in relation to a principle merely have an obligation not to undermine the implementation of that principle in regulating the conduct of insiders, provided again that it is reasonably just.

Waldron's approach promises to show how a natural duty to support just institutions can justify special obligations to others who are also insiders in relation to some set of principles and institutions. But it cannot explain why we have special obligations to fellow citizens, for the class of fellow citizens is not coextensive with the class of insiders: some insiders, for example, those who are merely long-term residents, are not fellow citizens. In this respect it faces the same difficulty as the other attempts to derive the special obligations to fellow citizens from general principles of justice.

---

[32] R. Dworkin, *Law's Empire* (London: Fontana, 1986), p. 193.
[33] J. Waldron, 'Special Ties and Natural Duties', *Philosophy and Public Affairs*, Vol 22, 1993, p. 13.   [34] *Ibid.*, p. 16.

I have not surveyed all possible attempts to derive special obligations to fellow citizens in particular from general principles of justice, and I have no transcendental argument to show that any such attempt *must* fail. There is, however, a pattern to the difficulties encountered by the approaches I have considered. Each fails to explain why the relevant obligations are owed to fellow citizens rather than to the residents in a given territory. As I pointed out earlier, the authors I have considered may not be troubled by this failure; they might deny that the distinction between citizens and residents does have any moral significance (except perhaps in so far as the two groups have different opportunities to participate in a polity, created by different sets of legal and political rights). In the next section, however, I shall defend an approach which, like commonsense morality, does attach moral significance to the distinction, and which I think shows how various special obligations to fellow citizens can be derived from the good of citizenship rather than from principles of justice.

3.   Grounding special obligations in the good of citizenship

The most obvious way of attempting to show that citizenship has special moral significance, and that special obligations to fellow citizens can bind independently of what justice requires, is from an account of the good of citizenship. In this way, I suggest, we make space for a distinctive republican conception of political community, the realization of which requires not only that citizens converge on the principles of justice which underlie their major institutions, but also that they fulfil their special obligations to one another, grounded in the good of citizenship. In order to show how these special obligations might be grounded in the good of citizenship, I propose to begin by looking at the way in which another class of special obligations might be grounded in a different good, viz. how the special obligations of friendship might be grounded in the good of friendship.[35] I shall draw upon Joseph Raz's brief but suggestive discussion of this issue.

Raz makes three central claims about the nature of friendship:[36] first, friendship is a non-instrumentally valuable relationship;[37] second, part of what it is for two people to be friends is for each to be under certain obligations to the other, and these obligations are justified by the moral

---

[35] I do not mean to suggest that there is a single model for the justification of special obligations. I agree with Samuel Scheffler that it is difficult for any single model to account for all special obligations, given their apparent diversity. See S. Scheffler, 'Families, Nations and Strangers', The Lindley Lecture, University of Kansas, 1994, p. 3.

[36] See J. Raz, 'Liberating Duties', *Law and Philosophy*, vol. 8, 1989, pp. 18–21.

[37] Raz uses 'intrinsic value' to mean non-instrumental value, but I shall follow the practice I defended in Chapter 2, of drawing a sharp distinction between the two.

good of friendship;[38] third, these special obligations are internally related to the good of friendship, i.e., they are part of that good. We might expand on these claims. Friendship is morally valuable for its own sake because it involves the expression of mutual concern; it allots a central role to altruistic emotions such as sympathy and compassion, and a willingness to give oneself to another.[39] Part of what it is for two people to be friends is to be under a moral obligation (other things being equal) not to betray each other's confidences or to use those confidences manipulatively, and to have responsibilities towards each other to provide comfort and support when needed.[40] (A good friend is one who, amongst other things, complies with the various obligations he has to his friends.)

On Raz's view, the obligations of friendship are internally related to the good which justifies them; they are partially constitutive of the moral good of friendship since this relationship is specified in part by those duties. As a result, these obligations cannot be adequately conceived as the means of realizing the good of friendship, for that good includes the fulfilment of the obligations. Raz resists the objection that this justification of the special obligations is viciously circular: the justification consists in placing them in a wider context (i.e. the relationship as a whole) to which they contribute and which is non-instrumentally valuable.[41] That wider context gives reasons for accepting the obligations. Raz's view has the virtue of preserving the intuition shared by many defenders of special obligations that obligations of friendship are not contingent upon any role they might play in maximizing general well-being, but are grounded in the nature of friendship itself.

Can a comparable account of the good of citizenship be developed? Consider the following proposal. Citizenship has non-instrumental value because in virtue of being a citizen a person is a member of a collective body in which they enjoy equal status with its other members and are

---

[38] Raz employs the language of duty rather than the language of obligation, but I do not think that anything turns on this, since he has elsewhere treated them as equivalent. (He does, however, maintain that there are reasons to distinguish between 'A has an obligation or duty to x' and 'A ought to x', and for assigning the former a special role.) See J. Raz, 'Promises and Obligations', in P. Hacker and J. Raz (eds.), *Law, Morality, and Society: Essays in Honour of H. L. A. Hart* (Oxford: Clarendon Press, 1977), pp. 210–28.

[39] See L. Blum, *Friendship, Altruism and Morality* (London: Routledge and Kegan Paul, 1980), ch. 4.

[40] Here it needs to be emphasized that much of what is valuable about friendship cannot be understood in terms of the recognition of obligations or duties. Indeed it would often be appropriate for one friend to be offended by another if they discovered that they had acted solely from a sense of duty rather than because they cared about them. The language of responsibility is perhaps more appropriate here because to say that one acted on behalf of a friend because one felt responsible for them carries with it no conversational implication that one's actions were not done out of concern for the friend.

[41] Raz, 'Liberating Duties', p. 21.

thereby provided with recognition of their equal worth. This collective body exercises significant control over its members' conditions of existence (a degree of control which none of its members individually possesses). It provides them with opportunities to participate directly and indirectly in the formation of these laws and policies. Part of what it is to be a citizen is to incur special obligations – these obligations give content to what it is to be committed or loyal to fellow citizens and are justified by the good of the wider relationship to which they contribute. In particular, citizens have an obligation to each other to participate in public life, and an obligation to give priority to the needs of fellow citizens so that they can also participate fully in the life of the collective, and can truly be said to possess equal status. A good citizen is, in part, someone who complies with these various obligations and responsibilities, and in doing so realizes the good of citizenship. (Each of these obligations, it might be argued, is qualified by a *ceteris paribus* clause.[42])

This account of citizenship, like those considered in section 1, conceives citizenship as a moral rather than merely legal notion. (And it can do so whilst preserving the distinction between being a citizen and being a good citizen.) So understood it means something different from mere membership of a state. A person may be a member of a state even though she lacks equal status with other members, and even if she is deprived of the opportunity to participate politically. Under these circumstances, she is not a citizen of the state in the moral sense I intend. (Think here of black South Africans prior to the dismantling of apartheid.) When citizenship is understood purely in terms of membership of a state, it is defined in different ways by different states. Moreover, a state may distinguish between different categories of membership of a state in terms of different packages of rights, involving various combinations of rights of residence, employment rights and political rights. For example, a person might be granted the (temporary or permanent) right to reside in a territory and seek employment within it without having any political rights. This is the plight of so-called guest workers.

If citizens are to constitute a republican political community in the moralized sense, their equality of status must preclude systematic exploi-

---

[42] I do not mean to suggest that friendship and citizenship are analogous in all important respects. Clearly there are important differences between them. Friendship (in general) is a voluntary relationship, whereas citizenship (in general) is non-voluntary; a person may cease to be a friend by persistently failing to fulfil the obligations of friendship, whereas a person does not cease to be a citizen of a state simply by neglecting her duties. The core of the analogy is unaffected by these observations, however. Citizenship, like friendship, is non-instrumentally valuable, and obligations of citizenship like obligations of friendship, are part of the good of that relationship as well as being justified by that good.

tation and oppression, and they must fulfil their special obligations to one another (i.e., be good citizens), which encode what it is for them to be mutually concerned. What institutions and policies are needed to provide equality of status, and indeed the opportunity to participate in political life, is a matter of dispute between different theories of citizenship which I shall not attempt to resolve. For example, some would argue that a welfare safety-net is insufficient, and that a citizens' unconditional basic income is required. Others agree that a mere safety-net is insufficient, but argue for the importance of a commitment to full employment, with the educational and retraining programmes that would involve.

According to the moral notion of citizenship I am describing, citizenship is in tension with permanent absence from the state's territory, since part of the point of the notion of citizenship is to pick out a relationship in which an individual is part of a collective which shapes his or her conditions of existence. When a person is permanently absent from the territory over which the collective body exercises control, it is no longer his or her conditions of existence which are being directly shaped by the collective (although this can be a matter of degree for such a person may have estates in that territory and pay taxes). To be a citizen of a state in the moral sense is to have equal status (including, usually, equal political rights), and normally to reside within the territory of that state.[43]

The moral notion of citizenship I have outlined would explain why citizenship, as opposed to merely residing together in the same territory, has non-instrumental value. Mere long-term residents do not possess the same political rights as citizens and do not have the same status as them. Although resident non-citizens may influence public affairs in profound ways, for better or for worse, they are not part of the collective which makes law and policy, and do not have the same kind of opportunities as citizens in relation to these matters. The state may have special obligations to its residents, and long-term residents may have special obligations towards each other, but if so, I suggest that these obligations will be justified by other means, for example, by the idea that the fulfilment of them is necessary for equal well-being or for protecting the vulnerable. Special obligations of this sort are unlikely to be justified by the value of merely residing together in the same territory, for at best that has merely instrumental value or value as a necessary condition for achieving other valuable things.

[43] I mean to leave it an open question whether citizens may possess equal status even when some of them enjoy special rights. On certain assumptions special rights can be reconciled with a fundamental equality of status. See Kymlicka, *Liberalism, Community and Culture*, esp. ch. 9; Young, *Justice and the Politics of Difference* esp. ch. 6.

4.   The liberal worry revisited

I hope to have shown that there is a republican conception of political community which is distinct from the dominant liberal conception. According to the republican conception which I have been developing, citizens form a political community only if they recognize, and act upon, the special obligations they owe to each other, obligations which are grounded in the good of citizenship and which are distinct from obligations of justice.[44] But does this conception of political community face the same objection as one which requires citizens to converge on the idea that political participation is an essential ingredient of the good life, viz. that such a community could not be sustained without the oppressive use of state power?

Although the republican conception of political community I have described supposes that political participation is a good, it need not make the highly contentious claim that political participation is the most important ingredient of the good life, nor that it is an essential part of the good life, and it does not require citizens to converge on such ideas in order for it to be realized. The republican conception does maintain that each citizen incurs various special obligations, fulfilment of which contributes to the good of citizenship. But it can allow that citizens may lead a good or satisfying life without fulfilling those obligations: a bad citizen may still realize a range of other goods and excellences. (Compare: a person who does not live up to the obligations of friendship is a bad friend, but may still lead a satisfying or good life, i.e. one which realizes a range of other goods and excellences.) In other words, the republican conception does not insist that political participation is 'the privileged locus of the good life' and can allow that political participation is one good amongst several.

The republican conception of political community need not take a very different view of how conflicts between community at the level of the state and below it should be resolved from that taken by the dominant liberal conception. Republicans *are* liberals in my broad sense (see Introduction), even though they do not endorse the dominant liberal conception of political community. They are committed to a set of basic rights; they

---

[44]   Even though these special obligations are grounded in the good of citizenship, rather than derived from principles of justice, might they nevertheless not be obligations of justice? There is no good reason to take this view. Justice may require a state to confer citizenship on stateless persons or others who want it, and it may require that members of a state receive various rights and opportunities, but it does not follow that the special obligations which are part of citizenship are also obligations of justice. (It may also be the case that there is some convergence between what justice requires and what the special obligations require, for example, both may converge on the idea that needy citizens should receive priority when policy is formulated.)

can allow that the authority to adopt some particular account of these rights depends upon its being the outcome of an inclusive political dialogue; and they will tolerate violations of those rights only in special circumstances, such as when enforcing those rights would be likely to result in greater injustice. When differences do arise between the dominant liberal approach and the republican approach in relation to these matters, they are likely to have their source in republican attempts to enforce citizens' special obligations to one another, or foster the capacities which dispose citizens to fulfil these special obligations.

The dominant liberal conception can acknowledge the importance of public service in various ways, but it need not suppose that citizens have an unconditional obligation to participate in public life. For instance, it may take the view that such an obligation is merely conditional: to participate if not enough others do so, and public institutions are in bad health. In practice, this may make a difference to the relative willingness of those who subscribe to the dominant liberal approach to force citizens to vote or to serve on juries, and to insist on a robust civic education. The republican approach is not committed to enforcing citizens' special obligations or to requiring children to undergo a demanding civic education but its acceptance of an unconditional obligation to participate in public life may sometimes lead it in that direction. It may also sometimes promote a degree of intolerance towards those communities (such as the Amish in the United States) which desire to cut themselves off from public life, and see public service as a barrier to the realization of their own conceptions of the good, not merely as irrelevant to those conceptions. But even when republicans favour enforcing citizens' special obligations, this need not be oppressive, for it can still leave plenty of space for individuals to lead their own lives and for communities to sustain their own practices.

It might nevertheless be thought that enforcing citizens' obligations is objectionable, even if not oppressive, on the grounds that the obligations of citizenship are not fully susceptible to public justification. It is reasonable to reject the more demanding of them at least. Like Brian Barry, however, republicans might allow that political decisions not concerning matters of justice may appeal to controversial ideas of the good, so long as they are made by fair procedures.[45]

5.   Conclusion

This chapter has endorsed a criticism of the dominant liberal conception of political community which has been developed from a republican

---

[45] See Barry, *Justice as Impartiality*, pp. 143–5.

perspective. In Chapter 5 I shall consider the liberal-nationalist claim that in order to realize the dominant liberal conception of political community, citizens must share a national identity, so liberals must take a more restrictive view of what kinds of communities they can allow to flourish below the level of the state. The idea that citizens need to share a national identity in order to realize political community has similar consequences for the republican conception: according to the liberal-nationalist critique, active citizenship is likely to be widespread only in the context of a national community.

5 National community: the benefits of a sense of belonging together

In this chapter I shall consider a challenge which applies not only to the dominant liberal conception of political community but to other liberal conceptions as well, and which maintains that a stable liberal political community cannot be realized unless citizens share a national identity – in effect, form a national community. According to this view, when conflicts arise in a liberal polity between national community and communities below the level of the state, they should be resolved in favour of the former. In the version I shall consider, this challenge comes from a perspective friendly to liberalism, which I shall call liberal-nationalism. The charge it makes against anti-nationalist liberals is that they fail to appreciate what is required in order to realize their ideals of political community, and as a result are too permissive towards communities below the level of the state.

Many anti-nationalist liberals have feared that fostering a shared national identity would require assimilating minority cultures, which can only be achieved (if it can be achieved at all) by oppression. This does not meet the liberal-nationalist's argument that a liberal political community cannot be sustained unless citizens share a national identity, but it explains why, even in the light of it, many liberals have been reluctant to support policies for fostering a national identity. In the first two sections of this chapter, I shall set out the liberal-nationalist case and argue that fears about its implications have often ignored the possibility that a policy of assimilation might be moderate in its aims, and pursued by subsidizing and promoting the dominant culture in various ways rather than using simple coercion. Fostering a national community need not require an oppressive intolerance of communities below the level of the state, and need not seriously affect the flowering of diversity at that level.

Although I deny that liberal-nationalism is an oxymoron, I shall not ultimately defend it. Instead I shall suggest that the liberal-nationalist challenge can be answered to a large extent, for there is reason to think that stable liberal institutions can be secured in the absence of a shared national identity. I shall argue that these institutions may be viable, provided citizens possess what I call a sense of belonging to their polity, even when they lack a shared national identity. Of course, this is partly an empirical matter so it cannot be settled by philosophical reflection alone; by formulating the relevant hypotheses as clearly as I can, and by considering some of the evidence which bears upon them, I try to make a strong case for their serious consideration.

But I shall not endorse the dominant liberal conception of political community (or even what I have called the republican conception) as a *regulative* ideal. Indeed I propose that a widespread sense of belonging to a polity structured by liberal institutions is a better ideal in practice than the dominant liberal conception which requires convergence on principles of justice if it is to be fully realized. In making a case for inclusive political community of this kind to be a regulative ideal, I shall illustrate how it may be possible to foster a widespread sense of belonging amongst citizens who subscribe to different principles of justice, and who are members of diverse cultural groups, by accommodating them in various ways and giving them various forms of legal and political recognition.

I.   Sharing a national identity

The liberal-nationalist in my sense argues that a shared national identity is important for the realization of various values which liberals usually endorse, such as respect for individual rights, democracy, and social justice.[1] But what is it for a group of people to share such an identity? Notoriously there is considerable disagreement on this question.

The most basic difference of opinion is between 'subjectivists' who maintain that sharing a national identity is simply a matter of people *believing* that they belong together for some special reason (perhaps because they believe that they have a distinctive shared culture, history, language or way of life)[2], and 'objectivists', who argue that in order to

---

[1] I shall treat this, stipulatively, as the defining thesis of liberal-nationalism. Those who are ordinarily regarded as liberal-nationalists advance it, but also defend a broader set of theses. See especially Tamir, *Liberal Nationalism*; Miller, *On Nationality*.

[2] See E. Hobsbawm, *Nations and Nationalism since 1780: Programme, Myth, Reality*, 2nd edn (Cambridge: Cambridge University Press, 1990), p. 9; J. S. Mill, *Considerations on Representative Government* (Chicago: Henry Regnery, 1962), p. 307; 'Coleridge', in *Collected Works of John Stuart Mill, vol. x; Essays on Ethics, Religion and Society* ed. J. M. Robson (University of Toronto Press, 1969), pp. 134–6. Although Mill defines nationality in terms of the possession of common sympathies, he thinks that in practice these sympathies are created by various factors such as shared history and language. See also Y. Tamir, 'Reconstructing the Landscape of Imagination', in S. Caney, D. George, and P. Jones (eds.), *National Rights, International Obligations* (Oxford: Westview, 1996), but compare her *Liberal Nationalism*, p. 66; B. Barry, 'Self-Government Revisited,' in D. Miller and L. Siedentop (eds.), *The Nature of Political Theory* (Oxford: Oxford University Press, 1983), p. 136. The fellow feeling and common sympathies or sentiments which both

share a national identity people must really possess distinctive common characteristics, such as a shared culture, history, language, or way of life.[3] Subjectivists accuse objectivists of conflating the issue of what it is for a group to be a nation with the explanation of how nations emerge.[4] Objectivists argue that it is impossible for a group of people really to share a national identity if they do not actually have anything in common.[5] On the face of it, however, neither of these arguments is persuasive. Objectivists needn't confuse the issue of what it is for a group to constitute a nation with the reasons why nations emerge, and subjectivists can simply insist that nations are wholly imagined but still real rather than imaginary.[6]

I suspect that there is no overall best account of what it is for a group to constitute a nation, and that which account should be adopted in a particular context will depend upon one's aims. The choice between the two different kinds I have distinguished is not crucial given my purposes in this chapter. As I hope will become clear in what follows, the liberal-nationalist's thesis is best understood as follows: that the realization of various fundamental liberal values requires citizens to have a sense of belonging together. By a sense of belonging together, I mean a belief amongst them that there is some special reason why they should associate together which appeals to something other than, say, that they happen to live in the same polity. (Both subjectivists and objectivists accept that the members of a nation must possess a sense of belonging together, but according to subjectivists, conationals need share a culture, history or language only in so far as this is necessary in order to generate or sustain that sense.)

Mill and Barry regard as essential to a shared national identity could in principle fall short of a sense of belonging together in my sense, for that requires believing there to be some special reason for associating together. But to the extent that, say, fellow feeling does fall short of a sense of belonging together, it would be a mistake to regard it as sufficient for shared nationality. For example, concern for others simply because they happen to be members of the same state, even if that is humanly intelligible, does not on its own make for a shared national identity, even on subjectivist accounts. So I shall assume in what follows that both Mill and Barry believe that a shared national identity is constituted by a sense of belonging together in my sense.

[3] See for example, J. Haldane, 'Identity, Community and the Limits of Multiculture', *Public Affairs Quarterly*, vol. 7, 1993, p. 210; Miller, *On Nationality*, pp. 21–7.

[4] See Tamir, 'Reconstructing the Landscape of Imagination', p. 88; Barry, 'Self-Government Revisited', pp. 136–7.

[5] Miller, *Market, State and Community*, pp. 244–5; D. Miller, 'Reflections on British National Identity', *New Community*, vol. 21, 1995, p. 153. Miller is an objectivist in my sense, although in his sense he is not since he holds that sharing a national identity depends in part upon people's belief that they do and an objectivist in his sense must deny that this is so.

[6] The idea that nations are imagined communities is Benedict Anderson's: see his *Imagined Communities*, especially pp. 5–7.

Why should it be supposed that a sense of belonging together is a necessary condition in practice for the realization of liberal values? There are at least four claims which are relevant here. First, it has been argued that a shared national identity is required in the modern world in order for the citizens of a state to avoid alienation from their political institutions. Second, it has been maintained that liberal institutions cannot be, or are unlikely to be, stable or enduring unless citizens share a national identity. Third, that a shared national identity is a precondition for the existence of the kind of trust which makes compromise possible in the face of conflicting interests. Fourth, that a shared national identity is a necessary condition for a politics of the common good, including widespread support for redistribution on grounds of social justice. As I shall go on to show, each of the arguments rests crucially on the idea that when people share a national identity, they have a sense of belonging together. The second, third and fourth arguments are variously related and mutually reinforcing: for example, part of the case for saying that the stability of the liberal state requires a shared national identity might rest upon the claim that such an identity makes compromise and the pursuit of the common good possible.

David Miller defends a complex version of the first argument. He maintains that, in the modern world, in order to avoid alienation citizens must be able to locate themselves socially and, furthermore, be able to identify with the collective which makes most of the major decisions that significantly affect their conditions of existence and which gives them the greatest possible control over these conditions. In practice this will be possible only if there is a non-political unity of the kind provided by a shared national identity, for only then will citizens attach importance to shaping their social world *together*.[7] In Miller's view, it is only if citizens have a sense of belonging together that they will value participating together politically. According to this view, without a shared national identity the liberal conception of political community is threatened, for it requires citizens to identify with their major institutions. (The republican conception of political community is threatened in a further way, for it requires active citizenship; if Miller is right, active citizenship is feasible in the world today only when citizens share a national identity.)

The idea that (in general) the stability, unity or order of liberal institutions requires a shared national identity is defended by John Stuart Mill in *Representative Government*. Mill believes that '[f]ree institutions are next to impossible in a country made up of different nationalities' mainly on the grounds that 'the united political opinion, necessary to the working of

---

[7] D. Miller, 'Socialism and Toleration', in S. Mendus (ed.), *Justifying Toleration: Conceptual and Historical Perspectives* (Cambridge: Cambridge University Press, 1988), pp. 241–2; *Market, State and Community*, pp. 234–6. Cf. Scruton, 'In Defence of the Nation', p. 308.

representative government, cannot exist' in the absence of fellow feeling.[8] Where there are different nationalities, there are different determinants of political judgement, and different politicians have the trust of different sections of the population. No army can be relied upon to uphold the good of all the citizens, as opposed to the good of one group. In consequence Mill seems to think that in order for liberal institutions to be enduring, citizens need to possess a sense of belonging together.[9]

Brian Barry puts forward a version of the third argument, maintaining that the interests of different groups within the state will inevitably come into conflict, and that if one group is to sacrifice its interests for others, then it must be assured that those groups will on future occasions reciprocate. They have that assurance only if they possess common sentiments or fellow feeling. In other words, Barry appears to think that a sense of belonging together provides the basis for the social trust which is essential for the smooth functioning of liberal institutions.[10]

David Miller goes one step further, arguing that a politics of the common good (not just reciprocal compromise in the face of conflicting interests) requires the existence of a shared national identity.[11] He maintains that people need a sense of belonging together if they are to meet politically 'not as advocates for this or that sectional group, but as citizens whose main concerns are fairness between the different sections of the community and the pursuit of common ends'.[12] He also believes that a sense of belonging together is necessary in order for there to be widespread support for redistribution on grounds of social justice.[13] His main

---

[8] Mill, *Considerations on Representative Government*, p. 309; see also T. H. Green, *Lectures on the Principles of Political Obligation* (London: Longmans, Green and Co, 1941), sections 122–3; M. Canovan, *Nationhood and Political Theory* (Cheltenham: Edward Elgar, 1996), ch. 3; E. Barker, *National Character and the Factors in its Formation* (London: Methuen, 1927), pp. 16–17. Lord Acton rejects Mill's thesis, arguing that liberty and stability are better preserved by the existence of more than one nation in a state. When different nations exist under the same sovereignty, there is a need to balance interests and restrain policy, and this guards against corruption and absolutism. See Lord Acton, 'Nationalism', in J. Figgis and R. Laurence (eds.), *The History of Freedom and Other Essays* (London: Macmillan, 1922), esp. p. 289. As Barker points out, however, Acton's claims are not borne out by history.

[9] Roger Scruton has recently arrived at the same conclusion as Mill, that the stability of liberal institutions must rest upon the existence of a shared national identity, via a somewhat different route. See Scruton, 'In Defence of the Nation'. See also J. Gray, *Enlightenment's Wake*, pp. 22–3.

[10] See Barry, 'Self-Government Revisited', pp. 141–2. See also note 2 above.

[11] Miller, 'Socialism and Toleration', p. 247; *On Nationality*, pp. 93–4. See also Tamir, *Liberal Nationalism*, pp. 117–20. Barry also endorses the idea: see Barry, 'Self-Government Revisited', p. 141.   [12] Miller, 'Socialism and Toleration', p. 247

[13] *Ibid.*, p. 243; *Market, State and Community*, p. 237. See also Canovan, *Nationhood and Political Theory*, ch. 4; Bell, *Communitarianism and its Critics*, pp. 137–8; Tamir, *Liberal Nationalism*, p. 121. Buchanan addresses a related thesis: see A. Buchanan, *Secession: The Legitimacy of Political Divorce from Fort Sumter to Lithuania and Quebec* (Boulder, CO: Westview, 1991), p. 51.

argument for this idea seems to be that people give greater weight to need than other considerations in matters of distribution to the extent that they see themselves as bound to the beneficiaries by common ties.[14] (In his most recent writings, however, Miller makes it clear that he thinks the mere existence of a shared national identity is neither necessary nor sufficient for redistributive policies to be widely endorsed. The character of the national identity also matters: only if the identity is 'solidaristic' can it play the necessary role.[15])

The idea that a shared national identity is required in order for there to be widespread support for redistribution on grounds of social justice will not threaten those liberal conceptions of political community which deny that justice has redistributive implications. But it does bear upon any conception of political community, liberal or otherwise, the realization of which requires the redistribution of resources amongst citizens.

2.   Assimilation

The various arguments for the importance of a shared national identity which I have presented appeal centrally to the idea that when people share a national identity they possess what I have called a sense of belonging together. In combination, these arguments lend support to the idea that when cultural diversity threatens to undermine a sense of belonging together, the state should pursue a policy of assimilation to undermine those communities below the level of the state that stand in the way of a shared national identity.[16] If a viable liberal political community cannot

---

[14] Miller, 'Socialism and Toleration', p. 243; *Market, State and Community*, p. 237. There does seem to be a non-sequitur here: from the fact that people give more weight to need than, say, merit when they see themselves as bound together to the beneficiaries, it does not follow that they will only give significant weight to need under these circumstances. But it might nevertheless be thought that Miller's thesis here has independent plausibility.

[15] Miller, *On Nationality*, p. 94. There is a danger of partly trivializing the claim here (as Miller is aware: see *ibid.*, p. 96, note 23) by defining a solidaristic national identity as one which involves a commitment to redistribution. What is it for a national identity to be solidaristic other than for compatriots to be mutually concerned, part of which would include a willingness to support redistribution? For further discussion of Miller's claims, see my 'The State, National Identity and Distributive Justice', *New Community*, vol. 21, 1995, pp. 241–54.

[16] The arguments do not, however, point unequivocally in the direction of a policy of assimilation. When the source of cultural diversity is the co-existence of a number of different nations within the same state, it might be thought that the arguments give reason for allowing them political independence of some kind. In many cases, however, granting national minorities political independence is unlikely to solve the problem given the intermingling of peoples and, indeed, may cause more harm than good. Even those theorists who are most sympathetic to national self-determination acknowledge that serious constraints need to be placed on the circumstances under which it is justified. See Miller, *On Nationality*, ch. 4; A. Margalit and J. Raz, 'National Self-Determination', *Journal of Philosophy*, vol. 87, 1990, pp. 439–61.

be achieved in the absence of a shared national identity, liberals would need to place stronger constraints on cultural diversity than those defended in Chapter 3. Liberal critics of liberal-nationalism have often responded that such a policy cannot be justified because it is fundamentally oppressive. According to these liberals, liberal-nationalism is an oxymoron. The guiding idea here is familiar in form at least: sharing a national identity would require convergence on controversial ideals and that can only be achieved, if it can be achieved at all, by oppression.

In order to assess the idea that the assimilation required in order to foster a shared national identity is necessarily oppressive, we need a clearer understanding of its nature. I shall call a policy one of assimilation if, and only if, it aims to produce an outcome in which members of some cultural community abandon at least some of their customs and practices.[17] It might be objected that when assimilation is defined this broadly everyone will agree that it can be non-oppressive. Even liberals wholeheartedly opposed to nationalism will be in favour of some assimilation policies understood in this way. As we saw in Chapter 3, when a minority engages in an unjust practice, liberals will want pressure put on them to abandon it, and in some cases will defend the use of force.

There is some truth in this charge. If liberalism can be defended against the accusation of cultural imperialism in the way I suggested in Chapter 3, then we are entitled to say that only assimilation policies which aim for more than the eradication of practices which violate basic rights are potentially oppressive. We therefore need to distinguish between different kinds of assimilation policies in order to identify the more problematic varieties, and to distinguish between the different means by which they might be pursued.

One important distinction is between what I shall call moderate and radical assimilationists. *Radical* assimilationists aim to create a polity in which members of minority cultural communities abandon all their distinctive customs and practices, including their distinctive linguistic practices, i.e., they aim to undermine those communities or, at least, to

---

[17] This definition does not respect a distinction that some have drawn between integration and assimilation. Roy Jenkins, for example, implicitly drew such a distinction in a speech in 1966 when he was British home secretary:
'Integration is perhaps a rather loose word. I do not regard it as meaning the loss, by immigrants, of their own national characteristics and culture. I do not think that we need in this country a melting pot, which will turn everybody out in a common mould, as one of a series of carbon copies of someone's misplaced vision of the stereotyped Englishman . . . I define integration, therefore, not as a flattening process of assimilation but as equal opportunity, coupled with cultural diversity, in an atmosphere of mutual tolerance'. R. Jenkins, *Essays and Speeches* (London: Collins, 1967), p. 267 (quoted by Sebastian Poulter in his 'Cultural Pluralism and its Limits', in B. Parekh (ed.), *Britain: A Plural Society* (London: CRE, 1990), p. 5).

destroy their current character. *Moderate* assimilationists, in contrast, aim to create a polity in which everyone is able to speak the same language (viz., the language of the dominant group) even if they have different first languages, and in which members of minority cultural communities abandon those customs and practices which are either unjust or in conflict with some of the central customs and practices of the dominant group. It is not implausible to suppose that moderate assimilation would be enough to provide the conditions needed for citizens to come to the belief that they belong together, and it is this belief which the liberal-nationalist thinks is vital.

What is it for two practices or customs to be in conflict? One practice or custom is in conflict with another if it is based upon, or presupposes, a belief that is inconsistent with a belief which the other practice or custom is based upon or presupposes. The paradigm case of this would be opposed religious practices: when two groups are deeply committed to different religions each of which regards the other as blasphemous. But there are other cases relevant to the predicament of liberal democracies. A central practice of the dominant group may presuppose the idea that people should choose their marriage partners, whereas a minority group may be committed to the idea that marriages should be arranged by the parents.[18] A central practice of the dominant group may presuppose the idea that a person should have at most one spouse, whereas a minority group may be committed to the idea that they should be allowed more than one.[19] In these cases the moderate assimilationist would argue that policies should be adopted with a view to bringing to an end the minority's practices.

It is these kind of cases and the assimilationist's apparently illiberal response to them that many have been troubled by. But the practical implications of moderate assimilationism are, in general, less severe than those of radical assimilationism. (Note, however, that this is partly an empirical matter for it depends on the nature of the central practices of the dominant group, and the thickness of the culture shared by it. Under some circumstances moderate assimilationism might converge with radical assimilationism.) It is clear that moderate assimilationism can tolerate, and indeed respect or even affirm group differences in many cases. For instance, it can celebrate the presence of other religions in a society,

---

[18] Here we need to distinguish between arranged marriages and forced marriages. There is no general reason for thinking that the former are unjust or involve a violation of individual rights: see Chapter 3, section 7.

[19] Liberals have sometimes objected that polygamy, when it takes its standard form of polygyny, is unjust because it discriminates against women (see J. S. Mill, 'On Liberty', in M. Warnock (ed.), *Utilitarianism* (Glasgow: Fontana, 1962), p. 224). But we can imagine forms of polygamy that did not discriminate in this way.

provided that the practices of these religions are basically just and not in conflict with the central practices, religious or otherwise, of the dominant cultural community. When the dominant cultural group shares no particular religion, or when it is committed to a religion which allows that there is more than one adequate spirituality or more than one path to God, moderate assimilationists will not be hostile to the presence of other faiths. There is no reason to think that conflict between the central practices and customs of the dominant cultural group and those of other cultural groups will always be pervasive.[20]

Radical and moderate assimilationists can use either coercive or non-coercive means (or both) to secure the results at which they aim, and the distinction between these two different means is crucially relevant to the question of whether assimilation policies can be defended. *Coercive* measures would include laws which prohibit members of a cultural community from engaging in their customs and practices. In their most extreme form, this might involve laws against practising particular religions, or against wearing certain kinds of dress, or using certain languages in public places. *Non-coercive* measures, in contrast, might include giving the customs and symbols of the dominant culture public status and respect (giving public holidays for festivals recognized by the dominant culture but not others); employing the language of the dominant culture in public affairs; requiring that state schools teach in that language, and educate children in the history, geography and literature of the dominant culture; subsidizing the dominant culture in various ways or giving tax cuts to those who participate in it.

When radical or moderate assimilation policies are pursued through coercive means, it is hard to avoid the conclusion that they are oppressive, except when they merely require cultural communities to abandon their unjust practices.[21] It is not obvious, however that non-coercive assimilation policies need be oppressive, especially when they take the moderate form. They need not even require the state to be non-neutral in the way that some liberals think is forbidden,[22] for the state can justify these policies by appealing to the importance of a shared national identity for

[20] Note also that radical and moderate assimilationism have very different implications in cases where minorities speak a different first language from that of the dominant community. Radical assimilationists will require minorities to abandon their first languages, whereas moderate assimilationists will allow them to continue using them (though they will require them to learn the language of the dominant community).

[21] Even then coercion may not be the justified response, for it may create more injustice, or be too costly, see Chapter 3.

[22] See R. Dworkin, 'Liberalism', in his *A Matter of Principle*. Not all those who think that the basic structure of society should be neutral between different conceptions of the good suppose that all of the state's policies should be neutral in this way. See Barry, *Justice as Impartiality*, pp. 143–4.

(say) cohesiveness and stability, rather than by arguing that the culturally specific commitments which it expresses are in some way superior.

It is not only liberals who have been suspicious of assimilation policies. Radicals committed to a politics of difference have also been opposed to them. Iris Young, for example, would maintain that assimilation, even when it is pursued non-coercively in its moderate form, will have oppressive consequences.[23] First, she claims that assimilated groups are in the position of being forced to learn the rules of a game which has already begun, and which they have played no part in devising. They are therefore unfairly disadvantaged by it. Second, she claims that assimilated groups suffer from cultural imperialism. When a policy of assimilation is pursued, the privileged or dominant cultural community will see their community as objectively superior or universally valid, and discount minority cultures as inferior or as less than fully human. Third, she maintains that as a result of cultural imperialism and the devaluation of groups which deviate from the dominant norms, members of them come to suffer from an internalized sense of inferiority.

But a policy of assimilation need not be premised on the idea that the dominant culture is superior and hence need not be culturally imperialist. It might simply be premised on the idea that a shared national identity is important (for the sort of reasons entertained in section 2 of this chapter), and that the best prospect of fostering one is by a policy of moderate assimilation. It is true that assimilated groups are often in the position of being forced to abide by the rules of a game that they had no role in devising. But the terms of assimilation might in principle be arrived at by a political process in which all are effectively represented, and as a result might involve some *mutual* adjustment.

This still leaves the question of whether the costs imposed on cultural communities by non-coercive moderate assimilation policies are necessarily unfair.[24] Will Kymlicka has developed an argument which might be

---

[23] See Young, *Justice and the Politics of Difference*, esp. pp. 164–5. Young's initial characterization of assimilation is somewhat different from mine. She calls it 'the transcendence of group difference' (*ibid.*, p. 157), but her discussion makes clear that she would also regard what I am calling moderate assimilation policies as oppressive even when they are non-coercive.

[24] Young also claims that a policy of assimilation is likely to be ineffective or counterproductive. Although the kind of non-coercive policies I have described are unlikely to be effective in assimilating members of minority cultures in a short space of time, they may well be effective over a generation or two, and need not always provoke significant opposition. What kind of opposition they are likely to face will largely depend upon past history. If the group concerned has been unjustly treated in the past, a policy of assimilation may provide a focus for their grievances. And assimilation is more likely to face resistance from indigenous groups who believe that they have some right of self-determination than from an immigrant group which makes no such claims. (It may also be affected by external factors, for example, groups may regard assimilation as a

thought to imply that such policies are unjust, at least when they target members of indigenous groups. His argument rests upon the importance to individuals of their cultural membership, and upon the idea that (with indigenous groups at least) a cultural structure is part of the circumstances in which people find themselves rather than a consequence of their choices.[25] According to Kymlicka, people's options are embedded in cultural structures, and the demise of such a structure may leave a person unable to lead a meaningful life. A member of a minority cultural community may be disadvantaged simply by living in the midst of a dominant cultural community whose members make choices which adversely affect her, perhaps leading to the eventual disintegration of her cultural community. When a policy of assimilation is actively pursued, the costs of being a member of a minority cultural community are potentially much greater, and the disadvantages of being one take on a different character.

As we saw in Chapter 3, Kymlicka contrasts ethnic groups, which have formed largely as a result of voluntary immigration, with indigenous groups, which have a long historical presence in the territory they occupy. The members of cultural communities which have formed as a result of voluntary immigration have chosen to leave behind the cultural structures in which they grew up, and entered a country with new cultural structures. He suggests that they have no complaint on grounds of justice if they face disadvantages due to the fact that they are in a minority. And he does not appear to think that they would have any complaint on grounds of justice or fairness if the state pursued a policy of non-forcible assimilation. In contrast, it is clear that he thinks members of cultural communities which have resided in the same territory over generations would have a legitimate complaint on grounds of justice if the state attached serious costs to their continuing in their traditional ways of life or if it subsidized other ways of life simply in order to secure a shared national identity.

Even if we understand cultural membership in the way Kymlicka does, and attach the same moral significance to it, the contrast he draws between immigrants and indigenous groups is suspect. As I suggested in Chapter 3, the children of immigrant groups which have succeeded in partially recreating the cultural structures which they left behind are in an analogous position to members of indigenous groups – neither chose to be members of minority cultures. If he is to be consistent, Kymlicka should accept that in general members of minority cultures, whether constituted by indigenous groups or recent immigrants, have a complaint

betrayal of their relatives in the country from which they have emigrated and who have remained true to their traditional practices.)

[25] See Kymlicka, *Liberalism, Community and Culture*, especially chs. 8–9; *Multicultural Citizenship*, especially chs. 5–6.

on grounds of justice if they are *seriously* disadvantaged because of their cultural membership.

It is not obvious, however, that a policy of assimilation need seriously disadvantage members of minority cultural communities in a way which would make it a matter of justice. The cases with which Kymlicka is most concerned are those where the very survival of a culture is at issue; then the disadvantage faced by members of it may be very grave indeed, for it may be that they will be unable to find meaning in the practices of the dominant community or wider society. But if a policy of assimilation has as its effects the gradual erosion of minority cultures, accompanied by a gradual transformation in the identities of their members so that they can identify more and more with the dominant culture, it is unclear whether they face significant unchosen disadvantages. So Kymlicka's case for the importance of cultural membership, and for the injustice of any serious disadvantage that rests upon it, is compatible with long-term policies aimed at gradual assimilation. Young could not appeal to it to justify the idea that assimilation must have oppressive consequences.

Young is surely right, however, that assimilation policies will have morally relevant costs, even if I am right that these are not necessarily sufficient to justify speaking of oppression. First, even if an assimilation policy is publicly justified by appealing to the importance of a shared national identity, rather than to the superiority of the dominant culture, it will be harder for members of minority cultures who choose to continue in their traditional ways of life not to come to feel that these are being devalued, and hard for them not to suffer low self-respect or self-esteem as a result.[26] Second, in most cases the cultures of minorities will contain much that is of value, and the disappearance of those parts of their cultures that are incompatible with the central elements of the dominant culture may still represent the loss of something potentially enriching even for members of the dominant culture.[27] But these considerations, though significant, are unlikely to be sufficient to defeat policies of non-coercive moderate assimilation, if a shared national identity is as important for the liberal conception of political community as its advocates suggest.

---

[26] See Young, *Justice and the Politics of Difference*, p. 165.
[27] Ten emphasizes the first of these objections and the value of cultural diversity: see C. L. Ten, 'Multiculturalism and the Value of Diversity', in C. Kukathas (ed.), *Multicultural Citizens: The Philosophy and Politics of Identity* (St. Leonards, NSW: Centre for Independent Studies, 1993), pp. 9–10, 12–16.

3. A sense of belonging to a polity *versus* a sense of belonging together

In this section I shall try to make plausible the idea that the various benefits which a shared national identity is alleged to make possible might be secured in other ways that do not impose the moral costs which arise from even moderate non-coercive assimilation policies. My argument relies on drawing a distinction between a sense of belonging to a polity and what I have called a sense of belonging together.

Let me begin by simply stipulating what I mean by a sense of belonging to a polity: a person has a sense of belonging to a polity if and only if she identifies with most of its major institutions and some of its central practices, and feels at home in them. When a person identifies with those institutions and practices, she regards her flourishing as intimately linked to their flourishing. In order to be able to identify with something outside herself, a person must be able to perceive it as valuable, at least on balance, and see her concerns reflected in it. When a person feels at home in a practice or institution, she is able to find her way around it, and experiences participation in it as natural. In order to be able to feel this way, she must not be excluded from the practice or institution or be marginalized in relation to it.

Although I have stipulated what I mean by a sense of belonging to a polity, I hope that my account resonates considerably with what we ordinarily understand by this phrase. Someone may have a strong sense of belonging to a polity in my sense, even if they do not much like what their government is doing in their name, or indeed (like many liberal Israelis at the time of writing) feel exasperated with the course it is charting. This discomfort or exasperation is compatible with continuing to identify with its major institutions and with at least some of its central practices.

In principle at least, the citizens of a state could identify with their major institutions and practices, and feel at home in them, without believing that there was any deep reason why they should associate together, of the sort which might be provided by the belief that they shared a history, religion, ethnicity, mother tongue, culture or conception of the good. In other words, the citizens of a state might in principle have a sense of belonging to a polity without thinking that there is any real sense in which they belong *together*. (When I refer to a sense of belonging simpliciter in what follows, I shall mean a sense of belonging *to a polity* rather than a sense of belonging together.)

Even though there is a conceptual distinction here, it might be doubted whether it can do any work in practice. But the distinction at least enables us to formulate two empirical hypotheses. The first is that sometimes a liberal polity can be viable even if its citizens lack a sense of belonging together, so long as they have a sense of belonging to it. The second hypothesis is that even when the citizens of a liberal polity do have a sense of belonging together, it may nevertheless be their sense of belonging to it which is the most significant factor in explaining why that polity is enduring and stable.

The first hypothesis suggests one way of interpreting Charles Taylor's proposal that Canada might become a polity held together by the acceptance of a 'deep diversity' in which a plurality of ways of belonging were acknowledged;[28] in my terms the idea would be that Canadian citizens might come to possess a much more secure sense of belonging to the Canadian polity, based upon differential forms of citizenship, even if they were not under the illusion that they belonged together in the relevant sense. But Taylor is aware that his proposal is likely to be dismissed as utopian speculation, for it is hard to find any actual polity which is held together by the acceptance of deep diversity.

This reveals a difficulty with the first hypothesis more generally: it is not easy to find polities whose citizens possess a sense of belonging but not a sense of belonging together. I shall consider some candidates below, but note, to begin with, that the second hypothesis cannot be dismissed as utopian speculation, for confirming it would not require us to find a stable liberal polity the citizens of which lacked a sense of belonging together. It might nevertheless seem intuitively implausible: if the citizens of a state do believe that there is some special reason why they should associate together, surely that belief must be the most important part of the explanation for why that state is enduring and stable. But this response ignores the possibility that a sense of belonging together may in some cases be parasitic on a sense of belonging to a polity. Perhaps in some cases if a group of citizens began to lose faith in the fairness of the institutions which governed them, and ceased to identify with these institutions, they would also lose their sense of belonging together with the rest.[29] If the second hypothesis should not be dismissed as utopian, then neither should the first, for if the second hypothesis is true, then we can see how the first hypothesis *might* be true, even in the absence of unambiguous confirming instances. Let me move on to a brief consideration of three polities – the United States, Switzerland and Belgium – in

---

[28] C. Taylor, 'Shared and Divergent Values', in his *Reconciling the Solitudes: Essays on Canadian Federalism and Nationalism*, ed. G. Laforest (Montreal: McGill–Queen's University Press, 1993), p. 183.

[29] Something of this kind may have happened in the twentieth century in Belgium, when many Dutch-speakers began to feel alienated from its main institutions, see below.

order to see what support, if any, they might provide for one or both of the two hypotheses I have described.

Consider first the United States. In a general discussion of social unity, Will Kymlicka proposes that 'what matters is not shared values, but a *shared identity* . . . People decide who they want to share a country with by asking who they identify with, who they feel solidarity with. What holds Americans together, despite their disagreements over the nature of the good life, is the fact that they share an identity as Americans.'[30] But Kymlicka says little about what it is for people to share an identity. For my purposes, it is important to distinguish between two different ideas. First, the idea that people share an identity if they have a sense of belonging together, i.e., they believe that there is some special reason why they should associate together, such as that which might be provided by the belief that they have a common history or distinctive culture. Second, the idea that people share an identity if they have a sense of belonging to the same polity, i.e., identify with some of the same institutions and practices, and feel at home in them. Once this distinction has been made, it might be argued that Americans do not possess a sense of belonging together in the relevant sense and that what holds the United States together is a shared sense of belonging to the American polity, expressed, in part, by the way in which American citizens identify with various symbols, practices and institutions, such as 'the flag, the Pledge, the Fourth, the Constitution'.[31] Or less ambitiously, it might be maintained that even though American citizens do possess a sense of belonging together in the relevant sense, the most important factor in holding the United States together is a sense of belonging to the American polity.

David Miller takes the view that Americans share a national identity.[32] If he were right, this would undermine the idea that they lack a sense of belonging together of the relevant kind. According to his account, for citizens to share a national identity 'there must be a sense that the people belong together by virtue of the characteristics that they share'.[33] The idea of common characteristics is then cashed out in terms of a public culture, where:

A public culture may be seen as a set of understandings about how a group of people is to conduct its life together. This will include political principles such as a belief in democracy or the rule of law, but it reaches more widely than this. It extends to social norms such as honesty in filling in your tax return or queuing as a

[30] W. Kymlicka, 'Social Unity in a Liberal State', *Social Philosophy and Policy*, vol. 13, 1996, p. 131.
[31] M. Walzer, 'What Does It Mean to Be an "American"?', *Social Research*, vol. 57, 1990, p. 602.   [32] See, e.g., Miller, *On Nationality*, pp. 20, 72 n24, 94, 113.
[33] *Ibid.*, p. 25.

way of deciding who gets on the bus first. It may also embrace certain ideals, for instance religious beliefs or a commitment to preserve the purity of the national language.[34]

But in the American case, it is hard to see what shared principles, commitments or norms could provide the content of a distinctive American national identity. American institutions, public practices and ceremonies are distinctive, but does that really reflect distinctive principles or norms which govern how citizens are to conduct their lives together? The alternative is to say that Americans share an identity in the sense that they identify with these institutions, practices and ceremonies, but this does not mean that they share a distinctive public culture in Miller's sense, nor indeed that they believe they share one.[35]

Similar points could be made about Switzerland. Switzerland appears to create problems for the liberal-nationalist, for it seems that the Swiss lack a sense of belonging together of the relevant kind but nevertheless have managed to realize, at least to a considerable extent, liberal values. Miller again takes the view that there is a Swiss national identity.[36] There is surely a Swiss identity, if by that is meant a widespread sense amongst Swiss citizens that they belong to the Swiss polity, but do they possess a sense of belonging together in the relevant sense? In his study of the peculiarities of Switzerland, Jonathan Steinberg is ambivalent on this question. On the one hand, he says that although there is a sense in which 'the Swiss see themselves . . . as a fragile set of communities held together by a sort of *volunté générale*',[37] this view of themselves can not be quite right because the polity is held together by a complex set of institutions which are capable of registering, channelling and resolving conflicts.[38] This account of the unity of the Swiss state does not take us beyond the thesis that it rests upon a sense of belonging to the Swiss polity, fostered in part by a complex institutional machinery.

It is only when Steinberg catalogues 'Swiss values', viz. 'longevity in service, anonymity, a certain populist cosiness, a general awareness of how things are done according to the "unwritten rules"',[39] that he appears to move towards the idea that the Swiss state is underwritten by a

[34] *Ibid.*, p. 26.

[35] These claims are controversial. For a different view, see Walzer, 'What Does it Mean to Be an "American"?', especially pp. 606–14; P. Gleason, 'American Identity and Americanization' in S. Thernstrom (ed.), *The Harvard Encyclopaedia of American Ethnic Groups* (Cambridge, MA: Harvard University Press, 1980), especially pp. 55–7. But I am inclined to think that the idea that there is a shared American national identity has been advanced so confidently because an adequate distinction has not been drawn between what I am calling a sense of belonging together and a sense of belonging to a polity.

[36] Miller, *On Nationality*, pp. 94–5.

[37] J. Steinberg, *Why Switzerland?*, 2nd edn (Cambridge: Cambridge University Press, 1996), p. 249.   [38] *Ibid.*, p. 251.   [39] *Ibid.*, p. 251.

shared national identity. But one might wonder which part of the story he gives about the unity of the Swiss state is the most important: is it the institutional machinery, which fosters a sense of belonging, or the alleged shared values, which might provide Swiss citizens with a sense of belonging together of the relevant kind?

Belgium raises some of the same difficulties for the liberal-nationalist as does Switzerland. For despite its cultural diversity and apparent lack of any robust national identity, it has managed to sustain liberal values, to some degree at least. In recent decades Belgium has evolved a unique system of federalism based on 'the creation of complex institutional shock-absorbers which subject all problems to lengthy discussion, compromise and rational solution'.[40] By doing so, it seems to have managed to create and sustain a reasonably strong sense of belonging to the polity, and a willingness to engage in hard discussions concerning the direction of constitutional reform.

The historical evidence suggests that at the time of the creation of the Belgian state, in 1830, its citizens did possess a strong sense of belonging together. And Dutch-speaking Belgians did not feel that *they* belonged together (or with other Dutch-speakers), nor on the whole did French-speaking Belgians think that *they* belonged together (or with other French speakers).[41] But this was to change, largely it seems because of a failure to give Dutch-speakers due recognition: Dutch was not recognized as an official language alongside French until 1898, and Dutch-speakers were disadvantaged in various ways. By the beginning of the twentieth century, Dutch-speaking Belgians had come to think of themselves as a 'people', and some French-speakers, fearing the advent of a compulsory bilingualism which would adversely affect their interests, also came to possess a group consciousness.

Today some commentators claim to detect the residual presence of a shared national identity that coexists alongside the particular linguistic and regional identities, for example, in the outpourings of grief which were caused by the death of King Baudouin in 1993.[42] But these outpourings are also consistent with the idea that Belgians identify with the institution of the monarchy and that Baudouin was a popular incumbent, especially because of his attempts at bridge-building between the two communities. Public grief was not necessarily indicative of a widespread

[40] J. Fitzmaurice, *The Politics of Belgium: A Unique Federalism* (London: Hurst and Co., 1996), p. 4.
[41] See R. De Schryver, 'The Belgian Revolution and the Emergence of Belgium's Biculturalism', and J. Stengers, 'Belgian National Sentiments', both in A. Lijphart (ed.), *Conflict and Coexistence in Belgium: The Dynamics of a Culturally Divided Society* (Berkeley, CA: Institute of International Studies, University of California, 1981).
[42] Fitzmaurice, *The Politics of Belgium*, pp. 61, 267.

belief amongst Belgians that they belonged together in the relevant sense. And even if it were indicative of a weak sense of belonging together, what reason do we have for supposing that it is this sense of belonging together that is important today in binding the polity together, rather than a sense of belonging to it?

4.   Liberal-nationalist doubts

The liberal-nationalist is unlikely to be convinced by my argument so far. Her doubts are likely to focus upon the first hypothesis I distinguished, which holds that the benefits which a shared national identity is alleged to provide could in practice be secured simply by a sense of belonging in the absence of such an identity. (The second hypothesis, that even when a sense of belonging together exists in a liberal polity it may be less important in making that polity viable than a sense of belonging to it, does not by itself threaten the liberal nationalist's position.) Although I hope that the discussion in the previous section will have provided some support for the first hypothesis, it is nevertheless important to address the arguments presented in section 1, to explain why they do not demonstrate the need for the citizens of a viable liberal polity to share a national identity.

Liberal-nationalist worries may conceal two different but related issues. First, the issue of whether a sense of belonging to a polity on its own could ever be enough in practice to yield the benefits which a shared national identity is alleged to provide. Second, the issue of whether, even if a sense of belonging to a polity could be enough to yield these benefits, it could be achieved in practice without a shared national identity. It is the second of these issues that is raised by the argument that a shared national identity is required in order to avoid alienation in the modern world. If citizens have a sense of belonging to a polity, then they will avoid alienation from it, but the charge is that a sense of belonging is unattainable in the absence of a shared national identity. David Miller, for example, would maintain that citizens need to work together in shaping their social environment if they are to avoid alienation, and that in practice they need some deep reason for doing so which in the modern world can be provided only by a shared national identity: '[n]ationality gives people the common identity that makes it possible for them to conceive of shaping their world together'.[43]

But why should we be persuaded by that claim? Perhaps under some circumstances it will be impossible for groups of citizens to work together politically, for example, when they or their ancestors have been related to

---

[43] Miller, *Market, State, and Community*, p. 189.

one another as oppressor and oppressed. When a particular group of citizens believe that some institution or practice has been founded upon, and evolved on the basis of, their exploitation or suppression, they are going to find it hard to identify with it even if it is now friendly to them. Here the problem is their tarnished relationship, not the absence of a shared national identity.

Having reasons to value an institution in its current form, and not being marginalized by it, are insufficient to guarantee feeling at home in it or identification with it. But in many cases they may be enough, and then a shared national identity is unnecessary to provide people with the motivation to work together politically. Although certain kinds of considerations may make it impossible for groups to cooperate together, in general they will need no special reason to do so other than the fact that they share a common fate, a sense of which can often be provided *merely* by the recognition that they each belong to the same polity and are not excluded from, or marginalized by, its institutions and practices. A sense of sharing a common fate may also be enough to produce significant convergence on the good of citizenship, which is part of the republican conception of political community. Members of a polity would be inclined to see themselves as fellow citizens, subject to special obligations to one another, the fulfilment of which contributes to the good of citizenship, and which are also justified in part by that good.

Since I see no general basis for supposing that identifying with society's major institutions and practices, or feeling at home in them, requires sharing a national identity with those who are also subject to them, I shall simply put aside the worry that it does in what follows. Is there then any reason to expect the various alleged benefits of sharing a national identity to flow from a widespread sense of belonging to a polity? As we saw in the first section of this chapter, Mill contends that the stability, and perhaps the very existence, of liberal institutions relies upon a shared national identity. The precise nature of the relationship between the stability of the liberal state and the existence of a shared national identity is complex, but it is obscure why we should accept the thesis that without such an identity stable liberal institutions are next to impossible in practice. Why can not a sense of belonging to a polity play much the same role as a shared national identity in securing liberal institutions?

Other things being equal, a state will be more stable and less vulnerable to various forms of social unrest when such a sense of belonging exists. When people do not identify with the major institutions and practices of the polity or feel excluded from those practices, they are less likely to think that they have a stake in its stability or survival, and they will be open to cooption by external aggressors. But when they identify with those institutions and practices, then there is no reason to think that the polity will be any more unstable or vulnerable to external aggression than it would be when a shared national identity existed. Indeed a sense of belonging to a polity can provide the basis for patriotism, understood *simply* as a love of its central institutions and practices.

What should we say about the idea that a shared national identity is necessary for, or at least facilitates, the willingness to compromise in the face of conflicting interests? No doubt a shared national identity does provide a basis for trust between different groups in society, and hence facilitates compromise. But why can not what I call a sense of belonging to the polity also do so? When people from different groups in society identify with its major institutions and practices, they are more likely to accept the *authority* of those institutions to resolve any conflicts of interest that arise between them and to trust the institutions to do so.

Consider also Miller's thesis that a politics of the common good will predominate only if there is a shared national identity. That competes with an alternative thesis which I do not see that Miller has given any evidence to undermine, and which is itself intuitively plausible: that a sense of belonging to a polity is needed to underpin a politics of the common good, but a shared national identity is often unnecessary. If there is a widespread sense of belonging of this kind, then citizens will feel part of the polity of which they are members, and as a result are likely to have a sense of sharing a fate with others who are also part of it. That sense of sharing a common fate may often be enough to motivate support for policies which aim at the common good without there needing to be a deeper sense of belonging together, which a shared national identity would involve.

Miller is perhaps on firmer ground when he maintains that there is unlikely to be widespread support for redistributive policies on grounds of social justice in the absence of a 'solidaristic' national identity. But this is not for the reason he gives, viz. that people are more likely to give weight to considerations such as need when they are bound together by a shared national identity. For there to be widespread support for redistributive policies on grounds of social justice, there would need to be considerable convergence on principles of social justice, and it is not implausible to suppose that there is unlikely to be such convergence in the absence of a solidaristic common culture. But even if there is not convergence on principles of social justice, there may nevertheless be a widespread consensus on the idea that redistributive policies are warranted. Some will support these policies on grounds of self-interest, as an insurance against bad luck in the future. Some will support them because they believe that humanitarian considerations require them, even if they do not believe that they are requirements of justice. And some will support them because they are committed to the good of citizenship, and believe that people cannot be full citizens – possess effective opportunities to participate in political life, say – unless their basic needs are met. Some convergence on this last idea might be encouraged by the way in which a sense of belonging to a polity tends to generate a sense of sharing a common fate.

5.   Patriotic Identification

How does my claim that liberal regimes can be sustained by a sense of belonging to them compare with the idea that these regimes cannot flourish without widespread 'patriotic identification'? In order to address this question, let me distinguish three different possible accounts of why the citizens of a liberal polity identify with its major institutions.

(i) They identify with these institutions because they identify with the particular culture or way of life which those institutions express.

(ii) They identify with these institutions because they are subject to them and identify with the general principles which they embody.

(iii) They identify with these institutions because they are subject to them and identify with the particular, historically situated way in which these institutions embody values such as liberty, justice and democracy.

Each of these possible accounts of why the members of a polity identify with its major institutions could be treated as a general model for a kind of patriotic identification that is needed in order to sustain liberal institutions.

The model suggested by (i) is favoured by some liberal-nationalists who believe that the citizens of a state will identify with its major institutions only if there is a close fit between those institutions and some national way of life that they share. It seems too restrictive as a general account, however: why can't some or all of the citizens of a state identify with its institutions for other reasons, such as those suggested by (ii) and (iii)?

Some have thought that there is a straightforward reason for preferring (iii) to (ii) as a general model of what is required to sustain liberal institutions, viz. that identification with these institutions could not be sustained by identification with general principles in the way that (ii) requires. Maurizio Viroli, for example, argues that citizens would not identify with their institutions merely because they shared 'universal principles and values', for that would be 'too distant and too general'.[44] What is required instead is for citizens to be attached to 'a particular liberty and a justice that is part of their culture, that has for them a particular beauty, a particular warmth, a particular colour that is connected with particular memories and particular histories'.[45]

Viroli's argument can be persuasive only if we suppose that the relevant universal principles and values must be discovered or justified from some standpoint which is detached from the form of life in which they are embedded. If, on the contrary, these principles and values can be recovered from reflection on the form of life itself, then there is no reason to think that they will necessarily lose the particular 'beauty, warmth and colour' supposedly possessed by the institutions and practices which embody them. In this respect, compare Charles Taylor's discussion of patriotic identification. He defines it as 'a common identification with a historical community founded on certain values',[46] and suggests that in the United States this requires 'a commitment to certain ideals, articulated famously in the Declaration of Independence, Lincoln's Gettysburg Address, and such documents, which in turn derive their importance from their connection to certain climactic transitions of a shared history'.[47] Here there is no suggestion that ideals such as liberty are necessarily to be recovered or justified from some detached standpoint.

Despite the difficulty involved in keeping them apart, (ii) and (iii) do supply rather different models of patriotic identification.[48] For (ii) to provide an adequate account, it would have to be possible to derive citizens' reasons for valuing their institutions from some set of general principles, whereas this would not be required by (iii). When the distinction is understood in this way, Jurgen Habermas's version of 'constitutional patriotism' is perhaps the clearest example of the model based upon (ii).[49]

From the perspective I have been developing, the model of patriotic identification provided by either (ii) or (iii), like that provided by (i), is too

---

[44] M. Viroli, *For Love of Country: An Essay on Patriotism and Nationalism* (Oxford: Oxford University Press, 1995), p. 14.   [45] *Ibid.*, p. 175.

[46] Taylor, 'Cross-Purposes', p. 199.

[47] *Ibid.*, p. 196. Taylor seems to think that patriotic identification can have many different bases, however; elsewhere he seems to allow that valuing 'deep diversity' could be a basis for patriotic identification. See Taylor, 'Shared and Divergent Values', pp. 182–4.

[48] It might seem that (ii) and (iii) can be readily distinguished because (ii), unlike (iii), is vulnerable to the objection that it has no explanation for why citizens identify with *their* major institutions rather than any other institutions which embody the same principles. But that is not obviously so; according to (ii) identification is explained, in part, by the fact that citizens are subject to those institutions.

[49] See J. Habermas, 'Citizenship and National Identity: Some Reflections on the Future of Europe' in R. Beiner (ed.), *Theorizing Citizenship* (Albany, NY: State University of New York Press, 1995), pp. 264, 278–9.

restrictive. If (ii) were adopted as a model, it would require citizens to converge on a particular set of principles. But I want to allow that citizens may have very different interpretations of the ideals which they regard as embodied in their polity's institutions – different conceptions of freedom, equality and justice, for example – in such a way that they cannot be said genuinely to share principles. They might still value the same institutions, and identify with them in a way that is sufficient to sustain them, but for very different reasons.[50]

Understood in terms of (iii), patriotic identification requires a commitment to a polity's institutions that is based upon acceptance of a set of values which acquire their significance from their place in the history of that polity. In contrast, I want to allow the possibility that at least some citizens might identify with their institutions even if they did not identify with the historical processes which lead to their emergence, or did not accept the historical myths that are told about those processes. This is not unimportant in a world in which the history and development of many liberal-democratic institutions has been morally troubled. Fostering a sense of belonging of the kind needed to sustain particular forms of these institutions need not rely upon telling ourselves and our children falsehoods about the past.[51] It requires identifying with those institutions as they are here and now, not identifying with some process which is alleged to have brought them into existence.

6.   Inclusive political community

The liberal-nationalist maintains that most liberals misunderstand the conditions that are required in order for political community, as they conceive it, to be realized in practice. If this critique were successful, it would show that the dominant liberal conception of political community could not be realized in the absence of an overarching national community. I have argued that the liberal-nationalist's arguments are unsuccessful. But there is no doubt that the conditions required for the realization of the dominant liberal conception are highly demanding. So much so that we are entitled to some degree of scepticism about whether the convergence on a particular conception of justice required by it is genuinely possible in culturally plural democratic societies, such as those in Western Europe and North America. Even if it were possible to reach

[50] Here again there is a parallel with Taylor's idea that a liberal polity divided by history and culture might be held together by the acceptance of deep diversity: see Taylor, 'Shared and Divergent Values', p. 183.
[51] For example, Taylor argues that American parents have no legitimate objection to 'the pious tone with which American history and its major figures are presented to the young' ('Cross-Purposes', p. 198). But what if that tone were founded upon historical illusions?

agreement at some very abstract level on a set of basic rights, there would be no reason to expect convergence at any more concrete level. And we have reason to be pessimistic about the possibility of resolving in practice the kind of disputes which emerge from contractualist and contractarian approaches to determining principles of justice (see Chapter 3, section 1).

The idea that in order for a polity to realize liberal ideals, citizens must have a sense of belonging to it, suggests the need for a different vision of political community which might serve as a better regulative ideal. I shall call this ideal 'inclusive political community', where an inclusive political community has the following three main features: first, its members have a sense of belonging to it; second, its constitution is a product of an inclusive political dialogue which aims at consensus even when it does not achieve that outcome; third, its constitution protects the basic rights to which liberals are committed, on some reasonable interpretation of what they are. Let us consider the first of these features: what is involved in practice when the citizens of a state possess a sense of belonging to it?

A widespread sense of belonging cannot in principle be achieved without some convergence in evaluative judgements. But it does not require a shared conception of the good in any genuine sense. It requires that citizens with different cultural backgrounds and conceptions of the good should be able to regard most of the polity's major institutions (especially its legal and political institutions) and some of its central practices as valuable on balance, and feel at home in them. Their reasons for thinking these institutions and practices valuable may in principle diverge considerably, and hence there is no requirement that they share a conception of the good, or even a detailed conception of justice. For example, some may regard these institutions as merely instrumentally valuable because they promote their interests, whilst others regard them as non-instrumentally valuable because they see them as just (perhaps on the grounds that they provide the structure for a mutually beneficial scheme of cooperation).

Citizens need not share a view of how these institutions and practices emerged, of what the key figures or forces were in their evolution, or whether these figures and what they did are legitimate objects of pride. They need only endorse reasons, from their own perspective, for thinking these institutions and practices are valuable in their current form, and as a result come to endorse those institutions and practices. In other words, an 'over-lapping consensus' is required on the desirability of these concrete institutions and practices, although not on some single set of principles or values which might be thought to underwrite them. This overlapping consensus is less demanding, in one respect at least, than that required by Rawls's political liberalism: it does not need agreement on principles of justice to underpin it, for convergence on particular evaluative judgements, some of which might conceivably be derived from divergent principles of justice, would suffice.

An inclusive political community could contain significant illiberal minorities. The idea here is that members of these minorities might nevertheless identify with liberal institutions and the practices they structure, and feel at home in them, because on balance they endorse these institutions and practices and do not feel excluded from them. By definition, their reasons for endorsing these institutions could not be based on their acceptance of liberal principles. Rather, they would be based on the fact that these institutions allow space for a variety of their own practices to flourish (even though they also exclude some of those practices), and are the outcome of a political dialogue to which they have been able to contribute.

Would an inclusive political community be a genuine community? Members of it would participate in the same institutions and practices, so it does not seem illegitimate to claim that, to some degree, they share a way of life. In principle they might not share a thick set of values, but I suggest that their convergence on a range of particular evaluative judgements is sufficient to justify speaking of the shared values that are integral to community, without doing too much violence to the concept of community. Furthermore, since members of an inclusive political community have a sense of belonging to it, they identify with its practices and institutions even if their reasons for doing so differ, and in order to sustain that identification each must be acknowledged by the others as a member. Taken together these features are sufficient to justify the conclusion that an inclusive political community is a genuine community in at least the ordinary sense.

Does an inclusive political community come close to being a community in the moralized sense? In order to do so, its members would have to be mutually concerned, and relations between them would have to be just or non-exploitative. An inclusive political community protects the basic rights of its members, so (from the liberal perspective I am assuming) it is minimally just. It would also need to provide them with equality of opportunity: if people are to have a sense of belonging to their polity, they must not feel marginalized in relation to its institutions and practices. An inclusive political community need not go beyond a commitment to a minimum equality of opportunity, but it is compatible with more demanding ideals of equality (or ideals of giving priority to the worst off) and can facilitate mutual concern. As I argued in section 4 of this chapter, when a widespread sense of belonging exists redistributive policies might come to be supported on a variety of grounds. As a result of identifying with their central institutions and practices, and feeling at home in them, each member is likely to think that she has a stake in the flourishing of those institutions and practices, and to acknowledge that she shares such an interest with other members. There is no guarantee that this would lead to a genuine concern for each other's interests, but it could be a step along that path.

An inclusive political community that falls short of the dominant liberal conception of political community is perhaps not the best, for a community in which all citizens converged on a single set of principles of justice (or rather, the correct or best set, if there is one) to govern their major institutions would be better. And it would be better still were the republican conception of political community described in Chapter 4 to be realized. But my suggestion is that neither of these ideals is likely to be achievable in polities that exhibit the kind of cultural diversity present in most Western democratic countries. In other words, we need to distinguish between the ideal in principle and the ideal in practice, where the latter should (in most circumstances at least) be the regulative ideal; even if there are good grounds for holding that the republican conception of political community represents the ideal in principle, what I have called inclusive political community is the ideal in practice in societies which exhibit considerable cultural diversity.

Defenders of the dominant liberal conception of political community might reply that, properly understood, it does provide us with the ideal in practice, and even where it is not fully realizable it should nevertheless regulate institutions and policy-making. They might agree that in practice it is likely to be impossible to secure a full consensus on a single set of principles of justice, because some citizens are unreasonable or subscribe to unreasonable doctrines, but argue that polities should aspire to a universal consensus on principles of justice amongst reasonable citizens or amongst citizens who affirm reasonable doctrines. There will always be some who are unreasonable, or who subscribe to unreasonable doctrines; what is important is that those who are reasonable should come to converge on the correct or appropriate set of principles and identify with their institutions because the institutions embody these principles. It might be maintained that even when *this* ideal is not fully realizable, it is nevertheless the best regulative ideal, as well as the best ideal in principle. Rawls, for example, thinks that convergence on principles of justice should be sought only amongst those who hold reasonable comprehensive doctrines, and acknowledges that even then it is more realistic to expect convergence on a family of liberal conceptions of justice rather than on a single conception.[52] And he recognizes that even this prospect is a significant historical achievement, speculating that many polities may

[52] Rawls, *Political Liberalism*, p. 164.

have begun with a constitutional consensus (i.e., a consensus on basic political rights and liberties), sustained first as a *modus vivendi* and only later coming to rest on moral foundations.[53] However, in restricting the scope of the dominant liberal ideal of political community in this way, Rawls threatens to undermine its attractiveness as an ideal in practice. Let me explain.

Consider the idea that it is convergence amongst those who hold reasonable comprehensive conceptions which should be sought. Rawls begins by giving a permissive account of what it is for a doctrine to be reasonable: a doctrine is reasonable if it is an exercise in theoretical and practical reason, covering a range of aspects of human life, displaying consistency, coherence and intelligibility, and normally drawing upon some tradition of thought and inquiry.[54] But it becomes clear that his full account is much more restrictive. A doctrine is unreasonable if it does not acknowledge that there are 'burdens of judgement' which make possible disagreement between reasonable people, or if it does not acknowledge that it is unreasonable to use political power to repress other comprehensive doctrines that are not unreasonable.[55] This will exclude any comprehensive doctrine which has at least one of the following features: it denies the burdens of judgement; it maintains mistakenly that some doctrine is such that it cannot be reasonably rejected (even in the light of the burdens of judgement) and seeks its imposition; it maintains that the deliverances of faith can be legitimately imposed even though it is not unreasonable to reject them.[56] An overlapping consensus which ignores 'unreasonable doctrines' that have one or more of these features may be a more realistic prospect, but it is highly exclusionary, and this surely detracts from its being the ideal in practice.

One response might be to insist that it is such an ideal, on the grounds that unreasonable doctrines should be 'contained'[57] and not given the kind of recognition that seeking to include them within an overlapping consensus would provide. But I think that this response is a dangerous one and, to the extent that liberals offer it, they risk fostering a worse society than is feasible, by alienating those who are deemed to subscribe to unreasonable doctrines. We should bear in mind a point emphasized

---

[53] *Ibid.*, pp. 158–64   [54] *Ibid.*, p. 59.

[55] *Ibid.*, pp. 58–62. In fact it is not clear whether Rawls means to say that doctrines which do not meet these conditions are unreasonable, or merely that (even though they are reasonable) they could not be endorsed by reasonable people. For the purposes of my argument, however, these points amount to the same.

[56] This is the position of those Joshua Cohen calls 'non-rationalist fundamentalists': see his 'Moral Pluralism and Political Consensus', in D. Copp, J. Hampton and J. Roemer (eds.), *The Idea of Democracy* (Cambridge: Cambridge University Press, 1993), pp. 286–7.

[57] Rawls says that unreasonable doctrines should be 'contained' so that they do not undermine the unity and justice of society: see *Political Liberalism*, xviii–xix, cf. p. 64 n19.

by Robert Goodin, that when an ideal is unobtainable, the best achievable in practice may be quite different from it.[58] In the present case, I suggest that the best achievable in practice is likely to be an overarching sense of belonging to a society containing liberal institutions[59], and in the presence of cultural diversity this may require special provisions of the kind I shall discuss in the next section.

Strictly speaking my arguments have not shown that the dominant liberal conception of political community should not be a regulative ideal at all, but they do, I believe, provide strong grounds for holding that it at least needs to be supplemented by a different regulative ideal, namely that of inclusive political community, which is likely to be more important in practice. If it is not supplemented in this way, aiming to realize the dominant liberal conception of political community may actually lead to a worse state of affairs than aiming at the second best, for there will always be the danger of excluding those who there is no hope in practice of persuading to accept the liberal principles which are supposed to be justifiable to all in principle.

7.   Fostering a sense of belonging to a polity

What measures are needed to foster a sense of belonging and construct an inclusive political community? Some write as if enjoyment of equal status in society's major institutions, in particular possession of the same civil and political rights and formal equality of opportunity, would be suffi-cient to foster a sense of belonging.[60] But such claims have come to seem increasingly suspect in the light of the experience of societies (such as Britain and arguably the United States) where minority cultural commu-nities live in the midst of a dominant cultural community. In these circumstances, it is possible for everyone to have the same rights and formal equality of opportunity, but for members of a group to feel alienated from its central institutions or be marginalized in relation to many of the practices which are central to society.

The legal and political structures and policies of a state are bound to play an important role in determining whether its citizens have a strong sense of belonging to it. In the face of cultural diversity, there are two obvious ways in which they can contribute to doing so: first, by ensuring

---

[58] Goodin, 'Designing Constitutions', p. 641.

[59] I suggest that inclusive political community is an appropriate ideal not only for nation states (which contain a dominant community and, in practice, usually significant cultural minorities), but also for what Walzer calls 'immigrant societies', such as the United States. See M. Walzer, *On Toleration* (New Haven, CT: Yale University Press, 1997).

[60] Kymlicka refers to this approach as 'benign neglect': see Kymlicka, *Multicultural Citizenship*, pp. 3–4.

that members of different cultural groups are effectively represented within the polity's major decision-making bodies; second, by granting 'cultural communities' as much self-determination as they want and can be feasibly given.

Consider the first strategy. In order to foster a widespread and robust sense of belonging amongst diverse cultural communities, it is important for their members to be represented in the major law and policy-making bodies, and in the judiciary. The presence of members of cultural communities is an indispensable symbol of inclusion and equal status within the polity.[61] But the danger with 'group representation' is that it will have the opposite effect. Members of law and policy-making bodies will see themselves solely as defenders of the interests of the groups to which they belong, and possess no overarching loyalty to the polity as a whole. It is one of the difficulties of the consociational approach to fragmented societies, which favours group representation as a means of power sharing, that one of the conditions favourable to its success, viz. that there should be some overarching loyalty to the state as well as to particular ethnic and national groups,[62] tends to be undermined by the operation of the institutions which are set up to provide group representation.[63] If law and policy-makers regard themselves solely or primarily as representatives of particular national or ethnic groups, and ordinary citizens regard themselves solely or primarily as members of such groups, this is unlikely to foster their loyalty to the state as a whole.

What this suggests is that although it is important for members of different cultural communities to be present on decision-making bodies, they should not be conceived solely, or even primarily, as *representatives* of those groups.[64] Their presence should be seen rather as a symbol of inclusion and equal status within the polity. In practice, of course, the inclusion of members of different cultural communities on law and policy-making bodies is also likely to make their products more sensitive to cultural differences. This is not to make the indefensible assumption, rightly rejected by Anne Phillips, that 'shared experience guarantees shared beliefs or goals'.[65] It is merely to suppose that direct acquaintance

---

[61] Cf. A. Phillips, *The Politics of Presence* (Oxford: Oxford University Press, 1995), pp. 39–40.

[62] See A. Lijphart, *Democracy in Plural Societies: A Comparative Exploration* (New Haven, CT: Yale University Press, 1977), pp. 81–3. This is one of the seven conditions which Lijphart mentions that are conducive to the success of consociational democracy.

[63] See B. Barry, 'Political Accommodation and Consociational Democracy', in his *Democracy, Power and Justice: Essays in Political Theory* (Oxford: Clarendon Press, 1989).

[64] Much the same point is made by Anne Phillips in her 'Democracy and Difference: Some Problems for Feminist Theory', in W. Kymlicka (ed.), *The Rights of Minority Cultures* (Oxford: Oxford University Press, 1995), esp. pp. 296–7, and at greater length in *The Politics of Presence*.   [65] Phillips, *The Politics of Presence*, p. 53.

with a culture is more likely to make a person sensitive to the effects of law and policy on it.

The other obvious way of fostering a sense of belonging is to give cultural communities some degree of self-determination. This may serve to reduce feelings of resentment, and satisfy aspirations to self-government. If members of the community possess the degree of legal and political autonomy they desire, they will identify with the constitutional framework which provides for it. Members of a cultural community may desire some degree of legal and political independence so that they can express and protect their identity in spheres that are particularly important to it without feeling the need for full independence.[66] For example, national minorities may wish to set their own public holidays, use their own language for the conduct of some of their affairs, and subsidize traditions and practices particularly central to their identity, perhaps even by raising their own taxes. This need not undermine the existence of a sense of belonging to the wider polity, and indeed may even help to foster it.

Of course if full legal and political independence is desired by a substantial proportion of a cultural community, or by its most influential members, then granting some degree of autonomy may be likely to weaken rather than strengthen an overall sense of belonging. But there is no *general* reason to think that providing a group with some degree of self-determination will automatically foster in them such a desire when it does not already exist.[67] Whether a group that is given some degree of self-determination will come to desire more is likely to depend in part upon the history of its relations with the other groups in the polity and the extent to which it trusts those other groups.

Although granting some degree of legal and political autonomy to cultural communities makes sense under some circumstances, and need not undermine a sense of belonging to the larger polity, in practice the scope for it is seriously constrained when those communities are geographically dispersed. Some degree of communal autonomy is perhaps still possible when it comes to family law, however. A plausible case might sometimes be made for the members of different cultural communities to be subject to different systems of family law, within the constraint described in Chapter 3, that these systems should be consistent with some reasonable interpretation of the basic rights, to be judged in practice by

[66] See Miller, *On Nationality*, p. 116.

[67] Here I am perhaps in partial disagreement with Kymlicka who argues that granting self-government rights to national minorities is unlikely to serve an integrative function, except in the case of guaranteed representation at the intergovernmental or federal level. See Kymlicka, *Multicultural Citizenship*, p. 182.

the citizen body or its representatives. They would then be able to make their own law concerning, for example, how many marriage partners a person may have and what age they must be, which persons may marry, when a marriage counts as void, when divorce is permissible and what sort of settlements should accompany it, and who should get custody of children.[68]

Even when granting some degree of communal autonomy is impractical, however, there is still scope for accommodation through group differentiated laws and policies. Laws and policies may be framed so that they take account of cultural differences and the importance of a cultural community for its members, even though they are made and enforced by the same legal and political institutions. Accommodation of this sort is clearly required if members of minority cultures are to have a deep sense of belonging to the state. Consider some examples.[69] Laws which forbid trading on Sundays but allow Jewish businessmen to trade on Sundays, provided that they do not do so on Saturdays. Laws which require the wearing of crash helmets on motorcycles, but exempt Sikhs. Laws which forbid the carrying of knives in public places but allow Sikhs to carry them for religious purposes. Let us call such laws 'group-differentiated', since they prescribe different rules for different groups of people.[70] Group differentiated laws are not the only way of being sensitive to cultural differences (for example, abolishing blasphemy laws, or extending them so that they cover other religions, are other ways in which a legislative may be sensitive to cultural differences), but they are an important way nonetheless.

There are, in general, two related factors which can make it hard to achieve or sustain a widespread sense of belonging to a polity in the face of cultural diversity. First, when one or more of the culturally defined

---

[68] During the 1980s, the Union of Muslim Organizations of the UK and Eire drew up proposals for a system of family law to be applicable to all British Muslims. See Poulter, *English Law and Ethnic Minority Customs*, p. 58.

[69] *Ibid.*, examples are owed to Poulter.

[70] In a forthcoming book Brian Barry is unsympathetic to a rule and exemption approach to accommodating group differences (see B. Barry, *Culture and Equality* (Cambridge: Polity, forthcoming)). His basic argument is in the form of a dilemma which he thinks few actual examples are able to escape: either the case for some law is sufficiently strong that it justifies universal compulsion, or it is not sufficiently strong to do so, in which case it should not be adopted at all. In response I would claim that there is an important good which exemptions can secure to which he does not give enough weight, viz. a sense of belonging. Exemptions (at least collectively) may facilitate the emergence of a sense of belonging by in effect giving public recognition to the way in which laws bear heavily on a particular group which is already marginalized in various ways. So my claim would be that in a range of cases the importance of cultivating a sense of belonging outweighs the case for compelling some minority, even though that case is sufficiently strong to justify compelling the others.

groups within it has suffered a history of oppression or unfair treatment in which the state is implicated. Groups in such a position are likely to find it difficult to identify with public institutions and practices if in the past they played a role in their oppression or unfair treatment, even if those institutions have now been reformed. Second, when the particular character of public institutions reflects the dominant culture. In these circumstances, it will be hard for those who are part of other cultural communities to feel at home in the polity, and in some cases their lack of a sense of belonging can lead them to demand to be allowed to secede.[71] But neither of these general obstacles to a widespread sense of belonging provides grounds for assimilation policies, designed to promote a shared national identity. Instead they underline the importance of the various forms of public recognition, and policies of accommodation, which I have described, and which do not aim at assimilation. (Of course, we cannot always expect recognition and accommodation to quieten secessionist movements.)

Let me conclude this section by noting the obvious point that the problem of cultivating a sense of belonging has many dimensions to it: for example, those who are homeless or unemployed are likely to lack a sense of belonging to the polity even if they share the culture of the dominant group; those who suffer racial prejudice or discrimination are likely to lack a sense of belonging even if they share the culture of the dominant group. My focus, however, has been the particular difficulties associated with fostering a sense of belonging that are created by the coexistence of a diversity of cultural communities. These difficulties can not be insulated from others: in so far as some cultural communities are constituted by members of particular races or ethnic groups who have been discriminated against, and perhaps continue to experience discrimination, then it is unlikely to be cultural difference understood in isolation which makes it hard for them to feel they belong.

8.   Conclusion

In this chapter I hope to have shown that although the liberal-nationalist position needs to be taken more seriously than it often is, it ultimately fails: there is reason to think that a liberal polity can flourish provided that its citizens have a sense of belonging to it, even if they do not possess a sense of belonging together of the kind deemed to be important by liberal-nationalists.

But I have suggested that the dominant liberal conception of political

[71] Taylor's suggestion that past failures of recognition explain the desire for independence expressed by many Quebeckers can appeal to both of the general factors I have mentioned. See Taylor, 'Shared and Divergent Values', pp. 168–9.

community is too demanding in the face of cultural difference, and that what I have called inclusive political community would generally serve liberals better as a regulative ideal. The sense of belonging required by this ideal needs careful nurturing, particularly through the design of legal and political institutions. These institutions may foster a sense of belonging in some circumstances by providing group representation, a degree of legal and political autonomy, and by framing group differentiated laws. None of this requires support for policies of assimilation.

But some will say that providing these forms of accommodation and recognition is not enough to foster a widespread sense of belonging. Educational institutions must also promote mutual valuing between members of different cultural communities in order to foster identification with the major institutions and practices, and provide the conditions for people to feel at home in them. The final chapter of this part of the book explores that idea.[72]

---

[72] This chapter is based upon my 'Political Community, Liberal-Nationalism, and the Ethics of Assimilationism', *Ethics*, vol. 109, 1999.

6   Multicultural education for an inclusive political community

It might be thought that the kinds of legal and political recognition defended at the end of the previous chapter are unlikely to be sufficient to foster the widespread sense of belonging which an inclusive political community requires. For there to be such a sense of belonging, citizens must identify with at least most of their major institutions and some of their central practices, and feel at home in them. But it is possible for a person to identify with a practice only if she finds it valuable. In so far as the political, legal, educational, artistic and other central practices of a society reflect mainly the concerns and interests of the dominant community, this will make it harder for members of minority cultural communities to identify with them and feel at home in them.

Identification with these practices could be facilitated by two kinds of change. First, by members of the dominant cultural community coming to value the influence of traditions which are part of other cultures, with the result that the practices are transformed. Second, by members of minority cultures coming to value the traditions which inform society's practices as they stand currently. This line of thought leads naturally to the conclusion that the major institutions should not merely acknowledge in various ways the importance of cultural communities to their own members but also foster the mutual valuing of cultures. In practice, this would make most difference to the design of educational institutions, which, it might be supposed, would need to become multicultural.

But not everyone agrees that multicultural education is the best means of promoting the mutual valuing of cultures; indeed, some have regarded it as a recipe for cultural apartheid. What I propose to do in this chapter is distinguish two different models of multicultural education, which I call the neutralist and the pluralist models. I shall argue that the pluralist model, when it is constrained in various ways, is best suited to fostering a widespread sense of belonging. This constrained version of the pluralist model in effect includes within it an account of how, from the point of view of educational institutions, conflicts between fostering a sense of belonging amongst citizens (part of the ideal of inclusive political community) and protecting or promoting communities below the level of the state should be resolved. I then consider two serious objections to the constrained pluralist model, and where appropriate I modify it to meet them. The first of these objections maintains that the model is too restrictive because it prohibits forms of education that should be allowed; the second maintains that it is too permissive because it allows forms of education which should be prohibited.

1.   What is multicultural education?

Before we can consider the role that multicultural education might legitimately play in fostering a sense of belonging by cultivating the mutual valuing of cultures, we need to clarify what is meant by 'multicultural education' since it is an expression with a range of meanings. Minimally it is used to refer to two different aspects of an educational system. First, a sensitivity to cultural differences in the way the school system is *organized*. This might include, for example, exemptions for members of various groups from religious assemblies; provision of single-sex schools, or of single-sex groups in activities such as swimming and physical education in general; flexibility in the rules governing school uniforms; provision of some teaching in the mother tongue as well as in English; providing opportunities for prayer during the school day. Second, 'multicultural education' may refer to a sensitivity to cultural differences in the *content* of the curriculum. Such a sensitivity might take very different forms, but must minimally require acquainting pupils with cultures different from their own, for example, by teaching the religion, history and literature of more than one culture. Both of these aspects of what is meant by 'multicultural education' are important for fostering a widespread sense of belonging. It is the second aspect, however, which has the most important role to play in fostering mutual valuing, and which creates the most theoretical difficulties.[1] Let me begin by distinguishing two different ways in which a curriculum may introduce pupils to the ideas, practices and values of more than one culture.[2]

According to the *neutralist* model, teachers should not take a stand on

---

[1] In terms of educational practice and the politics of education, however, the organizational issues have been just as important: see M. Halstead, 'Ethical Dimensions of Controversial Events in Multicultural Education', in M. Leicester and M. Taylor (eds.), *Ethics, Ethnicity and Education* (London: Kogan Page, 1992), pp. 39–56; and R. Honeyford, *Integration or Disintegration? Towards a Non-racist Society* (London: Claridge Press, 1988), ch. 8.

[2] I do not mean to suggest that these ways are exhaustive of the possibilities.

which culture's ideas, practices or values are the best, or which culture's practices embody the correct values.[3] In order to clarify the neutralist model, it is best to say what it is *not* committed to. The neutralist model need not endorse cultural relativism, and is well advised to avoid doing so, given the conceptual difficulties such a defence of it would face;[4] it is not, for example, committed to the view that it is always inappropriate to judge a culture in terms of standards which that culture does not share. Instead it can hold the view that, for educational or political purposes, teachers should not give a critical assessment of a culture's ideas, practices or values. According to some variants of the neutralist model, teachers should introduce other cultures in their own terms, focus upon what might be thought valuable in them, set up a dialogue between pupils, and avoid settling disputes that arise about the merits of different cultures and their practices.[5] On other variants, it is held to be permissible for a teacher to present her pupils with criticisms of a culture's ideas and practices, and to describe these ideas and practices in terms which would be foreign to insiders, so long as she does not endorse these criticisms.

The neutralist model need not advance the absurd idea that all the world's cultures should receive equal attention or equal weight in the curriculum, nor indeed that every one of the world's cultures should receive some representation. It is compatible with privileging the ideas, practices and values of one particular culture, in the sense of devoting more time to the study of them, and with ignoring some of the others. As a result, the neutralist model is not committed to the view that the *effects* of teaching should be neutral, i.e. that instruction should make it no more probable that pupils will endorse the ideas and values of one culture than another. A teacher may know in advance that even if she is not critical of

[3] See B. Parekh, 'The Concept of Multicultural Education', in S. Modgil, G. Verma, K. Mallick and C. Modgil (eds.), *Multicultural Education: the Interminable Debate* (Lewes: Falmer Press, 1986), for a clear presentation of the neutralist model. The Swann Report's conception of 'education for all' also fits this model. See *Education for All: The Report of the Committee of Inquiry into the Education of Children from Ethnic Minority Groups* (London: HMSO, 1985), especially ch. 6, and the phenomenological approach it favours to religious education, pp. 470–6.

[4] See, for example, P. Zec, 'Multicultural Education: what kind of relativism is possible?', *Journal of the Philosophy of Education*, vol. 14, 1980, pp. 77–86; D. Cooper, 'Multicultural Education' in J. North (ed.), *The GCSE: An Examination* (London: Claridge, 1987), pp. 143–6.

[5] See Parekh, 'The Concept of Multicultural Education', p. 28. Peter Gardner has argued that the open-mindedness multicultural education requires of pupils verges on incoherence: see P. Gardner, 'Propositional Attitudes and Multicultural Education or Believing Others Are Mistaken' in J. Horton and P. Nicholson (eds.), *Toleration: Philosophy and Practice* (Aldershot: Avebury, 1992) pp. 67–90. But it is not clear that it does. It may merely require a willingness to entertain the idea that one's own beliefs might be false and there is nothing incoherent in that notion: see W. Hare, 'Open-mindedness in the Classroom', *Journal of the Philosophy of Education*, vol. 19, 1985, pp. 251–9.

some set of ideas, practices and values, pupils will reject them because they arrive at school with commitments they have acquired both at home and in the wider communities to which they belong. The neutralist model does not require that teachers compensate for the commitments pupils have acquired before they come to school or which they acquire outside of their formal education.

In contrast to the neutralist model, the *pluralist* model maintains that it is legitimate for teachers to evaluate the ideas of different cultures from some particular perspective, find them wanting and dismiss them. Different schools may teach from different cultural and evaluative perspectives, and reach different conclusions about the ideas and practices they study. For example, some schools may teach from the perspective of Catholic doctrine, others from the perspective of Islam. Some may teach from the perspective of Scottish nationalism, others from some more cosmopolitan standpoint. The pluralist model does not require that schools subject the commitments which inform their teaching to critical scrutiny; it allows these commitments to be taken for granted as premises of the education they provide.

Some defenders of multicultural education might deny that the pluralist model has anything to do with multicultural education – they endorse the neutralist model and suppose that each culture must be presented 'in its own terms' and that no authoritative assessment of a culture should be given. But there are advantages to using the expression 'multicultural education' more broadly, for the pluralist model, like the neutralist model, requires that the curriculum acquaint pupils with other cultures. The crucial distinction between the neutralist and the pluralist model is not in terms of the range of cultures to which the children are introduced, but in terms of whether their education is based upon, and shaped by, particular cultural or evaluative commitments.[6]

2. Multicultural education and integration

Let us say that a polity is *integrated* when most of its citizens have a sense of belonging, i.e., when they identify with the polity's major institutions and practices and feel at home in them. My proposal, then, is that multicultural education can play a valuable role in promoting integration. But a general criticism of multicultural education has been precisely that

---

[6] Michael Walzer is prepared to describe a *system* in which different schools teach from different cultural perspectives, and each school teaches only one culture, as multicultural (see M. Walzer, 'Education, Democratic Citizenship and Multiculturalism', *Journal of Philosophy of Education*, vol. 29, 1995, p. 185). That strikes me as potentially misleading since individual children within that system would not receive a multicultural education.

it stands opposed to integration. Ray Honeyford, for example, argues that multicultural education in Britain is premised on the belief that 'schools should function to maintain separate cultural identities and ideals',[7] and that it is incompatible with a policy of integration.[8] But Honeyford does not distinguish the two different models of multicultural education in the way that I have done, and it is important to do so if we are properly to assess his claim.[9]

It is not obvious that Honeyford's criticism applies to the neutralist model.[10] Defenders of that model believe that by being exposed to other cultures without authoritative criticism of them, pupils will come to value each other's cultures (perhaps with the result that their own cultural identities become transformed), and that this will play an important role in *fostering* a sense of belonging. Honeyford may think that when teaching practices conform to the neutralist model, pupils will simply cling in an uncritical manner to the familiar beliefs they have acquired at home. But it is far from obvious that the various exchanges between pupils and between pupils and teachers which the neutralist model permits will have this outcome.

Although the neutralist model is unlikely to undermine a sense of belonging in the way that Honeyford fears, it nevertheless faces difficulties in satisfying the desires of parents to give their children certain kinds of education, since it excludes any education which is shaped by a particular set of cultural commitments. Some parents, for example, will want above all to send their children to schools which are informed by a particular set of religious commitments, such as those contained in Catholicism or Islam. For this reason, the neutralist model is likely to generate resentment amongst parents who want their children to have the sort of education that is excluded by the model, and undermine a sense of belonging by making it impossible for those parents to identify with educational institutions.[11]

---

[7] R. Honeyford, 'The Gilmore Syndrome', *The Salisbury Review*, vol. 4, 1986, p. 13.

[8] The objection that multicultural education cannot foster the kind of integration which is needed for individuals to feel at home within a political community has also been formulated from a socialist standpoint by David Miller: see Miller, 'Socialism and Toleration', pp. 251–4.

[9] For a good discussion of Honeyford's general attack on multicultural education, see M. Halstead, *Education, Justice and Cultural Diversity: An Examination of the Honeyford Affair, 1984–85* (Lewes: Falmer Press, 1988), ch. 8.

[10] In fact Honeyford has a particular definition of integration which makes it a conceptual truth that the neutralist model is incompatible with integration. For Honeyford, integration just *means* leaving cultural recognition to the private sphere (see his *Integration or Disintegration?*, pp. 37–40). But that still leaves his more interesting claim that multicultural education creates or reinforces separate cultural identities in such a way that no overall sense of belonging is possible.

[11] The degree of resentment generated will undoubtedly depend upon other factors, such as

The observation that the neutralist model is inconsistent with an education informed by a particular set of religious commitments may also give rise to the worry that the model is incoherent. It demands that teachers should give no critical assessment of a culture's ideas, practices and values, and that their teaching should not presuppose the correctness of any particular culture's ideas or values, whilst being implicitly committed to a particular culture's (or subculture's) conception of what counts as a good education, viz. a secular or humanist one. This is not a genuine incoherence, however. What it shows is that the neutralist model has to be defended by an appeal to some set of ideals, whether they be educational or political.[12]

Indeed arguments for neutrality in education tend to mirror those for state neutrality in general.[13] There are two which are initially promising. First, that neutrality in education is required in order to respect the autonomy of the pupil. Second, that neutrality is required in order for educational institutions to be publicly justifiable, i.e., acceptable to all reasonable citizens. But neither of these arguments is likely to produce the desired justification of the neutralist model of multicultural education. It is hard to avoid the conclusion that respect for autonomy in the classroom requires the teacher to *promote* the ability to choose how to lead one's life by portraying as virtuous those who make such a choice, and by being critical of those who simply conform.[14] An attempt to square this with neutrality by maintaining that fostering such an ability would not involve making any judgement about the value of ways of life which do not value critical reflectiveness would be hard to swallow. Public justifiability is also unlikely to favour the neutralist model, for that model appears to trample on the deeply held and reasonable convictions of many citizens about what constitutes a good education.[15]

how the wider society views these religious communities, the extent to which they feel under threat etc.

[12] A. Gutmann, *Democratic Education* (Princeton, NJ: Princeton University Press, 1987), pp. 55–6.

[13] Note, however, that one might consistently defend state neutrality but reject educational neutrality even in state funded schools. For example, one might argue that the content of education should be determined by parents or educational experts. See M. Clayton, 'White on Autonomy, Neutrality and Well-Being', *Journal of Philosophy of Education*, vol. 27, 1993, pp. 105–6. Some also defend a restricted version of political neutrality which is consistent with non-neutrality in education. Brian Barry, for example, argues that it is permissible for education policy to be non-neutral provided that it is the outcome of neutral procedures: see *Justice as Impartiality*, pp. 143, 161.

[14] This of course leaves open the possibility that a good education is indeed one that fosters autonomy, and hence that such an education is incompatible with both the neutralist model and some forms of education which are permitted by the pluralist model. I shall consider this question in section 6.

[15] Of course, at best the argument for the neutralist model from public justifiability would apply only to state-funded schools.

The pluralist model is in a good position to satisfy the desires of parents for forms of education involving particular cultural commitments. It has no objection to religiously committed education, for example. Honeyford's worry that multicultural education will simply reinforce separate cultural identities might seem better founded in relation to the pluralist model, however. If particular schools are committed to particular cultures, will this not just reinforce separate cultural identities in such a way that a widespread sense of belonging becomes impossible? Many citizens will not be able to identify with society's major institutions and practices because these institutions and practices will be suffused with cultural commitments they do not share, and their own cultural commitments will simply be reinforced by their schooling. Furthermore, if children are educated from a particular cultural perspective, why should we suppose that they will come to value the other cultures to which they are introduced as part of their multicultural education? There is considerable force to these points, but they can be met, to some extent at least, by constraining the pluralist model in two ways.

First, by requiring that education be informed by a presumption, advocated by Charles Taylor, that cultures which have 'animated whole societies over some considerable stretch of time have something important to say to all human beings'.[16] It is not entirely obvious how Taylor wants to ground this presumption. For my purposes, it is best regarded as a tool for fostering a sense of belonging rather than as the outcome of anthropological research. Adopting it would not require schools to treat all long-lived and wide-ranging cultures as valuable. It would merely require them to work with a presumption that these cultures are valuable, which might, in the course of studying a particular culture, be overridden. If teachers are critical of some culture's ideas, practices or values, they must, from within their own pedagogical perspective, attempt to seek out what (if anything) is worthwhile in them. Furthermore, they must apply the values and standards implicit in their own perspective impartially.[17]

Second, the pluralist model needs to be constrained by requiring that children be taught in such a way that they become aware of themselves and each other as future fellow citizens of a *particular* liberal-democratic state, and (in so far as possible) acquire the capacities, virtues and knowledge necessary to be good citizens of that state. By being taught in this way, there is a reasonable chance that they will come to identify with

[16] C. Taylor, 'The Politics of Recognition', in A. Gutmann (ed.), *Examining the Politics of Recognition* (Princeton, NJ: Princeton University Press, 1994), p. 66.
[17] In practice it may be hard to decide whether a curriculum embodies Taylor's presumption. But there will be clear cases in which a curriculum does do so, and clear cases in which it does not.

its major institutions. Such an approach would involve insisting that children learn competence in the official language (or languages) of the state, that schools privilege its history, politics, geography and literature, and acquaint them with the scientific methods and theories which inform its social practices. But different schools would be allowed to teach the history, politics and literature of the state from different cultural perspectives, and would be allowed to reject the prevailing scientific theories, and even established scientific methods, on religious grounds.[18]

There is controversy about what an adequate civic education of this kind would involve, and some of the disagreements here surely reflect different views of what virtues a person needs in order to be a good citizen which the state need not, and perhaps should not, resolve. But an adequate civic education must require cultivating in children the ability to be impartial in various contexts, for example, to treat the interests of the citizens of the state as equally important in political matters, even if the state allows for different ways of construing what precisely that ability involves.[19] Amy Gutmann appears to take the view that a civic education should also require teaching people to deliberate rationally about ways of life.[20] But that seems mistaken. Good political deliberation requires the ability to understand enough about the different ways of life in the polity to know what the impact of different policies will be upon them, rather than the ability to make rational judgements about which of these ways of life is the best.[21]

Should the state also require schools to teach the history of the polity in a particular way, perhaps in a favourable light? William Galston has no qualms about requiring the teaching of a sanitised version of national history for the purposes of fostering civic commitment, in which inaccurate accounts of major figures and events are presented as true.[22] Besides the general worries one might have about *requiring* schools to teach falsehoods, we might also worry about how well such an education is suited to fostering a sense of belonging and building an inclusive political

---

[18] So, creationists would have to teach theories of natural selection even if they also taught that these were false.

[19] The effectiveness of civic education will depend, in part, on whether what is taught in schools is supported in the families and communities to which pupils belong. But even when this is not so, civic education may have some degree of success.

[20] Gutmann, *Democratic Education*, pp. 30–1. See also E. Callan, *Creating Citizens: Political Education and Liberal Democracy* (Oxford: Oxford University Press, 1997), sections 11–13.

[21] William Galston argues that fostering rational deliberation among ways of life goes beyond what the liberal democratic state requires in order to sustain itself, and that such a form of education is not publicly justifiable since it can be reasonably rejected by those who do not value the autonomous way of life. See Galston, *Liberal Purposes*, pp. 252–4.

[22] *Ibid.*, pp. 242–4. For a critique of Galston from a different perspective, see Callan, *Creating Citizens*, ch. 5.

community. Some families will not be able to accept these 'noble' accounts of the polity's past, or the way in which its treatment of their ancestors is portrayed, and teaching its history in this way is likely to be counterproductive.

The constraints I am defending on the pluralist model are stronger than they may appear, however. Consider the question of whether they would permit a culture or sub-culture to teach racist or sexist ideas. These constraints would prevent the teaching of such ideas if it would impair the ability of future citizens to reason impartially in political matters. On these grounds some racist or sexist ideas, for example, those which taught the inherent superiority of men over women, are likely to be ruled out. But other such ideas might be permitted, for example, those which taught that the proper role of women was to be wives and mothers, but that women are equal to men.[23]

The requirement that children be taught in such a way that they acquire the virtues necessary to be good citizens has further implications. The relevant virtues will surely include toleration and law-abidingness. The state should permit a range of different interpretations of these virtues, but even then there will be some cultures (or sub-cultures) who reject outright the idea that, say, toleration is a virtue, or whose interpretation of toleration is so eccentric that it has to be regarded as unreasonable. Within the range of reasonable interpretations, there may be some who defend toleration on the basis of the idea that there are 'burdens of judgement' which make reasonable disagreement possible, whilst others defend it on the basis of the idea that social peace requires, within certain constraints, a policy of 'live and let live' even in relation to crazy doctrines.[24]

Despite requiring constraints, the pluralist model is an attractive vehicle for integration precisely because it avoids a problem which besets not only a monocultural model of education, but also any form of multicultural education which requires that *all* children be taught from a particular perspective, informed by a particular set of cultural commitments, for example, the commitments of the dominant or national culture. (This problem also confronts any form of multicultural education which commits itself to objective educational standards, if there are any, which are not widely accepted.) Education in accordance with any such model is likely to cause some children who undergo it to suffer from

---

[23] Would teaching this idea be ruled out by the further requirement that the school system should provide its children with the capacities and skills necessary for equality of opportunity? In section 5 of this chapter, I argue not.

[24] In my view Callan is mistaken to insist that a particular interpretation of what it is for citizens to be reasonable, based upon acceptance of the burdens of judgement, should be cultivated through educational institutions. See Callan, *Creating Citizens*, especially ch. 2.

alienation and a pervasive sense of cultural dislocation. If children are educated from the perspective of a culture radically different from the one in which they have been brought up, then it will be difficult for them to make sense of their social environment and their location within it. Far from being conducive to cultivating a sense of belonging, such an education is likely to weaken it since it is plausible to suppose that a secure identification with society's major institutions and practices minimally requires a stable sense of one's own identity[25] (even when that identity is of a dual or hyphenated kind, for example, British-Muslim).

Although the pluralist model is likely to provide children with a secure sense of their own identities, it might be thought that in practice it would undermine an overall sense of belonging in two ways. First, by encouraging a form of cultural segregation in the educational system which was likely to lead to the spread of prejudice and discrimination.[26] Second, by making the situation worse for members of minority cultures who live in areas where there are not enough of them to justify their own publicly funded schools, and who therefore are forced to go to schools which teach from some other cultural perspective.

There are dangers here, but they are not as serious as they may initially appear, and there are various ways in which they may be reduced. The risk of spreading prejudice and discrimination is not as great as it may seem because the pluralist model requires that a school's curriculum be multicultural and, according to the proposal I have made, be constrained by a presumption of value. The risk that members of minority communities who do not reach a critical mass will be worse off under the pluralist model than the neutralist model is a genuine one. But parents would sometimes prefer their children to have (say) a religiously committed education than one which is neutral between theism and atheism, even when this would involve having them taught from the perspective of a religion different from their own.[27] When parents in some areas do not want to send their children to a particular religious school, then publicly

---

[25] See J. M. Halstead, *The Case for Muslim Voluntary-Aided Schools* (Cambridge: The Islamic Academy, 1986), p. 27; T. Modood, 'On Not Being White in Britain: Discrimination, Diversity and Commonality', in Leicester and Taylor (eds.), *Ethics, Ethnicity and Education*, p. 77. Modood bases his claim partly on research done by H. E. Park and H. A. Miller: see *Old World Traits Transplanted* (New York: Harper, 1921). The strongest challenge to the use I am making of it comes from the idea that the child's place within her community may provide her with a sufficiently stable identity that it need not be threatened by being educated in school on the basis of a different set of cultural assumptions (see Honeyford, *Integration or Disintegration?*, pp. 280–1). It is hard to believe that this is the case, however.

[26] T. McLaughlin, 'The Ethics of Separate Schools' in Leicester and Taylor (eds.), *Ethics, Ethnicity and Education*, p. 125. See also Swann *et al.*, *Education for All*, pp. 508–11.

[27] See T. Modood, 'Establishment, Multiculturalism and British Citizenship', *The Political Quarterly*, vol. 65, 1994, p. 62.

funded, religiously uncommitted schools should be made available to them. And it is reasonable to insist that separate religious schools should then receive public funding only if they provide an efficient means of educating children.[28] In other words, religiously uncommitted schools should be the 'default' public provision. (By defending such schools as the default provision, I am assuming that for various reasons it is in general worse for children to be forced to be educated from a religious perspective different from the one with which they are being brought up at home, than for children to be forced to have a religiously uncommitted education when they are being brought up in a religious environment at home.)

3.   Is the constrained pluralist model too restrictive?

The constrained pluralist model is well suited to fostering a widespread sense of belonging. In general it is also likely to provide support for the cultural community to which children belong. By allowing parents to educate their children at school in terms of the ideas and values of the culture in which they have been brought up at home, the pluralist model is likely to sustain (or at least, not radically undermine) existing cultural communities. But the constrained pluralist model does place some restrictions on what forms of education are permissible, and hence does restrict the ability of cultural communities to reproduce themselves by educating their children in their ways. In effect, the constrained pluralist model resolves any conflicts between fostering an inclusive political community (in which there is a widespread sense of belonging to a society with liberal institutions) and supporting communities below the level of the state by favouring the former.

Clearly the constrained pluralist model may come into conflict with satisfying the desires of parents to give their children particular kinds of education. For example, parents may not want their children to be introduced to other cultures because they fear that this will lead their children to grow away from them and reject their own culture, perhaps leading to the eventual disintegration of the cultural community (this is how Steven Macedo represents the arguments of the Amish community in the United States for exempting their children from the educational system[29]) and in some cases their fears may be well grounded. But

---

[28] For different interpretations of the efficiency requirement, see my 'The Public Funding of Separate Schools', *Journal of Franco-British Studies*, no. 23, 1997.

[29] S. Macedo, 'Liberal Civic Education and Religious Fundamentalism: The Case of God v. John Rawls?', *Ethics*, vol. 105, 1995, pp. 471–2. Note, however, that this is not the grounds on which many Muslims in Britain have objected to proposals for multicultural education, such as those contained in the Swann Report: see Halstead, *The Case for Muslim Voluntary-Aided Schools*, p. 25.

fostering the mutual valuing of cultures requires that children be at least introduced to the ideas, practices and values of more than one culture. If the importance of mutual valuing of cultures for fostering a widespread sense of belonging is granted, then there are strong reasons for saying that it should take priority over parents' desires to give their children a particular sort of education when the two conflict, and over the possible long-term collapse of a particular cultural community. It should be emphasized, however, that the pluralist model, even when it is constrained in the way I have suggested, is compatible with the satisfaction of a wide variety of parents' desires, and with the survival of a wide range of cultural communities. Indeed that is one of its attractive features.

There may be pragmatic reasons in some cases for exempting particular communities from the requirement that education should foster the mutual valuing of cultures by presenting children with the ideas, values and practices of a number of cultural communities to which their fellow citizens belong. If a community is self-contained, does not generate overt conflict with the wider political community, and in effect opts out of it in the way that, for instance, the Amish largely do, then this may provide a good reason for allowing them to send their children to schools which have a monocultural curriculum. There may also be pragmatic grounds for offering them public financial support so long as they provide a reasonably efficient way of educating children.

The constrained pluralist model I have been defending will also come into conflict with the desire of some parents to educate their girls solely for motherhood since it requires them to be given a foundation in the humanities and sciences as part of their preparation of citizenship.[30] Here it seems that there is also a strong independent argument for not allowing such a desire to be satisfied, since equality of opportunity is at issue. If girls are educated *solely* for motherhood, then they are not being provided with the abilities and skills which are necessary for equality of opportunity, on any reasonable understanding of what this involves. (But we should recall one of the conclusions reached in Chapter 3. If greater injustice would result from requiring a school to conform to equality of opportunity than would be permitted by not doing so, or if requiring that school to do so would lead to a great sacrifice of other values, then the school should be allowed to violate it. These cases are surely rare, however. The most plausible candidates are when the very survival of a cultural community would require allowing it to violate its children's

---

[30] Many liberals think that the conflict between respecting parents' wishes and providing girls with the capacities necessary for them to have equality of opportunity arises most acutely in Britain in relation to Muslim education (see Swann *et al.*, *Education for All*, pp. 504–7, 512–13). The issues here are complex, however: cf. Halstead, *The Case for Muslim Voluntary-Aided Schools*, pp. 27–8.

equality of opportunity, and its collapse would deprive its members of the possibility of leading a meaningful life.)

It might seem that the pluralist model becomes much less permissive once we introduce the further constraint that schools should in general be required to respect equality of opportunity, on the grounds that there will be many forms of education which are incompatible with it. There is some truth in this observation. Note, however, that a further proviso defended in Chapter 3 also applies here. When there is more than one reasonable interpretation of what equality of opportunity requires, cultural communities (represented by parents in this case), should be allowed to choose that interpretation which best suits their interests. This would permit schools to prepare girls for motherhood, so long as this was not at the expense of providing them with the skills and abilities necessary for other opportunities.

Of course parents may judge that it is in the best interests of their child to be sent to a school which does not simply educate her from the perspective of the cultural community to which she belongs. In these cases parents should be allowed to make that choice on behalf of their children. (The problems of fractured identity which can occur when children are educated from a different perspective to the one that is constitutive of the cultural community to which they belong are likely to be less acute when parents support, rather than undermine, whether implicitly or explicitly, the education the children are receiving at school.) The pluralist model is not driven by the interests of different cultural communities.

Nor indeed is the pluralist model wholly driven by the interests of parents. There are difficult cases in which the desires of parents come into conflict with those of their children,[31] for example, when children do not want the kind of religious based education that their parents would choose for them. Although the pluralist model gives a large role to parental choice, it should also aim to give proper weight to the interests of the child. In cases where the desires of parents and children are in conflict, institutional mechanisms are needed which give some weight to the desires of the child at least in the choice of secondary education. This brings me to the second set of objections, which maintain that the constrained pluralist model is too permissive because, even though it can give some weight to the desires of children, it allows forms of education which are radically at odds with their interests.

---

[31] See Susan Khin Zaw, 'Locke and Multiculturalism: Toleration, Relativism, and Reason', in R. K. Fullinwider (ed.), *Public Education in a Multicultural Society: Policy, Theory, Critique* (Cambridge: Cambridge University Press, 1996), p. 124.

4.   Is the constrained pluralist model too permissive?

There are at least two ways in which the pluralist model appears to threaten the child's interests. First, it might be thought that the child has an interest in acquiring true beliefs whereas the pluralist model allows them to be fed ideas and theories which can be known to be false. Second, there is a possible conflict between the constrained pluralist model and the cultivation of an adequate capacity for critical reflection (which I shall call a capacity for autonomy), which many philosophers of education have regarded as vitally important to the well-being of the child, for the model is compatible with the uncritical endorsement of the ideas and values of a particular culture. (In this respect, the pluralist model fares worse than the neutralist model.)

If children have an interest in acquiring true beliefs, why not exclude forms of education which teach what can be known to be false – for example, those which deny that the holocaust happened or which maintain that the earth was created but a few thousand years ago with its fossil record intact? There are grounds for holding that only when teaching some particular falsehood would undermine a sense of belonging should schools be excluded from presenting it as true. In certain circumstances there may be a strong case for stopping schools from teaching that the holocaust never happened because this would undermine a sense of belonging, but it is less clear that there could be similar reasons for preventing schools from teaching that creationism is true. Placing such a constraint on schools would alienate parents who reject evolutionary theory and, believing themselves to be right to do so, want their children to be taught from a creationist perspective. More importantly, there are serious dangers in allowing the state, or any group it appoints, to be the arbiter of what can be known to be false.[32] These risks, it seems to me, are outweighed only in cases where preventing schools from teaching known falsehoods is clearly necessary in order to prevent a sense of belonging from being undermined.

To this it might be replied that the alternative I am proposing is equally dangerous because it in effect grants *parents* the power to determine what is taught as true. There is some truth in this charge. But granting parents this power is less dangerous than giving it to the state, for different parents are likely to use their influence to support different kinds of education, and this makes it more likely that in later life children who have absorbed false ideas and theories will encounter others who have true ones and will be able to replace the false with the true.

[32] Mill, 'On Liberty', pp. 238–40, is the classic source for arguments against state-directed education.

This can motivate the second worry: that the constrained pluralist model permits forms of education that undermine the child's capacity for autonomy or do not cultivate it, making it unlikely that she will be able to entertain the possibility that her beliefs are false. Although there is a tension here, it is not necessarily acute. The pluralist model is not necessarily incompatible with cultivating the capacity for autonomy, however that capacity is understood, since it leaves open the possibility of educational approaches which subject the beliefs and values of the culture which informs the curriculum to critical scrutiny. Furthermore, when the pluralist model is constrained by the requirement that education must prepare children for citizenship, this would seem to require that it foster in them the capacities necessary for deliberating about political matters. It is likely that those capacities will also equip them for deliberating about other aspects of their lives.[33]

It is also important to note that an education in accordance with the pluralist model provides one of the necessary bases of autonomy by making possible the kinds of secure identity which are required for effective agency. Because the pluralist model allows children to be taught from the cultural perspective that has informed their upbringing at home, they are able to develop a secure sense of their own identity.[34]

But there do seem to be potential conflicts between the pluralist model and the development of a capacity for autonomy when schools do not encourage pupils to subject the presuppositions that inform the curriculum to critical scrutiny, or positively discourage them from doing so and attempt to close their minds. The acuteness of these tensions will vary depending upon how the capacity for autonomy is conceived.[35] But on any reasonable conception of what it is to possess that capacity, there will be conflicts. Then the question becomes: should forms of schooling be tolerated which do not promote, or even undermine the capacity for autonomy?

Some will say that no school should be allowed which fails to promote the capacity for autonomy. But what is it about this capacity which requires us to promote it whatever sacrifice that would involve?[36] Not its contributions to the well-being of the child; for even though the exercise

---

[33] See A. Gutmann, 'Civic Education and Social Diversity', *Ethics*, vol. 105, 1995, p. 573.

[34] Cf. McLaughlin, 'The Ethics of Separate Schools', pp. 113–15.

[35] See, e.g., Mark Halstead's distinction between weak and strong autonomy. According to Halstead, weak autonomy involves 'coming to see the point of moral or social rules for oneself . . . and giving one's consent to them', whereas strong autonomy requires that 'all assumptions should be challenged and that all beliefs must be open to rigorous criticism based on rationality' (Halstead, *The Case for Muslim Voluntary-Aided Schools*, p. 36).

[36] See my 'Liberalism and the Value of Community', *Canadian Journal of Philosophy*, vol. 23, 1993, section IV, for a more detailed discussion of this issue.

of autonomy may be a very important component of well-being, it has its costs, and there can be little doubt that people can lead worthwhile, even flourishing lives, without possessing or exercising full autonomy.[37] Indeed, under some circumstances requiring that education promote the capacity for autonomy may lead children to have less fulfilling lives because they may become estranged from their families. The wider effects of requiring the educational system to foster the capacity for autonomy should also give us pause for thought; it is likely to prevent some parents from giving their children the kind of education they would like, and in extreme circumstances may lead to the disintegration of a cultural community. Given the difficulty a person may encounter finding her way in an alien cultural environment, this might in extreme cases deprive her of the possibility of leading any worthwhile life.[38] So even if an ideal education is one which, in part, fosters the capacity for autonomy, there may be reasons for allowing schools which fail to promote it to exist. There will even be a case for providing such schools with public funding, on the assumption that any form of education which serves (or at least does not undermine) public purposes is entitled to public funding, provided that there is sufficient demand for it.[39]

These remarks are unlikely to satisfy those who believe that the child has a *right* to autonomy. But here we need to recognize that there are a number of interpretations of that right. Consider two possibilities. First, that the child's right to autonomy requires that she should not have anything done to her to which she could in principle reasonably object when (or if) she acquired the capacity to do so. Second, that the child's right to autonomy requires that she should have cultivated in her whatever capacities are necessary for her to act autonomously.[40] (These interpretations of the child's right to autonomy are not mutually exclusive; indeed it might be claimed that the full right to autonomy consists in the combination of them both.) Each of these interpretations would rule out some forms of education. According to the first, any education designed to produce commitment to a particular religious way of life would violate the child's right to autonomy, even if it also cultivated in her the capacity to choose to reject that way of life at some later stage, for she might in

---

[37] Here I am implicitly opposing Joseph Raz's claim that it is impossible for a person to flourish in an autonomy supporting environment unless they are to a significant degree autonomous (see Raz, *The Morality of Freedom*, p. 391). I give some arguments against Raz's claim in my 'Liberalism and the Value of Community', pp. 236–8.

[38] See Raz, *The Morality of Freedom*, pp. 423–4.

[39] See my 'The Public Funding of Separate Religious Schools'.

[40] Joel Feinberg endorses this idea: see his 'The Child's Right to an Open Future', in W. Aiken and H. LaFollette (eds.), *Whose Child? Children's Rights, Parental Authority and State Power* (Totowa, NJ: Rowman and Littlefield, 1980), pp. 124–53. See also D. Archard, *Children: Rights and Childhood* (London: Routledge, 1993), p. 131.

principle reasonably object to having had that education in the first place.[41] According to the second formulation of the child's right to autonomy, any education which does not actively develop her capacity for autonomy would violate her right to it.

But each of these formulations could, it seems to me, be reasonably rejected. The first derives much of its power from our intuitions about what is wrong with a range of practices. Consider clitoridectomy during childhood, which was discussed briefly in Chapter 3. This practice does not prevent girls from acquiring the capacity to subject their beliefs and commitments to critical scrutiny. So if a child's right to autonomy ruled out only those practices incompatible with her developing a capacity for critical reflection of this sort, there could be no complaint on grounds of autonomy against clitoridectomy. Yet it does seem that such a practice violates a girl's right to autonomy. One possible explanation of why it does appeals to the idea that the girl does not (because she could not) consent to clitoridectomy. Examples such as this suggest that respect for the child's autonomy requires not just that she should not be subject to practices which prevent her from acquiring the capacities necessary for full autonomy, but also that she not be subject to various other forms of treatment. And it might be maintained that religious instruction falls into that category.

This is a hard position to sustain, however. Why should we suppose that religious instruction violates the child's right to autonomy? If the point is just that it involves imparting a particular 'comprehensive' conception of the good, then respect for autonomy, so understood, would be highly restrictive. It would seem to rule out cultivating in children virtues such as kindness and generosity, or a particular aesthetic sensitivity, and prohibit feeding a child fish, meat or even dairy products (to the extent that this presupposes the permissibility of exploiting fish and animals for this purpose).

Why not instead interpret the child's right to autonomy so that it requires consent only to practices which involve (or carry a significant risk of) serious injury, and to practices which would deprive the child of the possibility of pursuing what she might reasonably come to regard as an important good? This is a weaker requirement, for it would imply that the child should not be subject to certain forms of treatment, such as clitoridectomy, but would allow parents, or schools on behalf of parents, to cultivate in her particular conceptions of the good. Clitoridectomy may involve serious health risks (even when it is performed under hygienic

---

[41] See M. Clayton, 'Educating Liberals: An Argument about Political Neutrality, Equality of Opportunity, and Parental Autonomy' (D.Phil thesis, Faculty of Social Studies, University of Oxford, 1997), ch. 4.

conditions) and deprives girls of the future possibility of experiencing forms of sexual pleasure that they might reasonably come to regard as an important good. For these reasons, it is plausible to maintain that respect for autonomy would require the consent of the child to this operation, and hence that it cannot be justified. But it is not true in general that religious instruction or cultivating a particular conception of the good carries with it the risk of serious injury or deprives the child of the possibility of what she might reasonably come to regard as an important good. So the idea that the child's right to autonomy requires that she should not have anything done to her to which she could in the future reasonably object can itself reasonably be rejected.[42]

Could the second formulation of the right to autonomy also be reasonably rejected? Someone who rejects the idea that the child's right to it requires that she should have cultivated in her whatever capacities are necessary for her to be autonomous need not deny that the child has a right not to have her mind closed. And it seems to me that it is not *unreasonable* to suppose that the child's right to autonomy, as far as education is concerned, is exhausted by this requirement, which would permit forms of education which did not promote her capacity for autonomy. (This requirement might be regarded as grounded in the deeper idea that the child should not be subject to an education which would deprive her of the possibility of pursuing what she might reasonably come to regard as an important good.)

In Chapter 3 I argued that cultural communities which reject liberal principles should be allowed to interpret those principles in the way which is most beneficial to their practices, provided that this interpretation is reasonable. In the case of education, this suggests that parents should at least be allowed to select an interpretation which permits schools to foster religious belief provided that they do not thereby close their pupils' minds. This would permit some forms of education which do not cultivate the child's capacity for autonomy or even those which undermine it. Indeed it is hard to see how an education which meets the other conditions I have imposed on the pluralist model could itself be responsible for closing the minds of pupils. (Bear in mind that these constraints include the idea that children should be prepared for citizenship in a culturally plural society, and that the school curriculum should operate with a presumption of the value of long-lived, wide-ranging

---

[42] Some will argue that the use of children for pornography would be objectionable even if there was no risk of physical or emotional injury, and that we cannot make sense of why such use violates the child's right autonomy unless we appeal to something like the first formulation of the right: see Clayton, 'Educating Liberals', ch. 4. But would the use of children for sexual gratification violate their autonomy if it could be guaranteed that they would suffer no harm of any kind, even if it were objectionable on other grounds?

cultures, which requires that they introduce these cultures impartially from their perspective.)

This minimal interpretation of the right to autonomy requires that there be a morally relevant distinction between not developing a child's capacity for autonomy and closing her mind, and also a morally relevant distinction between (on the one hand) not intervening to prevent a causal process which, if left alone, will result in the closing of the child's mind and (on the other hand) being actively involved in a process which leads to the closing of the child's mind. These distinctions are hard to draw, not least because to speak of closing a person's mind is to use a vague metaphor. But to my knowledge no one has shown that it is unreasonable to hold that they are genuine and of basic moral significance.

5.   Multicultural education and anti-racism

Some have criticized multicultural education on the grounds that it does not constitute an adequate response to racism and thereby fails to provide the educational conditions necessary for minority communities to avoid marginalization and exclusion. This is of obvious relevance to any defence of multicultural education, like mine, which maintains that it fosters the widespread sense of belonging that is required by an inclusive political community. The criticism comes in a mild and a strong version. The mild version maintains that multicultural education does not go far enough. It should be directly concerned with fighting racism. Teachers and pupils need to be educated so that they have an awareness of racism, are fully attentive to their own racial prejudices, and understand the causes of racism, i.e., education should involve a form of consciousness raising. The strong version maintains that multicultural education not merely does not go far enough but is positively harmful for at least two reasons: first, it undermines the fight against racism by defusing feelings that potentially could be harnessed in that fight; second, it misidentifies the causes of racism, understanding it 'primarily as the product of ignorance and perpetuated by negative attitudes and individual prejudices'.[43] In its most extreme form, the strong version of the criticism maintains that multicultural education is a conscious way of 'buying off' ethnic minorities.[44]

The strong version of the criticism seems unfair. There does not seem to be any good reason to suppose that in general multicultural education

---

[43] B. Troyna, 'Beyond Multiculturalism: Towards the Enactment of Anti-Racist Education in Policy Provision and Pedagogy', *Oxford Review of Education*, vol. 13, 1987, p. 311. Cf. also his 'Multiracial Education: Just Another Brick in the Wall?', *New Community*, vol. 10, 1982–3, pp. 424–8.   [44] See Modgil et al. (eds.), *Multicultural Education*, p. 8.

will reinforce racism. It need not defuse resistance to racism, and indeed, as Bhikhu Parekh points out, to some extent at least it provides a weapon against racism since one way of engendering respect for members of different races is often to teach about the different cultural communities to which they belong. By becoming acquainted with other cultures, children may come to see the way in which the cultures of minorities have been misrepresented, and at the same time come to see those cultures as deserving of respect.[45] Although some theories of multiculturalism may presuppose an inadequate understanding of racism and its causes, they need not do so. Indeed, theories of multiculturalism need not presuppose any theory of racism and its causes, and need not even make the claim that multicultural education is part of the fight against racism.

In support of the milder criticism, however, it might be argued that multicultural education should go further and tackle racism directly, i.e., fighting racism should be a central aim of the educational system. The question then becomes: should multicultural education be supplemented with an educational programme specifically designed to combat racism? It might be argued that such a programme is necessary in order to eradicate or reduce racism, and furthermore that only if racism is counteracted will the conditions exist for fostering the widespread sense amongst citizens that they belong together which is required for them to form an inclusive political community.

It might be replied that this proposal contains a conceptual confusion. Antony Flew points out that race and culture are analytically distinct notions; race or colour seems to be a genetic or biological notion, whilst culture clearly is not.[46] Critics of multiculturalism who maintain that it does not go far enough in fighting racism cannot be convicted of a straightforward conceptual confusion, however. There are obvious empirical connections and correlations between race and culture, or at least between colour and culture; for example, the vast majority of Muslims in Britain are of a particular race or colour. And, in practice, racial prejudice might take the form of supposing, with no good reason, that the culture of members of different races is inferior.[47] As a result, it need not be confused in practice to suppose that racism might be countered in part by

---

[45] See Parekh, 'The Concept of Multicultural Education', pp. 30–1. Some are sceptical about whether introducing pupils to other cultures will do anything to combat racism: see Cooper, 'Multicultural Education', pp. 146–8.

[46] See, especially, A. Flew, 'Education: Anti-racist, Multi-ethnic and Multicultural', in I. Mahalingham and B. Carr (eds.), *Logical Foundations* (Basingstoke: Macmillan, 1991), p. 200; Honeyford, *Integration or Disintegration?*, pp. 74–5.

[47] Honeyford is right to point out that racism can mean either racial discrimination or racial prejudice: see Honeyford, *Integration or Disintegration?*, p. 21.

a particular kind of multicultural education, nor to suppose that it should be supplemented by racism awareness courses.

Problems are created, however, by the fact that what racism is – what kind of actions, policies, beliefs and attitudes are racist – is a matter of reasonable dispute and public debate, as indeed are theories about the causes of racism. Antony Flew, for example, thinks that racism means *simply* 'the advantaging or disadvantaging of individuals for no other or better reason than that they happen to be members of this particular racial set and not that'.[48] Flew thinks that other definitions of racism rest upon conceptual confusions, for example, a confusion of culture and race. A society may be multiracial but not multicultural and vice versa, and members of a culture may be intentionally disadvantaged by a policy without that constituting racism, so long as they are not disadvantaged because of their race.[49] Others, however, will argue that racism may occur when some policy (action, procedure, practice, custom) has the effect of disadvantaging most of those in a racial minority, perhaps because of their cultural membership, even when this is not intended by policy-makers. That is how they make space for the notions of unintentional and institutional racism.

I do not want to enter into the debate about what constitutes racism. The point I am seeking to make is that what counts as racism is contested, and there are different reasonable viewpoints on the matter, one of which is Flew's. This is not itself an uncontentious claim, for some (including Flew) will maintain that there is only one reasonable definition. But that is a hard position to sustain. If I am right that there are a number of reasonable accounts of the nature of racism and its causes, there are serious dangers in requiring schools to teach compulsory racism awareness classes, since these are likely to be predicated on just one.

Even if racism awareness classes survey accounts of racism and its causes, they run a serious risk of alienating members of the dominant culture rather than enlightening them. Many parents will not want such classes (perhaps because they are racists or because, working with a particular account of racism, they do not believe it is a serious problem) and may resent their children having to go to them.[50] Far from fighting

---

[48] A. Flew, 'The Monstrous Regime of "Anti-racism"', *The Salisbury Review*, vol. 7, 1989, p. 16; Flew, 'Education', p. 195.

[49] Flew identifies racism with racial discrimination, although of course it can mean racial prejudice: see his 'Education', p. 196. Someone who never disadvantages members of a particular race, but who supposes that they are inferior with no good reason, is guilty of racism, i.e., racial prejudice. Even if we accept Flew's view, it might be argued that being disadvantaged because of membership of some cultural community is unfair since membership of it is a matter of brute luck; it does not much matter whether you call that disadvantage 'racism'.   [50] Cf. Honeyford, *Integration or Disintegration?*, p. 4.

racism, or fostering an overall sense of belonging, *compulsory* anti-racist classes may reinforce racism or undermine a sense of belonging. (Of course, the pluralist model need have no objection to the existence of schools which adopt a distinctively anti-racist perspective in the education they provide; the objection is to requiring all schools to do so.) In short, although racism is likely to hinder the cultivation of a widespread sense of belonging, it is not best fought by making anti-racism classes a compulsory part of a national curriculum.

6.   Conclusion

I have argued for what I have called the pluralist model of multicultural education, on the grounds that a constrained version of it offers the best prospect of fostering a widespread sense of belonging. These constraints respect parental choice by allowing them, within very broad parameters, the kind of education they desire for their children. But it will not allow every parent's desires to be satisfied. It will rule out a number of kinds of curriculum: those which do not privilege the history, politics and literature of the liberal-democratic state to which they belong, or teach the scientific understandings which permeate its practices, and do not prepare children for citizenship in it; those which do not operate with the presumption that historically extended cultures which have sustained whole societies have value; those which do not introduce children to the ideas, practices and values of more than one culture. Each of these constraints is significant. Some parents will want any atheistic or secular culture represented as valueless, with no attempt to assess it fairly even from their own cultural perspective. Some parents will want their children to be introduced solely to their own culture because they fear that acquainting them with other cultures will lead them to reject it. Some parents will not want their children to be given a basic education in the humanities and sciences, preferring instead to prepare them for a particular role, such as motherhood. If my arguments are good, these choices should not generally be available to them.[51]

It should be clear that I am not defending the constrained pluralist model on the grounds that all the forms of education it permits are ideal. My claim is that those permitted by it are tolerable, and that the model constitutes the best response to the fact that there is massive disagreement about what constitutes a good education, given the importance of foster-

---

[51] On these matters, my conclusions are broadly similar to Mark Halstead's, though I reach them via a different route: see M. Halstead, 'Voluntary Apartheid? Problems of Schooling for Religious and Other Minorities in Democratic Societies', *Journal of Philosophy of Education*, vol. 29, 1995, pp. 268–71.

ing the mutual valuing conducive to a widespread sense of belonging.

If the arguments of this chapter and the last are successful, I have made a case for treating inclusive political community as a regulative ideal. The members of an inclusive political community identify with most of its institutions and some of its central practices, even though they have different principled commitments, and feel at home in these practices because they are not excluded from them or marginalized by them. Fostering a sense of belonging of this kind may be feasible even in the absence of a shared national identity.

Part 3

Political community and the limits of global community

7   The ideal of global community and the principle of non-intervention

Very few states can boast that their citizens come close to forming an inclusive political community, let alone that they measure up to the more demanding liberal and republican ideals of political community. Many polities fall short of being inclusive political communities either because they exclude some from the political process or because they lack liberal institutions (or both). At the very best, these polities are communities in the bare ordinary sense: their citizens share some values, a way of life, identify with their major institutions and practices, and acknowledge each other as members.

Some theorists have thought that we should at least operate with a *presumption* that the citizens of different states form communities, and that such a presumption is sufficient to underwrite a general principle of non-intervention in their internal affairs. But even if this presumption is justified, it is clear that political communities in the ordinary sense may be governed by grossly unjust institutions and practices (judged from the broadly liberal perspective I have been presupposing), and then the principle of non-intervention prevents others from coming to the aid of the victims, acting from a liberal ideal of global community. In effect the principle of non-intervention resolves conflicts between allowing political communities (in the ordinary sense) to maintain their unjust institutions and practices, and promoting a liberal vision of global community (in the moralized sense), in favour of the former. This chapter argues instead that, sometimes at least, these conflicts should be resolved in favour of the latter.

I.   Global community

The ideal of world or global community is not without difficulties, so we need to begin by considering its basis. It has a long history and can be traced back at least as far as the Cynics and Stoics. Diogenes the Cynic is reputed to have said that he was a citizen of the world when anyone asked him where he came from.[1] Within Christian and socialist traditions of thought, where the ideal has been further developed, it has sometimes been expressed in terms of a brotherhood of man. If we cavalierly put aside the apparent sexism of that notion, and the geographical and doctrinal restrictions which were usually placed on it, it is a vision of human beings bound together at least partly by recognition of their common nature, concerned for each other, and living together without systematic exploitation or injustice. In the abstract this ideal is not state-centred, but it does not prejudge the question of whether global community can be realized in the presence of separate states, nor indeed whether a world state would be required to sustain it.

The idea that human beings are predisposed to sin has often led Christians to be more sceptical than socialists about the possibility of realizing such a community in this world. St Augustine, for example, maintained that God chose 'to make a single individual the starting-point of all mankind' so that 'the human race should . . . be bound together by a kind of tie of kinship to form a harmonious unity, linked together by the "bond of peace"'.[2] As a punishment for their disobedience, however, Adam and Eve were condemned to mortal existence and man's nature was transformed for the worse: 'bondage to sin and inevitable death was the legacy handed on to their posterity'.[3] Augustine distinguished in an allegorical way between the City of God and the City of the Devil: residents in the former live by the spirit, whereas residents in the latter live by the flesh. He claimed that each seeks its own kind of peace, but earthly as opposed to heavenly peace will always be unstable because of man's predisposition to sin. Irrespective of whether Augustine's pessimism is well founded, it is clear that 'the brotherhood of man' represents a vision of community in the moralized sense, and provides an ideal which can be used to measure existing relationships.[4]

More generally, there are potentially many different kinds of global community in the moralized sense,[5] and these different kinds are available

[1] Socrates is supposed to have said the same. See D. Heater, *World Citizenship and Government: Cosmopolitan Ideas in the History of Western Political Thought* (Basingstoke: Macmillan, 1996), pp. 6–7. This book also contains a useful account of the origin of cosmopolitan ideas. For a recent presentation of the ideal of world community, and a defence of the idea that we should think and act as 'citizens of the world', see M. C. Nussbaum, 'Patriotism and Cosmopolitanism', in J. Cohen (ed.), *For Love of Country: Defining the Limits of Patriotism* (Boston: Beacon Press, 1996), pp. 2–17.

[2] Augustine, *City of God*, p. 547.   [3] *Ibid.*

[4] Indeed Augustine's very concept of peace seems to be moralized, for he says that 'the peace of the unjust, compared with the peace of the just, is not worthy even of the name of peace' (*ibid.*, p. 869).

[5] See C. Brown, 'International Political Theory and the Idea of World Community', in K.

in different conceptions depending on which theories of justice or exploitation they presuppose. So, for example, there are religious ideals of global community, some of which are liberal in nature because they give a high priority to a range of individual rights in the design of global institutions and practices, whilst others are non-liberal because they are shaped by ideas of decency and respect for God which leave no space for the recognition of such rights. My concern is with liberal conceptions, whether they be religious or secular in inspiration. Some of these maintain that the liberal ideal cannot be realized without a transfer of resources from rich to poor across the world, on the grounds that this is required by global justice. In keeping with the approach I have taken in the rest of the book, I shall stand back from these controversies in so far as it is possible to do so.

The very idea of a world or global community faces an initial challenge, in the form of the thesis that a community, by its very nature, requires 'outsiders', i.e., some who do not belong to it. David Miller, for example, insists that 'communities just are particularistic. In seeing myself as a member of a community, I see myself as participating in a particular way of life marked off from other communities by its distinctive characteristics'.[6] If this were part of the nature of community, the very idea of world community would be conceptually incoherent (unless, perhaps, non-human animals are implicitly taken to be the outsiders). According to my analysis in Chapter 1, however, it is not a conceptual truth that community requires outsiders; community in the ordinary sense involves sharing values and a way of life, identifying with the group and mutual recognition, all of which are possible in principle in the absence of outsiders.

Richard Rorty has different worries about the conceptual coherence of the ideal of global community, at least when it is understood in terms of identifying with others because they share a common human nature. For Rorty there is no antecedently existing common human nature that might come to be recognized or given due acknowledgement. But even if he were right, this would not undermine the possibility of a 'non-essentialist' ideal of global community. Indeed Rorty appears to accept this, for he does not deny that attempts to exhort global solidarity are valuable. He argues merely that we should see these as 'urging us to create a more expansive sense of solidarity than we presently have',[7] not as appealing to the moral significance of some common human essence.

There are others who are more radical than Rorty in one respect

---

Booth and S. Smith (eds.), *International Relations Theory Today* (Cambridge: Polity, 1995), p. 99.
[6] D. Miller, 'In What Sense Must Socialism Be Communitarian?', *Social Philosophy and Policy*, vol. 6, 1989, pp. 67–8.   [7] Rorty, *Contingency, Irony, and Solidarity*, p. 196.

because they reject the idea that humanity can ever be a morally relevant category. Peter Singer, for example, believes that it is always indefensible to regard mere membership of the species homo sapiens as morally significant.[8] In response, it might be argued that communities are not in general objectionable simply because they are founded upon morally irrelevant features; indeed most communities are founded on them. But in so far as ideals of global community are intended to be fully inclusive, they are vulnerable to the charge that they exclude on morally irrelevant grounds if they make species membership a criterion for inclusion. This is not an insuperable problem for these ideals, however, for they can make personhood instead a criterion for inclusion, i.e., possession of what those such as Singer are willing to concede are morally relevant capacities, such as the capacity for rationality or self-consciousness. This would exclude some human beings, but potentially include some non-human animals.

Even though the ideal of global community is coherent in principle, there may be various doubts about its status in practice, that is, whether it can be a significant or even coherent regulative ideal. For a start, one might wonder whether the identification with humanity it requires is ever likely to be strong. Even if outsiders are not a conceptual requirement for community, they often provide a considerable part of the motivation for identifying with a group. Indeed it might be thought that the primary motivation for identifying with groups derives from a powerful need to feel that one belongs to something smaller than the human race.[9] In Chapter 2, section 4, I suggested that we should hesitate before endorsing the idea that there is an unvarying universal need to feel that one belongs; nevertheless, identification tends to be at its strongest when there are outsiders and, moreover, when groups are in conflict with one another. Notwithstanding these points, however, identification with humanity as a whole need not compete with other identifications; global community does not require the absence of narrower group identifications and loyalties. And there is plenty of evidence to suggest that people do on occasions act because they identify with humanity as such.[10]

There is a further difficulty with treating global community as a regula-

[8] See P. Singer, *Practical Ethics*, 2nd edn (Cambridge: Cambridge University Press, 1993), ch. 3.

[9] This is perhaps connected with Chris Brown's worry that global community adds nothing to the constitution of individual human beings that is not provided by narrower groupings: see his 'International Political Theory and the Idea of World Community', esp. pp. 103–4. If there is a need to feel that one belongs, this need can be met, perhaps better met, by groups smaller than the human race. See also J. McMahan, 'The Limits of National Partiality', in McKim and McMahan (eds.), *The Morality of Nationalism*, p. 120, for related worries.

[10] See, e.g., K. Monroe, M. Barton and U. Klingemann, 'Altruism and the Theory of Rational Action: Rescuers of Jews in Nazi Europe', *Ethics*, vol. 101, 1990.

tive ideal, which arises out of two other conditions which would need to be met before it could be realized to any degree. This difficulty is partly conceptual and partly empirical in nature. Given the great diversity of value systems and ways of life, is it possible, without oppression of a kind which could only be sustained by a world state, to satisfy at the global level two of the minimum conditions for the existence of community, that is, some degree of shared values and some shared way of life? (This is the global analogue of the liberal claim, met in Chapter 3, that if community at the level of the state requires convergence on comprehensive doctrines, it could only be achieved by the oppressive use of state power.) If the shared values and common life necessary for global community could not be forged and sustained without oppressive measures, then global community is an incoherent ideal for us in practice, for it is, by its nature, incompatible with systematic injustice. It is not enough here to point out that I have restricted my attention to *liberal* conceptions of global community, for it still seems to be an open question whether a global consensus on the rights that are partially constitutive of a liberal outlook could be forged or sustained without oppressive measures.

In response, liberals can maintain that even though there is a great variety of traditions of thought around the world, each provides its own resources for justifying some or all of these rights and this makes possible an unforced consensus.[11] (They can allow that the differences between traditions are likely to mean that interpretations of those rights on which convergence is possible will differ markedly. Working from different traditions of thought, a variety of reasonable interpretations of them may be possible.) Debates over whether there is a set of distinctive Asian values, for example, have made it clear that there are resources within Buddhism, Confucianism and Islam for constructing defences of various individual rights. This is consistent with recognizing that there are also elements within these traditions which stand against that project, and with recognizing that in some cases the moral demands made from within these traditions are not naturally expressed in terms of rights. Political resistance to the rhetoric of individual rights may also mask the possibility of a deeper consensus on at least some of those rights, even though that consensus would have to be constructed from within different traditions of thought. However, it is a substantive question, which of the individual rights that liberals generally affirm could potentially be the object of an

---

[11] See J. R. Bauer and D. A. Bell (eds.), *The East Asian Challenge for Human Rights* (Cambridge: Cambridge University Press, 1999), especially the papers by Charles Taylor and Joseph Chan. See also A. Swidler (ed.), *Human Rights in Religious Traditions* (New York: Pilgrim Press, 1982), for accounts of the resources within different religious traditions for the justification of human rights.

unforced global consensus. (I will address this issue later in this chapter.)

Even if convergence were to occur globally on a set of individual rights, this would not necessarily generate the shared way of life which is essential for community of any kind. Cultures are not insulated from each other, however. Multiple memberships and areas of overlap mean that common ground is expanding without the use of oppressive means. The development of global markets has been facilitated by new forms of technology which have simplified transactions between those separated by large geographical distances. And the apparent emergence of a global civil society, even though very rudimentary, has made it more appropriate to regard human beings as participants in a shared way of life. These trends should not be exaggerated, as they are by those who speak of a 'global village'. But even if human diversity does pose an insuperable obstacle to a fully-fledged and coherent regulative ideal of world community, we can meaningfully consider the value and significance of potential *aspects* of community at the global level (see Chapter 1, section 2), such as identification with humanity, concern for fellow human beings and justice between all. Since that possibility would remain open, not much is gained by pursuing this objection any further. Those who remain unconvinced that global community is a coherent regulative ideal should substitute 'aspects of global community' when I mention global community in what follows.

Liberal ideals of global community can be explored in different ways, from different starting points. For example, we might begin from some very abstract claims about individuals being the ultimate unit of moral concern for everyone everywhere, and ask what institutional scheme is best suited to accommodating that idea.[12] This approach might lead to the endorsement of an institutional scheme very different from the ones with which we are familiar. Alternatively, we might begin from where we are now – that is, in the midst of a system of separate states, whose sovereignty remains significant despite increasing economic interdependence (and the emergence of new kinds of political units, such as the European Union) – and ask how various barriers to realizing liberal conceptions of global community might be removed or weakened, here and now.

If these approaches are to be coherent, the differences between them cannot be as stark as this initial characterization suggests. The first approach has to take into account existing institutional structures, and their defects as they have been revealed in practice. And the second approach needs some conception of global community to guide it; flesh-

---

[12] See T. Pogge, 'Cosmopolitanism and Sovereignty', *Ethics*, vol. 103, 1992.

ing out that conception will require taking a stand on abstract issues in moral theory, to do with what are the ultimate units of moral concern. But there remain differences in emphasis and degree between the two approaches, even when they are stripped of their excesses. In Chapter 8, some examples of the first approach will be considered, in the context of a discussion of how world peace might be achieved or promoted. In the remainder of this chapter, however, the approach is more down to earth. I begin from the assumption of a system of independent but sovereign states, which pay lip service to the principle of non-intervention, enshrined in Articles 2(4) and 2(7) of the United Nations Charter, even when they violate that principle.

2.   The principle of non-intervention and the concept of humanitarian intervention

As I have already observed, judged from a broadly liberal perspective, political communities in the ordinary sense often behave unjustly, in a systematic way, towards some of their members. So long as this continues, it is impossible to realize a liberal conception of global community (in the moralized sense) for this would require the absence of any systematic injustice, as liberals conceive it, between persons. Indeed it might seem that a liberal conception of global community can be effectively promoted in many cases only by intervention in the internal affairs of those states which are acting unjustly towards their members. In effect, the principle of non-intervention resolves a range of intrinsic conflicts between preserving the character of particular political communities (in the ordinary sense) and promoting a liberal conception of global community (in the moralized sense), in favour of the former, for it permits political communities to act unjustly, in a systematic way, towards their own members, and prevents others from coming to their aid, acting from some liberal ideal of global community. My aim is to challenge the principle of non-intervention, and to show that in a range of cases 'humanitarian intervention' can be justified. In these cases the conflict between political community and liberal ideals of global community should be resolved in favour of the latter, not the former.

Let me begin by stipulating a definition of humanitarian intervention which I will go on to defend: humanitarian intervention occurs when one or more actors (perhaps under the auspices of an international body such as the UN) intervene with the use of military force in a territory that is beyond their jurisdiction in such a way that the *only case* which can be made for intervening *in that way* is based upon the need to help some group who are being oppressed within the territory. When intervention is required in order to remove a threat to international peace, or to repulse an act of external aggression, it will not count as humanitarian on this definition if it does not go beyond what is required in order to remove that threat to international peace, or repulse that act of external aggression, even if it is actually motivated by humanitarian considerations, and even if a case could be made for intervention of this kind on humanitarian grounds. For the definition says that, in order to count as humanitarian, an intervention must be such that the only case which can be made in favour of the particular form it takes is humanitarian in character. According to the proposed definition, motives do not determine whether an intervention counts as humanitarian. This at least has the merit of removing one of the difficulties which surrounds identifying an intervention as humanitarian.

The principle of non-intervention as it is normally understood rules out most humanitarian intervention when it is defined in these terms. There are two potential exceptions. First, when law and order has broken down irretrievably. Whether the principle of non-intervention rules out intervention in these cases will depend on whether states are defined by territory alone or partly in terms of some other criterion such as a degree of success in preserving law and order. If the latter, then a complete break-down in law and order would mean that the state had ceased to exist and the principle of non-intervention would be irrelevant. The second potential exception is the use of military force at the request of a state which is no longer in full control of events in its territory and needs help to protect some group there. Although important, these two kinds of case do not cover all of those where intervention may be necessary to prevent oppression.

The definition of 'humanitarian intervention' which I have proposed is narrower than some others, for it covers only the use of military force. Importantly, it does not include much of what Oliver Ramsbotham and Tom Woodhouse call 'non-forcible humanitarian intervention',[13] for example, the use of military personnel and expertise to keep the peace where they can do so without the use of force, or non-military assistance which takes the form of providing food or medical supplies. What counts as an adequate definition of humanitarian intervention will be determined, in part, by one's theoretical purposes. Ramsbotham and Woodhouse's broad definition serves their purposes well, for they want to draw attention to the potential choice between a variety of different possible collective responses to human suffering, and the way in which these responses may interact and often reinforce one another. In contrast, I

[13] See O. Ramsbotham and T. Woodhouse, *Humanitarian Intervention in Contemporary Conflict: A Reconceptualization* (Cambridge: Polity, 1996), especially pp. 113–21.

restrict the subject matter in the way I do in order to focus on the hardest kinds of action to justify, for the conflict between liberal ideals of global community and the principle of non-intervention is most acute when the use of military force is the only way in practice of helping an oppressed group, and when the only case which can be made for the use of such force, in the way proposed, is of a humanitarian nature. If forcible military intervention on behalf of an oppressed group can sometimes be justified solely on humanitarian grounds, then other kinds of non-forcible intervention or influence (for example, non-forcible military intervention, economic sanctions or pressure, medical aid against the wishes of the government) will also be justifiable, where appropriate, in relevantly similar cases.

One consequence of my definition is that, in the world as it is now, states and derivatively the United Nations, are the only potential agents of humanitarian intervention, for only they possess the military force necessary for it.[14] But we should not rule out the possibility that, if a practice of humanitarian intervention were to be legitimized, the United Nations might recruit a volunteer military force directly rather than through its members,[15] or that non-governmental organizations (NGOs) might deploy military personnel for humanitarian purposes.[16]

The definition of humanitarian intervention that I have given still allows for a variety of forms of it: humanitarian intervention may aim merely at the immediate relief of suffering;[17] or it may aim to restore the status quo or some minimal political order; or it may aim to change the structures which cause, and perhaps are partially constitutive of, the oppression of the suffering group.[18] In particular cases, no doubt, one of these forms of humanitarian intervention might be more effective than the others at promoting liberal ideals of global community.

I shall consider three main approaches to justifying the principle of

---

[14] On broader definitions of humanitarian intervention which allowed non-military forms of intervention to count, NGOs would of course be major actors.

[15] See B. Urquart, 'For a UN Volunteer Force', *New York Review of Books*, 10 June 1993.

[16] In a semi-serious way, Bernard Williams mentions (without advocating) the possibility of a private relief agency which commanded military forces and which, with the cooperation of other states, could intervene on humanitarian grounds: B. Williams, 'Is International Rescue a Moral Issue?', *Social Research*, vol. 62, 1995, pp. 74-5.

[17] Contrast Bhikhu Parekh's definition of humanitarian intervention, which would not cover intervention that aimed merely to relieve suffering. In his view, humanitarian intervention must always aim to create peace and order. See B. Parekh, 'Towards the Just World Order: The Aims and Limits of Humanitarian Intervention', *Times Literary Supplement*, 26 September, 1997, p. 14.

[18] For a related set of distinctions, see A. Natsios, 'NGOs and the Humanitarian Impulse', *Ethics and International Affairs*, vol. 11, 1997, pp. 133-6; D. Mapel, 'When is it Right to Rescue? A Response to Pasic and Weiss', *Ethics and International Affairs*, vol. 11, 1997, p. 146.

non-intervention in the face of demands for humanitarian intervention. (These approaches are not mutually incompatible, and indeed may be combined as part of an overall argument against permitting humanitarian intervention.) The first approach, which will be considered in the next section, maintains that states should respect the communal autonomy of each other's citizens, and this requires strict adherence to the principle of non-intervention. The second approach, to be considered in section 4, defends non-intervention by arguing that legitimizing a practice of humanitarian intervention will be at best ineffective and at worst counter-productive. The third approach, which will be considered in section 5, maintains that states have no legitimate authority to engage in humanitarian intervention.

3.   Respect for Communal Autonomy

Some believe that a robust principle of non-intervention can be justified by appealing directly to the importance of respect for communal autonomy. Note, however, that a theory of what is required by respect for communal autonomy cannot by itself justify non-intervention in cases where there is no relevant community in existence. There is at least one important type of case here – when different groups within the state are at war with one another and the institutions of civil society have broken down to such an extent that there is no shared way of life which unites them.[19] This type of case need not be too troubling for a defender of the principle of non-intervention, however, for he or she can maintain that it is relatively rare in practice and can be treated as an exception to the principle. (Nor does it bear upon the issue of how conflicts between political community and liberal ideals of global community should be resolved, for if there is no political community, there can be no such conflict.)

Some further obstacles, however, would need to be overcome before respect for communal autonomy could succeed in justifying a robust principle of non-intervention. Far from underwriting non-intervention, respect for communal autonomy might seem to *justify* humanitarian intervention when a government is repressing its own community. Michael Walzer argues that in these cases we should nevertheless work with a strong presumption that there is a union or fit between a govern-

[19] No doubt a good degree of caution is required before we declare that there is no community which coincides with the state's borders, but it is hard to argue that we can *never* be sure. Even Walzer who is hesitant about making judgements of this kind acknowledges that 'when a government turns savagely upon its own people, we must doubt the existence of a political community to which the idea of self-determination might apply' (M. Walzer, *Just and Unjust Wars* (Harmondsworth: Penguin, 1978), p. 101).

ment and its 'people'. In his view, respect for communal autonomy will count against intervention unless a lack of such fit is 'radically apparent':

> Foreigners are in no position to deny the reality of that [fit] or rather, they are in no position to attempt anything other than speculative denials. They don't know enough about its history, and they have no direct experience, and can form no concrete judgments, of the conflicts and harmonies, the historical choices and cultural affinities, the loyalties and resentments, that underlie it.[20]

But Walzer surely over-states the case here. As David Luban points out in response, there may be many people with specialist knowledge of a community's history and culture who could advise about the fit, or lack of it, between government and community.[21] It would be ill-conceived to defend the idea that we should in general presume such a fit by arguing that we can never know a culture properly unless we belong to it. Even if that scepticism were justified, it would not preclude taking advice from 'insiders'.

The next obstacle to defending a principle of non-intervention by appeal to the importance of communal autonomy is the difficulty in showing that the autonomy of a community deserves respect when its government is systematically violating what liberals regard as the rights of its citizens. This difficulty arises even if these violations are in keeping with the character of the community so that we can speak of some sort of fit between government and community. These are the hardest cases, however, for they raise the question of which of the rights that liberals usually endorse in their own domestic contexts are universally applicable. When a case can be made for the universal applicability of some or all of a set of individual rights, this poses a potentially serious challenge to the principle of non-intervention when it is defended by appeal to the import-ance of respect for communal autonomy. For why should communal autonomy be thought so important that it should be respected even when such rights are being violated, perhaps in a massive way? The way in which self-determination enables a group to express and protect those practices and traditions central to its identity may be sufficient to show that its political independence is instrumentally valuable, and to the extent that its members desire this independence for its own sake then it may have further value. But these considerations seem unlikely to justify a principle of non-intervention in the face of massive violations of (univer-sally applicable) individual rights.

Those who ground their theories on the importance of respect for

---

[20] Walzer, 'The Moral Standing of States', p. 220.
[21] See D. Luban, 'The Romance of the Nation-State', in Beitz *et al.* (eds.), *International Ethics*, p. 241.

communal autonomy often do allow the legitimacy of some humanitarian intervention, but argue that it is justified only in a very limited range of cases. In his seminal discussion of the issue, Walzer restricted legitimate humanitarian intervention to actions or policies which 'shock the moral conscience of mankind',[22] which he thought covered only massacre and enslavement.[23] But why not also permit humanitarian intervention to prevent the widespread use of torture against political opponents, for example?[24] Like enslavement and massacre, routine torture can throw into question the very existence of a political community and it is hard to deny that it violates a universally applicable individual right. Even if there were a community whose traditions sanction the use of torture, it is hard to see why respect for it should, by itself, outweigh the enormity of the moral crime which is being committed. For Walzer's position to be plausible, he would need to provide us with a justification for restricting humanitarian intervention to cases of massacre or enslavement.

Even if Walzer's class of cases is too restrictive, there is good reason to be wary of proposals which would license very extensive intervention. For example, those who would sanction intervention to reform societies which do not provide people with the right to vote, or hold political office, are vulnerable to the charge of cultural imperialism, for a case can be made for saying that these rights are not universally applicable. There are surely legitimate forms of government which do not protect those rights but nevertheless do not systematically violate any of the other rights which liberals usually regard as basic.[25] In these cases, respect for communal autonomy seems to be a conclusive reason against intervention.

The way forward here seems to require identifying a special class of rights which are genuinely culturally universal, in the sense that they can be given a justification from within each of the major traditions of thought. Respect for these rights could then be seen as a precondition for good standing in the international system, entitling states to the respect for their community's autonomy provided by adherence to the principle of non-intervention. Violations of these rights, at least on a large enough scale, could be seen as enough to deny a state the protection afforded by that principle, even if there were often other reasons which made intervention unwise or unjustifiable. In 'The Law of Peoples', John Rawls seems to pursue a strategy which is consistent at least with this one. He

---

[22] Walzer, *Just and Unjust Wars*, p. 107.
[23] Walzer later expanded the list to include mass deportation: see his 'The Moral Standing of States', pp. 225–6, and his 'The Politics of Rescue', *Social Research*, vol. 62, 1995, p. 60.
[24] See J. Slater and T. Nardin, 'Non-Intervention and Human Rights', *Journal of Politics*, vol. 48, 1986, p. 91.
[25] For the point that liberal-democracy is but one form of democracy, see B. Parekh, 'The Cultural Particularity of Liberal Democracy', *Political Studies*, vol. 40, 1992.

rejects the idea that only liberal states are entitled to protection by the principle of non-intervention, arguing that another class of states, viz. hierarchical states, also has the necessary standing.

A hierarchical state has three main features.[26] First, it is peaceful and gains its legitimate aims through diplomacy and trade. Second, it is guided by a conception of justice which is based upon some conception of the common good, which it seeks to promote impartially, and which imposes moral duties and obligations on all members of societies. Furthermore, its political institutions 'constitute a reasonable consultation hierarchy' which allow its citizens as members of associations and corporate bodies to express their dissent and have their views respected. Third, it respects human rights, that is, 'the right to life and security, to personal property, and the elements of the rule of law, as well as the right to a certain liberty of conscience and freedom of association, and the right to emigration'.[27] In Rawls's view, hierarchical states are 'members in good standing in a reasonable society of well-ordered peoples', and are thereby entitled to the protection afforded by the principle of non-intervention: 'By being in place, [human rights] are . . . sufficient to exclude justified and forceful intervention by other peoples, say by economic sanctions or in grave cases, by military force.'[28]

Rawls appears to believe that there are practices which a liberal state should tolerate in other societies which it should not tolerate within its own borders. As we saw in Chapter 3, he believes that a liberal state should not tolerate violations of basic rights *within* its territory, unless eradicating them would lead to greater injustice. In contrast, he seems to think that it should tolerate violations of these basic rights *beyond* its borders, except in some cases when those basic rights are also human rights. How then does Rawls's class of human rights differ from the class of basic rights which are to receive constitutional protection in liberal societies? There are two main differences. First, some of the basic rights do not appear in any form on the list of human rights. The right to political liberty, i.e., the right to vote and be eligible for political office, is not counted by Rawls as a human right. Second, some human rights are attenuated versions of the basic rights. So, for example, although there is a human right to 'a certain liberty of conscience', which requires that no religions be persecuted, this is compatible with an established religion which provides political privileges to its adherents. Hence it does not extend as far as the basic equal right to liberty of conscience, at least as most liberals conceive that right.[29]

[26] See J. Rawls, 'The Law of Peoples', in H. Shute and S. Hurley (eds.), *On Human Rights: The Oxford Amnesty Lectures* (New York: Basic Books, 1993), pp. 60–3.
[27] *Ibid.*, p. 68.   [28] *Ibid.*, p. 71.   [29] *Ibid.*, p. 63.

Although Rawls has not presented us with a theory of intervention, his approach might seem to promise a better basis than Walzer's for identifying the kind of practices which might justify humanitarian intervention. 'Outlaw' states which violate human rights are candidates for humanitarian intervention, even if there are other reasons which count against intervention in their affairs in particular cases. By according moral standing to some non-democratic states, Rawls respects the important intuition (shared by Walzer) that there are legitimate forms of government other than the liberal-democratic, and that even non-democratic forms of government may be unobjectionable. But how might Rawls's position be developed? At present, it lacks a clear basis for identifying or justifying the human rights which are to be regarded as 'a special class of rights of universal application',[30] and it lacks an account of when violations of human rights are sufficient to merit humanitarian intervention.

Let me consider the first of these difficulties. As Peter Jones has observed, it is unclear how Rawls proposes to justify his claim that states in good standing in the international system must respect his list of human rights.[31] Perhaps Rawls is simply stipulating that respect for these rights is a conceptual requirement of truly well-ordered societies, including hierarchical states. But that strategy would be simply question-begging,[32] for it gives us no reason to suppose that well-ordered societies, so understood, are the only societies in good standing in the international system. However, it seems to me that extending the framework developed in Chapter 3 (for judging when the state should refrain from enforcing basic rights within its borders) to inter-state relations generates an approach which is broadly compatible with Rawls's position in 'The Law of Peoples' but which is also capable of supplying some of its missing pieces, including an account of why we are entitled to impose various moral requirements on states which they must meet to be in good standing.

In Chapter 3, I argued that the authority to adopt one set of basic rights rather than another, in the face of disagreement over which is best, can derive from its being the set which emerges from an inclusive political dialogue. States are entitled to permit violations of these basic rights within their borders in two circumstances: when forcibly preventing them would result in greater injustice; or when the costs of forcibly preventing them in terms of misery and suffering, or the alienation of a minority

---

[30] *Ibid.*, p. 70. Rawls says that basic human rights 'express a minimum standard of well-ordered political institutions for all peoples who belong, as members in good standing, to a just political society of peoples' (*ibid.*, p. 68). But this does not provide us with much by means of which to identify them.

[31] See P. Jones, 'International Human Rights: Philosophical or Political?', in Caney, George and Jones (eds.), *National Rights, International Obligations*, p. 192.

[32] See *ibid.*, pp. 194–5.

group, would be great, and other measures short of coercion could reasonably be expected to be successful in ending these violations in the longer term. I also argued that respect for communal autonomy requires that communities which have 'societal cultures' should be permitted to live by whatever reasonable interpretation of the basic rights they see fit. How could this framework be extended to the international domain?

In the international case, there is not at present anything close to an inclusive political dialogue which could vest states with the authority to intervene beyond their borders. In section 5 of this chapter, I shall suggest that they may nevertheless possess the legitimate authority to do so. But in order to avoid the danger, or at least the charge, of cultural imperialism, some judgement would need to be made concerning what set of rights could, in the presence of good faith, be the object of a reasoned global consensus in the light of the very different cultural resources to which argumentative appeal might be made, and is made in practice.[33] Of course, there are societies that do not employ the language of human rights, but their moral traditions may nevertheless contain the resources to justify the existence of various moral constraints that can be expressed in terms of rights without doing violence to their own understanding of those traditions, for example, a right not to be murdered.[34] I should add that I leave open the question of whether there is a set of rights which can be given a philosophical justification that in some sense transcends the resources contained in particular cultures to justify them. Even if that were possible, to impose them solely on the grounds that they can be given such a justification would invite the charge of cultural imperialism (even though *ex hypothesi* that would be misconceived), and raise questions about the legitimate authority to impose them.

Extending the framework described above to inter-state relations would then imply that states should intervene on humanitarian grounds to end the violation of those rights which (even in the light of the very different cultural resources to which argumentative appeal might be

---

[33] See C. Taylor, 'Conditions of an Unforced Consensus on Human Rights', in Bauer and Bell (eds.), *The East Asian Challenge for Human Rights*. The 'good faith' clause in my formulation is designed to take into account the way in which hostility between different cultures may make it hard to reach consensus in practice, even when the resources exist within those cultures for an unforced consensus. The requirement I am envisaging falls short of the idea that there should be some universal dialogic community: see A. Linklater, *The Transformation of Political Community: Ethical Foundations of the Post-Westphalian Era* (Cambridge: Polity, 1998), esp. pp. 85–100. I assume that the charge of cultural imperialism can be answered in the absence of a universal dialogic community, even if such a community would provide the securest defence against that charge.

[34] Given the weight of the arguments in favour of the idea that the political rights associated with liberal-democracy, such as the right to vote and to be eligible for political office, are culturally particular, a consensus of this kind would be unlikely on the idea that a failure to respect these rights was sufficient to deprive a state of good standing.

made) could in the presence of good faith be the object of a reasoned global consensus, except under two circumstances: when engaging in it would lead to greater injustice, judged in terms of the violations of these rights, or when its costs would be so great that measures short of military force should be used if they have some reasonable chance of success in the longer term. In order to take due account of the importance of communal autonomy, the extended framework should also require that in judging whether an intervention would lead to greater injustice, whatever reasonable conception of those rights would cast the offending state in its best light should be employed. Indeed there is no case for intervention if states are working with reasonable interpretations of these rights, even if they depart from (what is believed to be) the best interpretations. This squares with Rawls's idea that hierarchical states are in good standing.

Let me move on to consider two objections to the idea that extending the framework would justify humanitarian intervention in a range of cases. The first of these, which I shall explore in the next section, takes 'the extended framework' for granted and considers the argument that, contrary to appearances, it underwrites a principle of non-intervention in international affairs. This argument maintains that legitimizing a practice of humanitarian intervention would be likely to lead to greater injustice, and that it is hard (perhaps impossible) to know in particular cases whether it will be successful, so in practice the framework will forbid it. The second objection, to be considered in section 5, maintains that it is fundamentally misconceived to extend to inter-state relations a framework which was developed to cover intra-state relations.

4.   The difficulties and risks of humanitarian intervention[35]

So far I have considered a defence of the principle of non-intervention which appeals to the importance of respect for communal self-determination. In this section I propose to consider what can be construed as an indirect defence of the principle, which predicts dire consequences from allowing a class of exceptions to it, and appeals to the difficulty of determining whether humanitarian intervention is likely to be successful.[36] If a practice of humanitarian intervention were likely to lead to greater injustice and greater suffering, or if there were grave difficulties

[35]   This section draws upon A. Mason and N. Wheeler, 'Realist Objections to Humanitarian Intervention', in B. Holden (ed.), *The Ethical Dimensions of Global Change* (Basingstoke: Macmillan, 1996). I am grateful to Nick Wheeler for his permission to adapt the material for my purposes here, although I of course take responsibility for the use to which it is put.

[36]   Caroline Thomas maintains on the basis of past interventions that 'most of the time intervention will do more harm than good' (C. Thomas, 'The Pragmatic Case Against Intervention', in I. Forbes and M. Hoffman (eds.), *Political Theory*, p. 92).

with determining in all or most cases whether it is likely to be successful, then the extended framework described in the previous section would appear to support rather than undermine a principle of non-intervention.

There are a number of general reasons that might be given for thinking that a practice of humanitarian intervention will either make matters worse or be ineffective, or be highly risky. First, there is widespread disagreement on what counts as injustice or oppression. It might be argued that a reasoned global consensus is next to impossible in practice on any rights. In the face of disagreement, widespread humanitarian intervention is likely to undermine world order, potentially creating more injustice in the form of rights violations. Second, even if agreement could be reached on what counted as oppression or injustice, whatever rules are devised to govern humanitarian intervention will be abused. Third, in practice it is impossible to know whether humanitarian intervention will be successful, so given the risks involved it should not be undertaken. The outcome of intervention is always highly uncertain and therefore it is unreasonable to embark upon it. Fourth, even if an intervention is successful in the short term, it is likely that the same oppression will occur again in the future, or that some other form of oppression will take its place. These arguments need to be developed further before they can be properly assessed.

The first argument points to widespread global disagreement on what counts as injustice or oppression, and maintains that this will inevitably mean disagreement about when humanitarian intervention is justified (and indeed on what counts as humanitarian intervention, since it is defined in terms of attempting to help the oppressed). Allowing a practice of humanitarian intervention in these circumstances would be likely to undermine world order: states will intervene to end what they *perceive* as injustice, leading to escalating tensions, and ultimately more wars between states, thereby resulting in greater injustice. Hedley Bull presented a variant of this argument. He emphasized that there is no agreement on the content of human rights, and suggested that this underwrites the reluctance of many statesmen to experiment with a right of humanitarian intervention.[37] His position seems to be that general well-being is better served by upholding the principle of non-intervention than by allowing humanitarian intervention in the face of disagreement about where and when it is justified.

The second argument really makes two different points, although they are sometimes run together. The first point is that states will intervene

[37] See H. Bull (ed.), *Intervention in World Politics* (Oxford: Oxford University Press, 1984), p. 193.

simply in order to further their own national interest whilst claiming a humanitarian motive. Thus Thomas Franck and Nigel Rodley once argued that the principle of non-aggression enshrined in the United Nations Charter is vulnerable enough to states abusing it in the name of self-defence, without a legal right of humanitarian intervention providing a further cloak for the unjustified pursuit of national self-interest.[38] Given the possibilities of abuse, humanitarian intervention may become simply a new form of imperialism and itself lead to greater injustice.[39]

It is worth distinguishing this point from another: that states will apply the rules governing humanitarian intervention selectively, intervening only when they can further their own national interest, and intervene successfully (given the scale of the problem and the resistance they are likely to meet). On this ground, it might be argued that humanitarian intervention is likely to be destabilizing and lead to greater injustice in other ways. It will occur unexpectedly because it is impossible to foresee where states will perceive an interest in intervening. It will lead to grievances that are apparently justified because one state will complain that it has been unfairly 'picked on', whilst others are equally blameworthy. This point differs from the first because it maintains that even when an intervention is genuinely humanitarian, abuse will occur because the practice of intervention will be selective, and will not occur in all cases when it would be justified.

The third argument, that in practice it is impossible to know that an intervention will be successful, can be supported by a number of observations.[40] First, it is very hard to gather the information necessary to make a prudent judgement about the possibility of successful humanitarian intervention: the political context in which an intervention takes place is complex and unfamiliar, making it difficult to evaluate the prospects of success of various different policy options. Second, the success of an operation is frequently dependent upon a multiplicity of factors that are out of the control of the intervening force. Since advocates of humanitarian intervention want to distinguish it from conquest or imperialism, they suppose that successful intervention will involve providing an oppressed group with the means to protect itself or enabling a society to rebuild its institutions. In practice, the former will often require helping to install a

---

[38] See T. M. Franck and N. Rodley, 'After Bangladesh: The Law of Humanitarian Intervention by Force', *American Journal of International Law*, vol. 67, 1973, pp. 275–305.

[39] See J. McMahan, 'The Ethics of International Intervention', in K. Kipnis and D. Meyers (eds.), *Political Realism and International Morality* (Boulder, CO: Westview Press, 1987), p. 92, for in my view a much too hasty dismissal of considerations of this sort.

[40] This argument is presented forcefully by Gordon Graham: see G. Graham, 'The Justice of Intervention', *Review of International Studies*, vol. 13, 1987, pp. 113–46, see especially p. 143.

government that is friendly to the oppressed group, whereas the latter will rely upon the ability of different groups to work with one another. Both of these are much more out of the intervening force's control than simple conquest. Third, it is hard to intervene successfully without destroying the institutions of government, and without alienating a sufficiently large section of the population so that effective non-military government becomes impossible.[41]

The fourth argument, that even if an intervention is successful in the short term, it is likely to be ineffective in the long term, because oppression will re-occur later or simply be replaced by a new form, was defended in one version by John Stuart Mill. Mill developed this argument in defence of the principle of non-intervention restricted in its application to so-called civilized societies, but it might also be employed in defence of such a principle applicable to all states. Mill argues that where a people, or some portion of them, is being oppressed by their government, there is no point in liberating them, for unless they are willing to liberate themselves it will only be a matter of time before their liberty is taken away again.[42]

These broadly consequentialist arguments in favour of the principle of non-intervention are powerful and do draw attention to the danger that humanitarian intervention can make matters worse, and to the difficulties in judging whether it is likely to be successful. They can be answered, however. There is radical disagreement over what counts as injustice and oppression, but it is not so radical that it rules out the possibility of any significant convergence. The risks and difficulties of humanitarian intervention do not justify a blanket prohibition when they are placed within the extended framework described at the end of section 3. According to that framework, states should refrain from humanitarian intervention when that would lead to greater injustice, judged from the perspective of those rights which could in the presence of good faith be the object of a reasoned global consensus, or when its costs would be so great that measures short of military force should be used instead if they offer a reasonable chance of success in the longer term. When that framework is combined with a measured assessment of the limitations and risks, I believe that it would permit and justify a practice of humanitarian intervention provided it is subject to various specific guidelines. Although these guidelines would overturn a strict principle of non-intervention,

---

[41] See T. G. Weiss, 'UN Responses in the Former Yugoslavia: Moral and Operational Choices', *Ethics and International Affairs*, vol. 8, 1994, p. 5.

[42] See J. S. Mill, 'A Few Words on Non-Intervention', in J. M. Robson (ed.), *Collected Works of John Stuart Mill, vol. 21, Essays on Equality, Law, and Education* (London: Routledge, 1984) especially pp. 122–3. See Walzer, *Just and Unjust Wars*, pp. 87–8, for a somewhat different reading of this argument.

they would leave in place a general presumption against intervention:

  (i) Humanitarian intervention should be permitted only in extreme cases, that is, mass murder,[43] enslavement or deportation (including so-called ethnic cleansing) and widespread institutional use of torture or rape.

 (ii) A state (or group of states) should be required to obtain the permission of an appropriate international body, perhaps the Security Council of the United Nations, before it acts. Unilateral action would be permissible but only if it was licensed by such a body.

(iii) This international body should work within a definite framework when considering whether to license humanitarian intervention in a particular case. It should specify that an intervention will not be licensed if it would be likely to lead to greater injustice, judged in terms of the rights which could (in the presence of good faith) be the object of a reasoned global consensus, for example, by causing disorder in neighbouring countries. It should also require that the intervention have clearly defined aims and a reasonable chance of success, and that less drastic measures be tried, unless there is good reason to think that they would fail and there is insufficient time to try them out.[44]

These guidelines do not provide, nor are they intended to provide, an algorithm which can be applied mechanically to determine when intervention is justified. They are designed to address the various worries about the effectiveness and risks of humanitarian intervention. They suppose that a rational consensus is possible in principle on the idea that mass murder, enslavement and mass deportation, and the institutional use of torture and rape, are grave moral wrongs. Although it is possible to disagree considerably over the definitions of these terms, and to disagree over the application of any agreed definition to particular cases (for example, can letting a group of people starve constitute mass murder?, is amputating limbs as a punishment a form of torture?), with some small measure of good faith agreement should be possible in a range of cases.[45]

No doubt states will undertake humanitarian intervention selectively. It is likely that in practice states will intervene only when they can further their national interest by doing so. (Of course, if these are to be genuine instances of humanitarian intervention, humanitarian reasons must con-

---

[43] I do not mean to restrict 'mass murder' to cases of genocide, for the notion of mass murder does not imply any racial or ethnic connection between those killed.

[44] Cf. C. Beitz, 'The Reagan Doctrine in Nicaragua' in S. Luper-Foy (ed.), *Problems of International Justice* (Boulder, CO: Westview Press, 1988).

[45] Whether the necessary good faith exists will, of course, depend upon specific historical circumstances. Whether it exists now is a matter of dispute.

stitute the only case which can be made for the particular form that intervention takes.) By and large this will not be destabilizing or lead to greater injustice, however, for it will be clear where national interests are at stake, and hence where interventions are likely to occur. In any case, the interventions, if they are to be legitimate, will have to be authorized by an international body such as the UN, so they will not be unpredictable.

The UN Security Council is not of course an impartial judge, so any decisions it makes about intervention would be bound to reflect to some extent the realities of international power. (Indeed any other politically feasible international body which might in the near future come to regulate humanitarian intervention would be likely to possess similar flaws.) But the hope is that morality could nevertheless play at least a limited role; even if humanitarian intervention did not always occur when it was morally desirable, it might nevertheless occur only when it was morally desirable. It is not clear that selectivity of this kind would in itself be an injustice. Only if humanitarian intervention were morally required in all cases where it was morally permissible would it follow that selective intervention was always unjust. Even then it would not be the fact of selectivity itself that was morally questionable, but rather the absence of humanitarian intervention in some circumstances in which it should occur.

The concern that in practice it is impossible to know that an intervention will be successful also has considerable force, but overstates the difficulties involved. There are many dangers attached to humanitarian intervention. For example, forces may become unwilling participants in a conflict from which they cannot extricate themselves. It is very hard to intervene with sufficient force to be successful without at the same time alienating a sizable proportion of the population, or without destroying the institutions which are necessary for government of any sort. But there surely can in practice be cases where we have good reason to think that humanitarian intervention will be successful, and the potential gains in terms of justice are such that the risk is worth taking.

Mill's claim that humanitarian intervention is ineffective because if a people is to remain free for any length of time, then they must free themselves, also seems to over-state the case against intervention. A love of liberty is not always enough to enable a people to escape tyranny, especially when that tyranny takes the form of mass murder. In these cases intervention would be justified not on the grounds that it is needed to liberate those who are being oppressed, but on the grounds that it is required to prevent their extermination.[46]

[46] Cf. Walzer, *Just and Unjust Wars*, p. 106.

A number of counter-objections to the proposed guidelines might be made. First, it might be argued that still no principled reason has been given for restricting intervention to cases of mass murder, enslavement, or deportation, and widespread torture or rape. Why draw the line around these rather than to include, say, imprisonment of dissidents or other forms of persecution which fall short of the required severity? The framework with which I have been working does provide principles of a sort for determining where the line should be drawn, although it is very difficult to know where it comes in practice. Intervention is permissible only if a state violates rights which could be the object of a reasoned global consensus. If allowing a more extensive practice of humanitarian intervention would lead to greater injustice, judged according to this set of rights, then the framework prohibits it. My judgement – and it is only a judgement – is that there are not the shared resources for a reasoned global consensus on a more extensive set of rights, and that in any case allowing a practice of intervention to protect the violations of other rights would, for the reasons considered, be likely to lead to more violations of the rights in the narrower set in the long term.

Second, it might be argued that even if humanitarian intervention is morally legitimate in some cases, it is better not to institutionalize it as a practice, or give it the sanction of international law. (This argument is similar in form to one which is sometimes presented in the debate over euthanasia: although euthanasia is morally permissible in some cases, it is better for it to remain illegal given the possibilities of abuse.) In response to this objection, it can be maintained that the institutional arrangements described would minimize the scope for abuse, and lead to less injustice than ones in which all humanitarian intervention is ruled out by international bodies such as the UN and regarded as a violation of international law.

The defence of a limited practice of humanitarian intervention considered in this section has extended a framework which was developed in Chapter 3 to guide the state's enforcement of basic rights within its borders. This approach might be regarded as fundamentally misconceived, however, on the grounds that states can never possess the authority to engage in humanitarian intervention, even in order to prevent violations of rights which could in the presence of good faith be the object of a reasoned global consensus. It is to this objection that I now turn.

5.   The state's authority to intervene

The question of whether states possess the authority to engage in humanitarian intervention has two different aspects. The first concerns whether a state has the legitimate authority to benefit the citizens of other states when this does not (at least on balance) benefit its own citizens. The second concerns whether a state which intervenes on humanitarian grounds in a territory which lies outside its jurisdiction lacks the legitimate authority to do so because it violates the sovereignty of the state which does have jurisdiction over that territory.

Consider the first aspect of the question. An initially plausible theory which threatens the idea that a state has the legitimate authority to engage in humanitarian intervention is the following: a state possesses the legitimate authority to pursue some policy or course of action if and only if that policy or course of action would, at least on balance, benefit its own citizens. But there are other theories of the state's legitimate authority which preserve what is attractive in the idea that such authority must rest upon the benefits it confers on its citizens but would permit a greater range of humanitarian intervention. Consider, for example, Joseph Raz's claim that 'the main argument for the legitimacy of any authority is that in subjecting himself to it a person is more likely to act successfully for the reasons which apply to him than if he does not subject himself to its authority'.[47] Raz's account allows that some of the reasons which apply to a person may derive from moral obligations which he is under, compliance with which may not benefit him (even if what benefits a person is construed broadly to include anything which promotes his well-being). So Raz's account can allow that the state may have the legitimate authority to engage in humanitarian intervention when it thereby enables its citizens to discharge their moral obligations to those beyond its borders.

In response, it might be argued that the state has special moral obligations to its own citizens, which it has no legitimate authority to override, and which would be violated by all, or at least most, cases of humanitarian intervention. Humanitarian intervention is a highly risky business (it usually involves putting at risk the lives of soldiers) and is highly costly in terms of resources. If states are morally obliged to give the interests of their own citizens priority, it would seem to follow that they can legitimately intervene only when the interests of their own citizens can be best promoted by doing so.[48]

Do states have special obligations to their own citizens? It is widely agreed that they do, and that these obligations have a certain kind of primacy.[49] (Some 'realists' go further and maintain that these obligations

---

[47] Raz, *The Morality of Freedom*, p. 71.
[48] This is the case that 'realists' characteristically put against humanitarian intervention: they argue that the state should pursue the national interest, and understand the national interest to be the interests of its citizens.
[49] For a clear presentation of this idea, see R. Jackson, 'International Community Beyond the Cold War', in G. Lyons and M. Mastanduno (eds.), *Beyond Westphalia: State Sovereignty and International Intervention* (Baltimore, MD: Johns Hopkins University Press, 1995), especially pp. 74–7.

are the only ones to which the state is subject.) But in my view the most plausible account of those special obligations makes space for some legitimate humanitarian intervention. Let me explain.

In Chapter 4 I argued that citizens have special obligations to each other. It would seem to follow that the state has special obligations to its own citizens, for the state is not entirely independent of them. If we suppose that citizens act collectively through the institutions of the state[50], then in doing so they are under an obligation to give priority to each other's interests in determining policy. This limits the extent to which the state can possess the legitimate authority to act in order to benefit the citizens of other states. But could it justify a principle of non-intervention?

I think not. In Chapter 4 I also tried to show that the best defence of special obligations to fellow citizens justifies them by appealing to the good of citizenship. Part of the good of citizenship consists in the fulfilment of these obligations, and some of these obligations require citizens to put each other first, to help provide each other with the conditions necessary to enjoy equal status and the opportunity to participate politically. But if this is so, it is implausible to suppose that these special obligations will leave no space for justified humanitarian intervention. If citizenship is a good, then it is a good for everyone. Even if that good is realized in part by citizens giving preferential treatment to each other in their collective deliberations, and can only be fully realized in that way, there still comes a point at which it can be better promoted or honoured by ceasing to give priority to one's fellow citizens, and perhaps even by securing the conditions under which others can lie in that relationship to one another. The considerations which speak in favour of the idea that states have special obligations to their citizens also support the idea that those obligations are limited.[51]

Citizenship is also just one good amongst several, and promoting, respecting or honouring these other goods may on occasion require giving them greater weight than citizenship and the obligations which are part of it. The good represented by beneficence towards strangers (and general obligations to aid or relieve suffering) may well outweigh the good of citizenship (and the special obligations of citizenship) in circumstances where the needs of strangers are much more urgent than the needs of

[50] The assumption that citizens act collectively through the state may hold only when the state is democratic or when its political institutions form what Rawls calls a consultation hierarchy.

[51] In Chapter 4, I argued that general principles of justice might also justify other kinds of special obligations, for example between residents rather than citizens. But since these special obligations would be derived from principles of justice, there is even more reason to think that they would permit and perhaps even require intervention in a range of cases.

fellow citizens. The good of citizenship, though important, will not always override other goods, and promoting or honouring these other goods may mean that intervention is not merely permissible but morally required.

Even if states need violate no special obligations to their own citizens when they intervene on humanitarian grounds in a territory that is beyond their jurisdiction, there is the further issue, mentioned at the beginning of this section, of whether they must nevertheless lack the legitimate authority to do so because they violate the sovereignty of the state which does have jurisdiction over that territory, assuming it has not given them permission to intervene.

It might seem that one state can be *justified* in intervening in another state's internal affairs even when they have not been authorized to do so by that state, and even if they lack the legitimate authority to intervene. Consider an analogy, based on a case which I adapt from Raz.[52] Suppose you know that a man has a life-threatening, infectious disease, and is about to enter a public place where he is likely to pass it on to others. Surely it would be justified for you to prevent him, by using force if necessary, even though you have not been authorized to do so and have no legitimate authority to do so. By analogy, even if one state has not been authorized to intervene in the internal affairs of another, and lacks the legitimate authority to do so, it may nevertheless be justified for it to intervene in some circumstances where it can bring about good.

But this analogy is vulnerable to the following counterargument. If you forcibly prevent an infectious person from entering a public area in order to protect others from the risk of contracting a life-threatening disease, you are justified in doing so only if, and in so far as, the legitimate authorities on this matter are not at that time in a position to act. When they are in a position to act, then their decision concerning what should be done is binding. You would not, for example, be justified in forcibly quarantining the person if the legitimate authorities judged that, contrary to your (even medically qualified) opinion, his disease was not infectious. So too, a state is justified in intervening beyond its borders in order to help those who are being oppressed only if there is no legitimate authority in a position to act to help them (or if it acts at the request of that authority). In cases where some state with legitimate authority *is* the oppressor, no other state is justified in intervening in its internal affairs.

Even this response makes a concession to humanitarian intervention, however. For it allows that intervention of this kind may be justified if the legitimate authority in a territory has broken down or is incapable of

---

[52] Raz, *The Morality of Freedom*, p. 25.

acting. But it would rule out intervention in the affairs of a state which could act to help the oppressed within its borders but for some reason fails to do so, or which is itself the oppressor.

The envisaged response relies on the idea that the state retains legitimate authority over those of its members it oppresses, or fails to protect when it could. Can this idea be defended? Suppose that the state's legitimate authority is founded on its ability to facilitate mutually beneficial cooperation, or on its ability to enable its citizens to act more successfully for the reasons that apply to them. Then we might suppose that the state lacks legitimate authority over those whom it oppresses if it is possible for them to establish an alternative authority which would be more beneficial to them, or if they would be better off in the absence of any authority, even when that would lead to chaos.[53] In extreme cases, an oppressed group might be better off without any coordinating authority, and then the existing state would lack legitimate authority over them. But even when that was not so, an intervening force might be in a position to facilitate the establishment of a new or reformed authority which could support cooperative activity in a way that was more beneficial to an oppressed group, and, by being in this position, make it the case that the existing state lacked legitimate authority over members of that group.

Some might object that these results merely show that the kind of theory of legitimate authority which I have been entertaining is far too individualistic. Could an alternative communitarian account, of the kind briefly considered in section 6 of Chapter 3, justify the idea that a state might retain legitimate authority over those it oppresses or fails to help, even if an intervening force could improve their situation? According to that communitarian account, a state possesses legitimate authority over its citizens only if they are members of a community for which the state is the vehicle of self-determination. But from this perspective it is hard to justify the idea that a state must have legitimate authority over *all* its citizens. If the state includes a number of different cultural communities but is a vehicle for the self-determination of only the dominant one, then the communitarian account will be unable to underpin the idea that it has legitimate authority over the members of the other minority communities. Furthermore, some citizens may reject, or distance themselves from, the cultural community on behalf of which the state acts, and it is unclear how, according to this communitarian theory, the state can retain an unproblematic authority over them. Those who are suffering injustice will often fall into one of these two categories, and so the communitarian theory will be unable to justify the claim that the state of which they are

[53] See McMahon, *Authority and Democracy*, pp. 128–9, 151.

members has legitimate authority over them. So even from this communitarian perspective, it is hard to sustain the idea that an intervening force must, in general, violate the legitimate authority of the state in which it intervenes.

In this section I have tried to answer the objection that no state has the legitimate authority to engage in humanitarian intervention. When the existing state in a territory lacks legitimate authority over some of its inhabitants, other states may be justified in intervening. In doing so, they need not violate their special obligations to their own citizens. But the idea that states have special obligations to their own citizens nevertheless shows that it would be a mistake simply to extend a framework that was designed for considering the question of when rights are to be enforced within the state's borders and apply it to the issue of intervention beyond its borders, for that would be wholly to ignore those special obligations.

Whatever the precise content of the special obligations which the state owes to its citizens, they will include some constrained obligation not to endanger their vital interests, to ensure that they have their basic needs met, and to provide them with whatever is required in order for them to be full citizens capable of participating in public life. But when these obligations have been fulfilled the state can legitimately act, and is perhaps even required to act, to prevent rights violations beyond its borders, and in extreme circumstances its special obligations to its own citizens can be overridden. So where does this leave us in relation to the extended framework described in sections 3 and 4?

According to that framework, the state should, beyond its borders, prevent the violation of those rights which could in the presence of good faith be the object of a reasoned global consensus, except in two circumstances. First, when it would be likely to lead to greater injustice (judged in terms of the set of rights which could be the object of a reasoned global consensus). Second, when it would be likely to be so costly that it would be better to pursue non-military options if there was a reasonable prospect of these being successful in the long term. This framework has to be modified in order to give a place for the special obligations that the state owes to its citizens: it can legitimately engage in humanitarian intervention but in assessing whether to do so it should give proper weight to those special obligations. The state has constrained special obligations not to endanger the vital interests of any of its citizens, to ensure that they have their basic needs met, and to provide them with whatever is required in order for them to be full citizens capable of participating in public life. Only if the needs of outsiders are much more urgent can the state be justified in overriding these obligations in order to assist those beyond its borders. I suggest that for affluent western democratic regimes at least, the guidelines for intervention developed in section 4 will not require serious amendment in the light of their special obligations to their own citizens. For the needs of groups who face massacre, enslavement, deportation, or the institutional use of torture or rape, are likely to be sufficiently urgent to justify the state overriding its special obligations to its own citizens.

This raises the further question of whether the obligations that citizens owe to outsiders are so demanding that they morally *require* them to be willing to put their lives at risk when this is needed to save others; perhaps people are morally required to save lives only when it is in their power to do so, and no great sacrifice is required. To do more than this, it might be said, is to act in a noble or saintly way, but it is not morally required. If so, there is no obligation, enforceable or otherwise, for individuals to be *involved* in risky humanitarian intervention. It would then be important for any soldiers involved to be volunteers who joined the armed forces in full knowledge that they might be asked to risk their lives for the citizens of other states (or stateless persons). In any case states owe it to their citizens, and especially their soldiers, to make a proper assessment of the risks involved, and the likelihood of such an intervention being successful.

Even if no individual citizen has an obligation to become involved in humanitarian intervention, it would not follow that the state has no obligation to do so either. But any obligation the state was under could then only be conditional – to participate if enough of its citizens were willing to volunteer. Furthermore, even if individuals have no obligation to participate in military interventions, they may nevertheless be under an enforceable obligation to contribute resources, in the form of taxes, to help those interventions.

6.   Conclusion

I have tried to show that the principle of non-intervention cannot justifiably be used to resolve conflicts between political community and liberal ideals of global community. The kind of priority which the principle of non-intervention gives to political communities cannot be justified. Respect for the autonomy of political communities is important, and the dangers and limits of humanitarian intervention are real, but a restricted practice of it can be defended. In Chapter 8, I shall consider another potential barrier to the realization of the liberal conception of global community: the idea that the structure of the state system makes global community, to any significant degree, impossible. If this were so, then the existence of independent political communities (in the absence of a world state, at least) would be in conflict with the promotion or realization of liberal ideals of global community.

8 Political communities, global solidarity and the state system

The troubled relationship between political community and liberal ideals of global community is helped by revising the principle of non-intervention so that it permits humanitarian intervention in some cases. But many theorists have thought that the relationship will always be fundamentally unhappy because 'the state system' places structural obstacles in the path of these ideals. The existence of a plurality of political communities in the absence of an overarching authority is seen as undermining the conditions necessary for the realization of liberal visions of global community.[1]

I shall not aim to resolve the issue of whether there is a systemic conflict of this kind.[2] Instead I shall try to clarify the way in which the 'anarchic' structure of the state system might be thought to stand in the way of liberal ideals of global community, and raise some doubts about whether it always constitutes a serious obstacle to them. I shall then entertain various alternative theories which place much of the blame elsewhere, in the nature or internal structure of the political units which make up the state system. Some of these theories recommend radical changes to those units, and blur the boundary between changing the structure of the system and changing the nature of its constituent parts. Unlike the previous chapter, which took for granted the state system and asked what changes to the rules governing it would give due weight to liberal ideals of global community when they conflict with political community, this chapter calls into question whether these ideals are compatible with that system. (Throughout the chapter I mean by 'a state system' a plurality of

[1] Global community, as I presented it in Chapter 7, differs from international community. Global community is primarily a relationship between individuals which in principle might exist in the absence of a state system, whereas international community is primarily a relationship between states, and as such necessarily presupposes the existence of a plurality of them. Given the alleged systemic conflict between liberal ideals of global community and the existence of a plurality of political communities, it is a substantive issue whether the former can be realized in the presence of a state system.
[2] In general, a systemic conflict occurs when a plurality of interacting communities undermines the existence, or current way of life, of some other community.

states which interact but are not subject in any ultimate way to an overarching political authority. Existing states are held to belong to a single system of this kind.)

1.   The international system as a state of nature

The problem of community in international relations (as one commentator calls it[3]) is often thought to arise from the anarchic character of the state system. That system is anarchic in the sense that there is no overarching authority to which states are subject in an ultimate way. In Hobbes's view parties in such a condition, which he calls a state of nature, are in a state of war, not because they are constantly fighting, but because they are constantly disposed to fight and are also known to be so disposed.[4] Hobbes thought that living in an international system in which there is no common power is much less grave for individuals than it would be for them to live without any state to protect them.[5] But his argument might appear to show that actual fighting between states is highly likely over time, and that in large measure this is due to the structure of the state system. Let me briefly reconstruct the steps by which a Hobbesian might arrive at these conclusions. I shall employ the least controversial premises that are needed to do so and I shall make little attempt to pin the resulting argument on Hobbes himself.[6]

First, the Hobbesian assumes that there is at least moderate scarcity of resources: not everyone can have what they want. Second, people generally have a strong desire to continue living, and a strong desire to meet their own basic needs; for some people in some circumstances, these desires may be overridden by their commitment to a cause, or their concern for the well-being of another, but generally speaking for most people in most circumstances these desires are overriding. Third, there are some 'dominators', or at least it is reasonable to believe that there are such people. Dominators are defined as those who are willing to conquer others in order to achieve their ends, even when they have no reason to believe that their own security is threatened. (For some dominators, domination of others may be an end in itself, or pursued for the sake of glory; for others, it may be based upon a desire to enlighten or improve those they subjugate.) Fourth, individuals are roughly equal in terms of power: even the strongest person can be defeated by the weakest if he or

---

[3] A. Linklater, 'The Problem of Community in International Relations', *Alternatives*, vol. 15, 1990   [4] T. Hobbes, *Leviathan* (Harmondsworth: Penguin, 1968), pp. 185–6, 91.
[5] *Ibid.*, pp. 187–8.
[6] My reconstruction is strongly influenced by Gregory Kavka's discussion in *Hobbesian Moral and Political Theory* (Princeton, NJ: Princeton University Press, 1986), esp. chs. 3–4.

she combines with others, or has surprise on his or her side.

On these assumptions it is rational for individuals in a state of nature to attack each other for a number of reasons: most importantly, in order to obtain and secure a reasonable level of well-being, it is rational for an individual to strike pre-emptively against another, regardless of whether he or his potential victim is a dominator, because in so doing he can secure himself against attack. If he defeats his opponent, he can obtain his resources, and may obtain control over him, and thereby reduce the risk of being defeated by others. When the number of dominators is small, or there is good reason to think so, it may be rational to risk laying low. But laying low is unlikely to be a successful strategy where there are a significant number of dominators, because over time it is likely that a dominator will engage in an unprovoked attack. So there is a point at which the number of dominators makes it unreasonable not to become an aggressor.

Note that this argument is not unduly cynical about human nature;[7] at most it relies on the idea that a proportion of human beings are dominators, not that all or even most fit this description. It may even be possible to generate a similar conclusion without assuming the existence of dominators. Given the difficulties in determining the intentions of others, and an overriding interest in survival, it would often be rational for individuals in a state of nature to assume that some of their number are dominators, even if there was no firm evidence to support this assumption. But if someone builds up their weaponry in order to guard against possible dominators, this can easily be misinterpreted as a preparation for aggression. If it is interpreted in this way, others may build up their arms or strike pre-emptively. So even in the absence of dominators, an overriding desire for security in a state of nature may lead to war.

To what extent can the same reasoning be applied to states in the absence of any overarching power? Some have doubts about whether it makes sense to attribute beliefs, desires and goals to states. These doubts are sometimes of a conceptual nature. For example, it might be argued that it is only individual persons who can act or possess beliefs, desires or goals. This is a hard position to sustain, however. As I pointed out in section 2 of Chapter 1, we do talk about collectives acting in quite mundane ways, for example, 'the jury found the defendant guilty', and there seems no equivalent way of re-describing these actions in terms of the actions of individuals. In one sense of course, it is the individual

---

[7] Does the second assumption ignore the way in which mothers especially, but parents in general, are often willing to take considerable risks with their own welfare, and to forego satisfaction of their basic needs, for the sake of their children? Perhaps. But then the relevant premise could be reformulated to apply to family units.

members of the jury who find the defendant guilty. It is their deliberations that lead to the verdict. But none of their actions or deliberations count as 'the jury finding the defendant guilty', not even the foreman's announcing the verdict in court.

Worries about the idea that states act may be more empirical in nature. Some doubt whether states are *unitary* actors; they argue that decision making emerges from individual deliberations that occur in different bureaucracies in such a way that we cannot regard it as the product of a sole actor.[8] It might be said, for example, that decisions are simply the outcome of a power struggle between the different bureaucracies in a state. But it is not obvious why we should regard the fact that decision making emerges in this way as undermining the view that states act, even though it is clearly of crucial importance in explaining why they act in one way rather than another. The following general account appears to be left open. The mechanisms which lead a state to act often involve a number of bureaucracies competing against each other (each offering its own perspective on the issues, and each bringing its own interests to bear upon them), but there is some action, attributable to the state as a whole, which is the outcome of this process. In explaining why the action was performed we can appeal to the various bureaucratic interests which came into play, and the strength of their support, but the action is performed by the state even when it results from the interplay of those interests.

For Hobbesian reasoning to have relevance to the condition of states in the absence of an overarching power, it needs to make sense to suppose that states have a desire for their own security which is in general overriding. That is not an implausible assumption even if we suppose that the decision making of states is deeply affected by the interaction between different bureaucracies and their relative power. For even if this is the case, it is plausible to suppose that when vital security interests are at stake these will prevail through that process because they will affect the interests of each of the different bureaucracies in the same way.

A Hobbesian theory of international relations can plausibly maintain that some states are dominators, or at least that it is reasonable for one state to believe that some of the others are dominators because of uncertainty about their future intentions and actions. If there are known to be a significant number of dominators, and states have an overriding interest in their own survival, it is rational even for those that are not dominators to build up their arms, adopt an aggressive posture and strike preemptively to enhance their absolute power and their power relative to others. (And given the risks involved, it is irrational for a state with an

[8] See, for example, G. Allison, 'Conceptual Models and the Cuban Missile Crisis', *American Political Science Review*, vol. 63, 1969.

overriding interest in its own security to deplete its resources by unnecessarily conferring benefits on the citizens of other states.) Even if there is no firm evidence that other states are dominators, it can often be a rational strategy to make this assumption, given the difficulties in understanding their behaviour. But if a state builds up its arms for purely defensive reasons, this can be misinterpreted by other states as a hostile act. Other states may then decide to build up their weaponry, or strike pre-emptively in order to defuse or end the perceived threat. So even in the absence of dominators, misunderstanding can lead to war.[9]

Within the discipline of International Relations, Hobbesian theories are regarded as part of the realist tradition, but it is conventional to distinguish between structural (or neo-) realism and classical realism in terms of whether the theory rests on a pessimistic view of human nature. Structural realists within international relations theory think that the structure of the state system explains why war is likely to occur, and why an often precarious balance of power is the best which can be expected.[10] Classical realists, in contrast, gave a central role to a pessimistic account of human nature.[11] Within this schema, Hobbesians are conventionally regarded as classical realists.

It is important not to overdraw this distinction, however, and the differences between the two 'schools' is often a matter of emphasis. Even Kenneth Waltz, who is regarded as the leading structural realist, acknowledges that in particular cases a full explanation of why states go to war will appeal to individual character and internal conditions.[12] What makes him a structural realist is his view that the structure of the state system explains why any 'accident', whether it be an irrational action, a piece of selfish-

[9] Nicholas Wheeler and Ken Booth take this to be the very essence of what they call 'the security dilemma': see N. Wheeler and K. Booth, 'The Security Dilemma', in J. Baylis and N. Rengger (eds.), *Dilemmas of World Politics: International Issues in a Changing World* (Oxford: Oxford University Press, 1992), pp. 29–31.

[10] See K. Waltz, *Man, the State and War: A Theoretical Analysis* (New York: Columbia University Press, 1959); *Theory of International Politics* (Reading, MA: Addison Wesley, 1979); S. Krasner, *Structural Conflict: The Third World Against Global Capitalism* (Berkeley, CA: University of California Press, 1985).

[11] Thucydides, Hobbes, Spinoza and Rousseau are generally regarded as the classical realists: see S. Forde, 'Classical Realism' in T. Nardin and D. Mapel (eds.), *Traditions of International Ethics* (Cambridge: Cambridge University Press, 1992). The heirs of this tradition include Morgenthau and Niebuhr: see H. Morgenthau, *Politics Among Nations: The Struggle for Power and Peace*, 2nd edn (New York: Alfred Knopf, 1954); R. Niebuhr, *Christian Realism and Political Problems* (New York: Charles Scribner's Sons, 1945).

[12] See Waltz, *Man, the State and War*, pp. 218, 229–30. But he believes that the structure of the state system is the underlying cause of war, even though he allows that human nature, or the internal structure of states may be the immediate cause of particular wars. For a sustained critique of this idea see H. Suganami, *On the Causes of War* (Oxford: Oxford University Press, 1996), especially ch. 1.

ness or some internal defect of a state, can bring about a war.[13] Just as structural realists can give a role to human imperfection in explaining the occurrence of war, so too classical realists can give an important role to structural considerations. Although Hobbes is conventionally regarded as a classical realist, his analysis of why the state of nature is a state of war makes essential appeal to its structure. And indeed if it does contain a pessimistic account of human nature, that is not essential to Hobbesian accounts in general, as my reconstruction illustrates.

Hobbes thinks that although states in the absence of a common power are at war (in his technical sense), this is not as bad for individuals as it would be were those individuals themselves in a state of nature because simply by adopting an aggressive posture states can often succeed in deterring attack and uphold the 'Industry of their Subjects'.[14] There are other differences between a state of nature composed of individuals and a state of nature composed of sovereign states that Hobbes does not emphasize sufficiently, which make actual conflict even less likely in the latter. First, fighting between states in a state of nature is likely to be much less frequent than fighting between individuals in a state of nature because states have geographically separated territories, which makes them less vulnerable to attack.[15] Second, there are generally high risks and few certainties in battles between states which are roughly equal in terms of power, which makes it reasonable for such states to be reluctant to go to war even when one sees a potential vulnerability in the other.[16] Third, states are often more unequal than individuals; even with surprise on its side, it is hard, sometimes practically impossible, for a weaker state to defeat a stronger state, unless it has a large number of allies. For that reason, there is not always a powerful incentive for strong states which are not dominators to conquer weak states, for it is not always necessary for their survival to obtain more power in this way.[17]

The Hobbesian account of international relations also tends to underestimate the possible benefits of cooperation.[18] There may be strong incentives for states to keep their agreements in the absence of a common power because they may need the help of the state with which they have made this agreement in the future. States are not as numerous as individ-

[13] Waltz, Man, the State and War, p. 231.   [14] Hobbes, Leviathan, p. 188.

[15] See M. Cohen, 'Moral Skepticism and International Relations', in C. Beitz, M. Cohen, T. Scanlon and A. J. Simmons (eds.), International Ethics (Princeton, NJ: Princeton University Press, 1985), pp. 30–1.

[16] See Kavka, Hobbesian Moral and Political Theory, p. 163.

[17] See C. Beitz, Political Theory and International Relations (Princeton, NJ: Princeton University Press, 1979), pp. 40–1; Cohen, 'Moral Skepticism and International Relations', p. 30.

[18] Kavka, Hobbesian Moral and Political Theory, p. 129; Beitz, Political Theory and International Relations, pp. 46–7.

uals, and they can soon run out of potential allies. If a state reneges on an agreement, this is also likely to become known by other states, and will mean that they will be less likely to enter into similar agreements with that state in the future. Similarly, in a range of historical circumstances there may be good self-regarding reasons for a state to abide by a norm of non-aggression: if that norm is accepted by other states, and a state violates it, then other states may penalize it in various ways; for example, impose sanctions or refuse to enter into trade agreements. In general, the structure of the state system is such that states often have good self-interested reasons to refrain from aggression and each can be motivated by the good of other states and their citizens without putting their own security at risk by the consequent depletion of their resources.

But even if for these reasons it is wrong to describe the condition of states which are not subject in any ultimate way to an overarching authority as a war of all against all in any ordinary sense, it remains the case that if dominators exist in significant numbers amongst the most powerful states, peace will be fragile and depend upon a 'balance of power', as neo-realists have claimed. At best, dominators will keep their agreements and refrain from aggression only so long as, and in so far as, it remains in their enlightened interest to do so. When a powerful state is a dominator, it is much less vulnerable than even powerful individuals would be in a state of nature, so it can afford to risk aggression. States which are not dominators will keep their agreements and refrain from aggression only so long as, and in so far as, they believe that this does not put their vital interests at risk. And there will be considerable scope for them to misunderstand the intentions of other states, given that defensive measures can often be misinterpreted as offensive and it is highly risky to give other states the benefit of the doubt. When the balance of power is disrupted, peace is likely to come to an end.

So there is reason to suppose that when a significant number of powerful states are dominators, the structure of the state system places considerable barriers in the way of realizing liberal ideals of global community, not just because it means that these states will make war when the occasion arises. Their existence in the state system means that it can be rational for non-dominators to make war against other non-dominators in order to build up their power, and for them to strike pre-emptively rather than give other states the benefit of the doubt. And even when there are no wars, the future prospect of war means that states may pose some risk to their own security by depleting their resources in order to benefit the citizens of other states. Those liberals who think that justice requires international redistribution of resources must therefore regard the structure of the state system as providing a further obstacle to realizing their ideals of global community when dominators exist in significant numbers.[19]

2.   From war to peace

I have argued that the structure of the state system places serious obstacles in the way of liberal ideals of global community when a significant number of powerful states are dominators. But what if none of the most powerful states is a dominator, and the incidence of dominators within the state system as a whole is small? Does the structure of the state system still constitute an obstacle to world peace? It does not appear to do so. If none of the most powerful states is willing to conquer others simply in order to further its own ends, and the incidence of dominators amongst weaker neighbouring states is low, then non-dominators would have little reason to build up their weaponry, strike pre-emptively, or conquer other states in order to become more powerful and deter aggression. Nor would there be any need for non-dominators to resort to such measures if dominators were relatively weak, few in number, and the other states were willing to come to each other's aid even when it was not in their interests (narrowly conceived) to do so.

Neo-realists would respond by pointing to the permanent possibility of misunderstanding and its potential (in the absence of a world state) to lead to conflict. But when there is an ethos of cooperation, and only a few relatively weak dominators, there is no reason to think that misunderstanding will regularly have this outcome. Under these circumstances states can afford to interpret each other's intentions charitably until the evidence becomes unambiguous. In order to defend the neo-realist's position, it would have to be argued that we can never know, or have sufficient reason to believe, that other states are not dominators, and that when there is room for doubt about the intentions of other states it is rational to assume that they could be dominators. The first proposition is unsustainable,[20] and the second is questionable in circumstances when we have good reason to believe that the most powerful states are not dominators, and that those states which are dominators are relatively weak and few in number.

This raises an obvious question: what changes might occur, or would need to occur, to reduce the incidence of dominators, especially amongst

---

[19] This argument can be overstated, however. Affluent states which already have considerable military power may often be in a position to give up some of their wealth without making themselves vulnerable. As Simon Caney shows, realists are often unjustifiably pessimistic about the scope for states to act, individually and collectively, on cosmopolitan ideals: see S. Caney, 'Cosmopolitanism, Realism and the National Interest', in G. Parry and H. Steiner (eds.), *Freedom and Trade* (London: Routledge, 1997).

[20] See Suganami, *On the Causes of War*, p. 50.

the most powerful states in the international system? (It would of course be a mistake to assume that a reduction in the number of dominators, or even their complete disappearance, would necessarily lead to permanent peace. War between peace-loving states may still result from misunderstanding, negligence, insensitivity, thoughtlessness or recklessness.[21]) I shall present five general answers to these questions, which I shall label 'the convergence view', 'the Kantian view', 'the national identification view', 'the Marxian view' and 'the dispersal of sovereignty view' respectively.

(a) According to *the convergence view*, dominators begin by honouring their agreements and refraining from aggression because, and only because, it serves their ends to do so. But over a number of years (perhaps centuries) as a result of their peaceful interaction with other states, sustained in part by a balance of power, dominators come to acquire a moral commitment to toleration and peaceful coexistence with other states even when they do not share their values.[22] As a result states which had been dominators lose their willingness to fight to achieve their ends when their own security is not at stake because cooperation and toleration are no longer treated solely as means to furthering their own 'self-regarding' interests or of effecting (what they regard as) an improvement in the values or ways of life of others.

In short, states develop a habit of obedience to principles of non-aggression and begin to follow them not only because it is in their interests to do so, but also because of their moral commitment to cooperation and toleration. They may, for example, come to respect other states as a result of endorsing what Thomas Pogge has called international pluralism – 'the idea that knowledgeable and intelligent persons of goodwill may reasonably favour different forms of (national) social organization'[23] – and ground their commitment to cooperation and toleration on this idea.

---

[21] On this, see *ibid.*, pp. 173–90. In general, Suganami stresses that war is a multicausal phenomenon – many factors contribute to the making of war and there are many paths to it (see *ibid*, p. 206).

[22] See J. Thompson, *Justice and World Order: A Philosophical Inquiry* (London: Routledge, 1992), pp. 36–9; T. Pogge, *Realizing Rawls* (Ithaca, NY: Cornell University Press, 1989), pp. 227–30. Pogge argues that the international order needs to move from being based upon a *modus vivendi* to being based upon genuinely shared values. In a later article, however, he also (quite consistently) defends a version of what I call the dispersal of sovereignty view; it is not just shared values that are needed for world peace but also a dispersal of the powers of sovereignty that are currently concentrated in states (see Pogge, 'Cosmopolitanism and Sovereignty').

[23] Pogge, *Realizing Rawls*, p. 230. Defenders of the convergence view need not maintain that widespread acceptance of international pluralism is the only way in which the relevant change might be brought about, however. Indeed it might be thought that convergence on the idea that communal autonomy is non-instrumentally valuable is better suited to effecting the change, even if that idea is mistaken.

The convergence view bears an obvious analogy to Rawls's account of how groups and individuals within the state might gradually achieve an overlapping consensus on principles of justice: they begin by accepting basic rights and liberties as a *modus vivendi*, then they move to a moral commitment to these rights and liberties.[24]

(b) According to what I call *the Kantian view*, for the population of dominators to be seriously reduced, states would need to change in terms of their political (and perhaps economic) organization: that is, they would need to become liberal democracies.[25] This is a revision of Kant's own account, for his position was that world peace required states to become republics. His notion of a republic is broader than that of a liberal democracy since republics may have non-democratic forms of government so long as these forms receive the consent of the people.[26]

The main idea behind the Kantian view is that in liberal democracies those who will be required to fight, and pay all the various costs of war, will have influence on the statesmen who make the decision to fight, and hence statesmen will be less willing to go to war.[27] As Kant himself put the point:[28]

If, as is inevitably the case under this constitution, the consent of the citizens is required to decide whether or not war is to be declared, it is very natural that they will have great hesitation in embarking on so dangerous an enterprise. For this would mean calling down on themselves all the miseries of war, such as doing the fighting themselves, supplying the costs of the war from their own resources, painfully making good the ensuing devastation, and, as the crowning evil, having to take upon themselves a burden of debt which will embitter peace itself and which can never be paid off on account of the constant threat of new wars.[29]

But it is not just that citizens bear the costs of war and in liberal democracies can exercise influence over their leaders. Toleration and mutual

---

[24] Rawls, *Political Liberalism*, pp. 158–68. Rawls's story is more complex since he also distinguishes between a mere constitutional consensus and an overlapping consensus proper.

[25] The Kantian view has been revived recently by Francis Fukuyama in *The End of History and the Last Man* (London: Hamish Hamilton, 1992).

[26] I. Kant, *Political Writings*, ed. Hans Reiss (Cambridge: Cambridge University Press, 1991), pp. 100–1.

[27] And as Michael Doyle points out, since representative democracies involve rotation of offices, this can help to prevent personal animosities between leaders from becoming the impulse behind wars: see M. Doyle, 'Kant, Liberal Legacies and Foreign Affairs', *Philosophy and Public Affairs*, vol. 12, 1983, p. 230.

[28] The Kantian view can also point to the way in which democratic accountability makes it hard for states to galvanize domestic support for humanitarian intervention – we have to face the possibility that one of the factors which makes war less likely also makes liberal ideals of global community harder to realize in another way.

[29] Kant, *Political Writings*, p. 100.

respect for individuals are part of the public culture of liberal democracies and are likely to come to inform inter-state relations as well, for leaders will be required to justify their decisions in the light of this public culture.

Liberal economic relations also encourage peace between liberal states; if it is accepted that prices are determined by the market, rather than by the state's control of production and distribution, then this removes one potential source of conflict.[30] (But defenders of the Kantian view can agree that Richard Cobden was unduly optimistic in supposing that free trade would 'act on the moral world as the principle of gravitation in the universe – drawing men together, thrusting aside the antagonism of race, and creed, and language, and uniting us in the bonds of eternal peace'.[31])

The Kantian view, as I shall understand it, is compatible with a number of different accounts of how the transition to widespread liberal democracy might occur.[32] It could be argued that as global interdependence increases, states will not be able to flourish unless they allow a relatively free market for producing goods, and that the kind of equality inherent in the market will generate a strong pressure towards democracy. Or it might be argued that the citizens of liberal democracies will encourage their leaders to put pressure on, or offer inducements to, authoritarian regimes to democratize. If a state or its citizens are committed to liberal-democratic principles and institutions, they will find it hard to avoid a commitment to promote these principles and institutions abroad.[33]

Kant himself thought that republics would need to organize themselves into a federal state in order for there to be a lasting peace. Unless such a federation were to come into existence, states would be in a state of nature and, like Hobbes, Kant thought that a state of nature was a state of war. Kant was keen to distinguish such a federation from a world state, however, because he thought it important for political communities to retain their sovereignty in order to avoid 'a soulless despotism', followed by a lapse into anarchy.[34] For Kant, the federation would simply be a voluntary alliance between sovereign states committed to peace. It would bear some resemblance to our United Nations.

(c) According to *the national identification view*, war is inevitable so long as the primary unit of the international system is the nation state. The

---

[30] Doyle, 'Kant, Liberal Legacies and Foreign Affairs', p. 231.
[31] Quoted by Linklater, 'The Problem of Community in International Relations', p. 144.
[32] Kant himself thought that the transformation of states into republics would be a natural one, since based upon both inclination and reason. See Kant, *Political Writings*, p. 112.
[33] See C. Brewin, 'Liberal States and International Obligations', *Millennium: Journal of International Studies*, vol. 17, 1988, pp. 331–7; A. Linklater, 'What is a Good International Citizen?', in P. Keal (ed.), *Ethics and Foreign Policy* (St. Leonards, NSW: Allen and Unwin, 1992), p. 38.   [34] See Kant, *Political Writings*, pp. 102, 113.

crudest version of this view maintains that people have a need to feel that they belong to some ethnic group, and that in modern times this need can only be met, or is best met, by ethnically defined nations. To this is added the idea that ethnically defined nations are prone to be dominators for a number of reasons. When the nation is coextensive with a state, any threat to 'the national way of life' may be experienced by its members as a challenge to their very identity, with the result that war is a permanent possibility. Members of a nation state may also regard some piece of territory that lies beyond its jurisdiction as part of their homeland, and irredentist demands can bring them into conflict with the state (or states) which at present claims sovereignty over that territory. National minorities within the state may attempt to secure political independence, and this may not only provoke civil war but also lead to instability in neighbouring countries, perhaps in such a way that they are drawn into the conflict.

Part of the crudest version of the national identification view has already been laid to rest in Chapter 2. It is implausible to suppose that there is a universal need to feel that one belongs to some ethnic group.[35] But more sophisticated variants of the national identification view are possible. For example, it might be said that in a variety of circumstances people experience a need to feel that they belong to some socially defined group, and that in the world today this need is most commonly and most readily satisfied by nations. Identification with nations tends to be particularly strong, and as a result the conditions which are conducive to various kinds of conflict will be common. When nations possess their own states, war between those states is likely to be the outcome in at least some cases, whether it results from irredentist claims or from perceived threats to national ways of life. When national minorities do not possess their own states, wars to secure independence are also likely because they will feel that their way of life is threatened by coexistence in the same state with larger communities. This tendency is aggravated when the state system is governed by a norm of national self-determination, i.e., the principle that nations are entitled to political independence, for national minorities will use this principle to legitimize their struggle.

The national identification view maintains that so long as the dominant unit within the state system is the nation state the seeds of conflict are present. It is compatible with a variety of proposals for how the reign of the nation state might be brought to an end. For example, it might maintain that the way forward is for international organizations such as the United Nations to continue to distance themselves from radical

---

[35] See also Benner, *Really Existing Nationalisms*, pp. 222ff.

interpretations of the principle of national self-determination, to legitimize the idea that state boundaries should remain as they are except in extreme circumstances, and to encourage states to make their borders more permeable so that immigration can dilute their national cultures. In general the idea would be that political units should come to be formed around political rather than national identities and whatever measures are needed to encourage this should be adopted.[36]

(d) *The Marxist view* comes in more or less sophisticated forms, but all of its versions maintain that an enduring peace is possible only if capitalism is abolished. The idea here is that capitalist states are dominators because they will always primarily be motivated to protect the vital interests of their capitalist class, and hence that they will go to war whenever that is necessary in order for them to do so. The Marxist view as I have characterized it need not be crudely reductionist, since it can allow that the state may act in ways that fail to promote the interests of the capitalist class, or even damage its interests, so long as in doing so it does not damage its vital interests.

Marx argued that war was often used to prevent the overturn of the capitalist system. In his view it was frequently a means 'to subjugate in each country the producers by pitching them against their brothers in each other country, a means to prevent the international cooperation of the working classes, the first condition of their emancipation'.[37] Marshalling the workers behind national causes enabled the state to protect the vital interests of their capitalist class, and indeed the interests of the capitalist class in other states, by preventing the solidarity necessary to destroy capitalism from emerging. War was in effect in the interests of the global capitalist class.

Alongside this account of why war occurred, Marx also observed that the capitalist class often sought to overcome economic crises (when the development of the productive forces come into conflict with the relations of production) by conquering new markets.[38] As Erica Benner has pointed out, this provides the seeds of a further Marxian account of why a global capitalist system is prone to war.[39] This account exploits the existence of a conflict rather than a harmony of interests in the global capitalist class, claiming that competition between different groups of capitalists leads to conflict between the states which represent their

[36] See McMahan, 'The Limits of National Partiality', in McKim and McMahan (eds.), *The Morality of Nationalism*, pp. 122, 131–5.
[37] K. Marx and F. Engels, *Collected Works*, vol. XXII (London: Lawrence and Wishart, 1975), p. 501.
[38] K. Marx and F. Engels, *The Communist Manifesto* (Harmondsworth: Penguin, 1967), p. 86.   [39] Benner, *Really Existing Nationalisms*, pp. 210ff.

interests. Lenin gives one particular account of how this might occur. According to him, capitalism in its advanced stages creates monopolies through a process of free competition.[40] As the need of these monopolies for more raw materials grows, the state as their representative conquers less-developed countries,[41] and eventually the world becomes divided out amongst the more developed states in proportion to their economic strength.[42]

According to the Marxist view more generally, capitalism is what stands in the way of peaceful coexistence between individuals. Indeed in its classical form, the Marxist view maintains that once capitalism is fully transcended the state system will be unnecessary; states exist to protect the vital interests of their capitalist classes both domestically and internationally. Once capitalism is defeated, there will be no need for them since coercive political power will be unnecessary. It is of course possible to endorse a revisionist account which sees capitalism as the main obstacle to peace, but which does not accept the utopian idea that once capitalism has been eradicated across the globe there will be no need for the state.[43] I shall use the label 'Marxist view' to cover revisionist accounts of this kind as well as the classical Marxist account.

(e) The *dispersal of sovereignty view* holds that for there to be an enduring world peace, the sovereign powers which are currently concentrated in nation states would have to be dispersed to both larger and smaller units,[44] for example, neighbourhood, town, county, province, state, region and perhaps the world at large. It locates an important cause of war in the structure of the state system, but in a very different manner to neo-realists: it maintains that liberal ideals of global community are incompatible with the state system in its current form because such ideals require the demise of geographically separated, fully sovereign states. By giving states exclusive control within their borders, the state system provides them with strong incentives to become dominators when by going to war they can extend the territory and resources over which they enjoy this control. By dispersing sovereignty, some of these incentives are removed since no one political unit has exclusive control over a piece of territory. This 'would decrease the intensity of the struggle for power and wealth within and among states, thereby reducing the incidence of war, poverty,

---

[40] V. I. Lenin, *Imperialism, the Highest Stage of Capitalism: A Popular Outline* (Moscow: Progress Publishers, 1968), pp. 14–27.   [41] *Ibid.*, p. 77   [42] *Ibid.*, p. 70

[43] For an example of this sort of account, see J. Hobson, *Imperialism*, 3rd edn (London: George Allen and Unwin, 1938).

[44] Pogge, 'Cosmopolitanism and Sovereignty', p. 58. See also McMahan, 'The Limits of National Partiality' in McKim and McMahan (eds.), *The Morality of Nationalism*, pp. 122–3; Linklater, *The Transformation of Political Community*, esp. ch. 6.

and oppression'.[45] The dispersal of sovereignty view requires the most radical changes to the state system of the views so far considered, except for those versions of the Marxist view which suppose that once capitalism has been transcended, there will be no need for states at all. It does not, however, go so far as to advocate the need for an extensive world state, although it entertains the possibility and desirability of creating a political unit of some kind with some powers at that level.

The existing form of the state system, which concentrates power in the hands of fully sovereign political units, also encourages citizens to identify strongly with a single political community. The extent to which citizens feel bound to outsiders is likely to be severely reduced. As a result the willingness of citizens to fight wars against other states is correspondingly greater and can be exploited by statesmen even when there is a public culture of tolerance. Even if liberal democracy were to spread throughout the state system, that willingness would continue to exist. (Here the dispersal of sovereignty view bears some resemblance to the national identification view.) But if individuals were members of a variety of different political units, as the dispersal of sovereignty view recommends, it would be unlikely that enough of them would be willing to identify themselves with a single one of these units in the way that would be required for them to be motivated to fight a war on its behalf in a single-minded way. The dispersal of sovereignty view is compatible with the continued existence of political communities, but they would be of a very different kind to the geographically separated and fully sovereign political communities that are part and parcel of the state system in its current form.

The dispersal of sovereignty view is also compatible with a number of different accounts of how the variety of different political units it envisages might be brought into existence. For example, it might be argued that they will emerge in the wake of a widespread commitment to the importance of democratic principles. New political units will gradually be forged as a result of a genuine commitment to the idea that all people, and only those people, significantly affected by some decision (when no individual or group has a right to make that decision on their own) ought to be given a say in it.[46] Or more realistically perhaps, 'globalisation' – increasing international interdependence and the declining power of individual states – may lead to the emergence of sub-national and trans-

[45] Pogge, 'Cosmopolitanism and Sovereignty', p. 48.
[46] Cf. *ibid.*, pp. 65–9; B. Holden, 'Democratic Theory and the Problem of Global Warming', in Holden (ed.), *The Ethical Dimensions of Global Change*, pp. 138–51. The bracketed part of the principle is intended to take account of Nozick's objections to the unqualified version of the principle: see Nozick, *Anarchy, State and Utopia*, pp. 268–71.

national social movements, and generate demands for the creation of smaller and larger political units to take over some of the powers currently vested in the state.[47]

These different views of what changes would have to occur to the 'units' which make up the state system in order for the incidence of dominators to be reduced have complex relations with one another. Some are mutually compatible. The Kantian view is not necessarily inconsistent with the convergence view, for a defender of the latter could in principle accept that the adoption of liberal-democratic institutions is a precondition for the emergence of a genuine non-instrumental commitment to cooperation and toleration. But the Kantian view is inconsistent with those versions of the convergence view which maintain that states with liberal-democratic institutions are in no better position to develop a genuine commitment to toleration and peaceful coexistence, or which maintain that an enduring peace is possible even amongst states which do not value or implement democracy.

The Marxist view is ultimately compatible with the essentials of the dispersal of sovereignty view; the abolition of capitalism might simply be seen as a precondition of the possibility of eventually dispersing those non-redundant powers of sovereignty which are currently concentrated in nation-states. But the Marxist view in general would regard the dispersal of sovereignty view as idealist unless it placed that kind of importance on internal economic organization in its account of what conditions are required for the realization of global community.

The Marxist view is fundamentally incompatible with the Kantian view, however, at least if the Kantian view (unlike Kant's own view) proposes a sufficient condition for global peace. From a Marxist perspective, the Kantian view fails to comprehend the class-based nature of all actual societies and the constraints the economic organization of these states places on foreign policy. In short, it fails to understand the dynamics of existing liberal democracies. (The Kantian view and the Marxist view, however, share the idea that the realist account of international relations misunderstands the way in which the internal structure of states

---

[47] For an analysis of the mechanisms by which globalization might bring this about, see J. A. Camilleri and J. Falk, *The End of Sovereignty? The Politics of a Shrinking and Fragmenting World* (Aldershot: Edward Elgar, 1992), esp. ch. 9; M. Horsman and A. Marshall, *After the Nation-State: Citizens, Tribalism and the New World Disorder* (London: HarperCollins, 1994), esp. pp. 171–83; D. Held, 'Democracy and the New International Order', in D. Archibugi and D. Held (eds.), *Cosmopolitan Democracy: An Agenda for a New World Order* (Cambridge: Polity, 1995), pp. 96–120.

– their forms of political and economic organization – deeply affects the character of those relations.[48])

The national identification view is also incompatible with the Kantian view when the latter is understood as proposing a sufficient condition for world peace. According to the national identification view it is not enough for states to become liberal democracies, for that might occur whilst they remained nation-states, and so long as they remain nation states, they may easily turn into dominators. The national identification view, however, is compatible with complex versions of the Marxist view which allow that nations can be a source of identification and potential conflict even in the absence of class differences. It is also compatible with the dispersal of sovereignty view, for it can maintain that dispersing sovereignty is one way of loosening the strangle-hold of the nation-state.

It should also be noted that the various accounts can be weakened so that each is understood to identify a change which would reduce the incidence of dominators in the state system. Then they are potentially all mutually compatible. For it can be argued that a non-instrumental moral commitment to cooperation and toleration, democratic internal structures, the demise of the nation state, the end of capitalism and the dispersal of sovereignty to a variety of overlapping political units, would each contribute to more peaceful global relations.

3. Progress towards global community

Are any of these accounts of what is required in order for the incidence of dominators to be reduced, and of how this might come about, remotely plausible? A fully informed answer to this question could only be provided by an expert in International Relations, which I do not pretend to be.[49] But even a casual glance at the evidence casts doubt on whether any of them could provide the whole story. Let me identify some strengths and weaknesses of the different views which can be discerned without specialist knowledge of the past causes of inter-state violence. My discussion of them will not give grounds for optimism about the full achievement of any liberal ideal of global community in the future, but, on the other hand, neither will it serve to rule out the possibility that such an ideal might be realized to a significant extent. Even if the nature or

---

[48] Structural realists are, of course, well aware that their approach gives little weight to the internal structure of states in explaining conflict between them, and believe that it is a mistake to think that it has any deep significance: See Waltz, *Man, the State and War*, chs. 4–5.

[49] For a recent study of the causes of war which is philosophically sophisticated, and gives references to the relevant empirical literature, see Suganami, *On the Causes of War*.

internal structure of particular political communities brings them into ultimate conflict with liberal ideals of global community, this conflict need not be so acute that it rules out any significant progress towards realizing one of these ideals.

As an analysis of what changes are required in order to reduce the incidence of dominators in the state system, the convergence view verges on tautology. If states developed a sufficiently strong non-instrumental commitment to cooperation and toleration, then they would cease to be dominators. But the convergence view faces a grave difficulty in making plausible the process by which states might come to value peaceful co-existence for its own sake. Rawls considers the analogous process by which individuals and groups within the state might come to attach non-instrumental value to basic political rights and liberties, having begun by valuing them merely as a means to their own ends. He in effect distinguishes three ways in which this might happen, depending on the precise relationship between these rights and liberties and the various comprehensive moral doctrines to which individuals are committed.[50] When the rights and liberties can be derived from an individual's comprehensive moral doctrine, there is no problem – an appreciation of the way in which they can be derived will suffice. In the second type of case, i.e., when there is no fundamental incompatibility between the two, but the rights and liberties cannot be derived from the comprehensive doctrine, he says we can nevertheless reasonably expect individuals and groups over time to come to see the non-instrumental good these rights and liberties accomplish. In the third type of case, i.e., when there is a fundamental incompatibility between the basic political rights and some comprehensive doctrine, Rawls suggests that citizens who adhere to that doctrine may nevertheless come to reject it and affirm the rights on moral grounds.

We might wonder whether all the mechanisms that Rawls has mentioned really do operate, and hence whether there is any point in looking for analogues at the international level. Indeed he has given us no general reason for thinking that those who affirm comprehensive doctrines which are incompatible with basic political rights and liberties will change those comprehensive doctrines, rather than simply continue to regard these rights and liberties as an evil necessary to further their own interests. Similarly at the international level, we have no general reason to think that those states which regard peaceful coexistence with others as a necessary evil will come to change their outlook over time. This lacuna makes it plausible for defenders of the other views I have canvassed to argue that

[50] Rawls, *Political Liberalism*, p. 160.

dominators are unlikely to undergo the changes in commitment Rawls envisages without a transformation of their internal structures. The Kantian view, for example, can argue that states are likely to attribute non-instrumental value to cooperation or toleration in their foreign policy only if they possess a liberal-democratic culture which is committed to them.

The Kantian view is available in different versions, some of which are better supported by the available evidence. To begin with we need to distinguish the idea that liberal-democratic states are peace-loving from the more general idea that democratic states are peace-loving. The Kantian view places most of its weight on the existence of democratic accountability. And it may be that the various forms of democracy which are not so closely associated with liberalism do just as well, or even better, at encouraging peace. So, for example, it might be argued that representative government, the dominant form of government in those states generally regarded as liberal democratic, does not encourage peace to the same extent as participatory forms of democracy, which make government more accountable to the people. Or it might be argued that forms of democracy that actually reject some liberal principles, such as freedom of religion or freedom to engage in consensual sexual relationships, can still have the necessary forms of accountability to make them strongly disposed to peaceful relations.

The idea that democratic states are likely to be peace-loving also needs to be distinguished from a related but different hypothesis, namely that democratic states tend to behave peacefully *towards one another*. This hypothesis makes no claim – and in some versions even denies – that democratic states (as opposed to non-democratic states) are less likely to go to war with non-democratic states.[51] If this hypothesis is true (and it appears to be the best confirmed of all the variants of the Kantian view), less weight needs to be given to the unwillingness of citizens to go to war because they will bear its costs (since these disincentives will exist even when war is contemplated with non-democratic states) and more to the commitment in the public culture of stable democratic regimes to the idea that democratic states should not fight one another.[52]

[51] Bruce Russett distinguishes sharply between the claim that 'democracies are *in general*, in dealing with all kinds of states, more peaceful than are authoritarian or other non-democratically constituted states' and the claim that 'democracies are more peaceful in their dealings with each other'. Arguing in favour of the latter and against the former, he contends that 'there are no clearcut cases of sovereign stable democracies waging war with one another in the modern international system'. See his *Grasping the Democratic Peace: Principles for a Post-Cold War World* (Princeton, NJ: Princeton University Press, 1993), p. 11, see also p. 16.

[52] This seems to be Russett's conclusion. He suggests that 'democratic norms' are more important than 'institutional constraints' in explaining why democratic states do not tend to go to war with one another: see his *Grasping the Democratic Peace*, pp. 92, 119.

The mechanisms to which the Kantian view appeals in explaining how the *transition* to liberal democracy might occur also stand in need of further elaboration. Although the governments of democratic states may put pressure on authoritarian regimes to change their internal structures, we should not be surprised if they fail to apply that pressure when business interests and jobs are at stake. Unemployment, like war, is unlikely to be popular with an electorate. And we have even less reason to expect private firms to refuse to trade with authoritarian regimes when there is money in it, unless they are prevented by the government from doing so. None of these observations undermine the most plausible versions of the Kantian view, however.

The national identification view, in contrast, does provide a fundamental challenge to the Kantian view, for it raises the question of whether democratic states might nevertheless be prone to conflict when they provide a focus for national loyalties. But it needs to take care in specifying the conditions under which national loyalties may, or are likely to, lead to conflict. Even if the nation-state is still the predominant political unit in the state system, it incorporates individuals and groups with a variety of perspectives, and as a result with a variety of different conceptions of 'the national life'. In consequence, as Erica Benner points out, what is perceived as a threat to national life by one group may not be by others.[53] Indeed one group may perceive a change as a threat to the nation's way of life which others perceive as an enrichment of it. More generally, national identification is a complex phenomenon (why is it strong under some conditions but not under others?) and may not be nearly so prone to produce conflict between states as this view maintains.

The most plausible version of the national-identification view defends the nuanced thesis that nation-states, democratic ones included, can under certain circumstances gain the support from their citizens which is necessary to go to war on behalf of national causes even when the security of the state is not threatened. Note that even if this nuanced but rather banal thesis were true it would not refute a weakened version of the Kantian view which claimed only that democracies are less likely than non-democracies to go to war, especially with other democracies, when their security is not threatened.

The Marxist view that capitalist states are prone to conflict because each will be moved to protect the vital interest of its capitalist class is hard to test, and for that reason hard to refute, at least in its sophisticated versions. In its crudest form, the Marxist view maintains that a capitalist state will always promote the interests of its capitalist class in foreign

---

[53] Benner, *Really Existing Nationalisms*, p. 227.

policy whenever it is possible to do so. The most plausible version, in contrast, allows that a capitalist state has some degree of autonomy to act against the interests of its capitalist class, whilst maintaining that it can never act so as to damage their vital interests. So, for example, a capitalist state may promote peace, and engage in foreign aid programmes without necessarily seeking to further the interests of its own capitalist class, when this does not damage that class's vital interests.

According to this sophisticated version of the Marxist view, whether capitalist states are strongly disposed to go to war will depend upon how often the vital interests of their capitalist class will require them to do so. Given the capitalist class's vital interest in the stability and order of the international system, there is a general reason for thinking that, on the contrary, capitalist states support peace.[54] Both crudely reductionist and sophisticated versions of the Marxist view must regard capitalist states as dominators, for they maintain that under at least some circumstances capitalist states are willing to go to war simply to further their own ends. But sophisticated versions can accept that these circumstances rarely occur and hence suppose that capitalist states are relatively peace-loving. They can regard capitalism as a contributory cause of war under some circumstances, without supposing that it makes war perpetually likely.

In the previous section I outlined the two mechanisms which Marxists have traditionally thought would lead capitalist states to make war in order to protect their vital interests. Do they undermine the revisionist idea that capitalist states are prone to peace not war? When ordinary citizens are relatively affluent, and have some stake in the capitalist system, their motivation to rebel against the capitalist class is weakened. As a result, one of the mechanisms by which Marxists have thought war occurs – as a means of undermining international solidarity against capitalism – becomes redundant. The other mechanism, i.e., capitalism's need to conquer new markets, also seems unlikely to lead to widespread confrontation, except when there is a deep global recession. How often these are likely to occur is a matter for economists to debate.

The dispersal of sovereignty view provides some good reasons for thinking that the potential for serious conflict would be diminished by spreading the sovereignty which is now concentrated in states to smaller and larger political units. We should allow, however, that some of the beneficial effects of dispersing sovereignty can be achieved in less radical ways. Citizens may be, and often are, members of communities above and below the level of the state, so the political community need not be their sole locus of identification, and other identifications may be more

---

[54] This is of course compatible with claiming that serious conflicts of interest between states will be resolved in the interests of global capital, as many Marxists today would argue.

significant to them. When they have multiple identifications, it is likely that they will be able to entertain the possibility of identifying with more encompassing groups, including humanity as such.

These observations are important, for one of the mechanisms the dispersal of sovereignty view describes for how political power might come to be spread across a number of overlapping political units looks somewhat utopian.[55] Widespread adherence to the principle that those directly affected by a decision should make it seems an insufficient basis for establishing the variety of political units which the dispersal of sovereignty view envisages coming into existence. Even if (as I argued in Chapters 5–6) a stable political unit does not require a shared national identity, there at least needs to be a sense of belonging to it. Of course in some cases there may be regional, neighbourhood or transnational identities which are the necessary basis of such a sense of belonging, but their existence cannot be taken for granted, and it is unclear whether the processes of globalization are likely to foster these identities. (And there is no general reason to think that, if there are such identities, making them the locus of decision-making would satisfy the principle that those who are significantly and directly affected by a decision should be involved in making it.) If the concentration of sovereignty is a cause of war, we should not suppose that it can be easily overcome.

4.   Conclusion

In the first section of this chapter I argued that the 'anarchic' structure of the state system places serious obstacles in the way of the liberal ideal of global community when powerful states are dominators. Under these circumstances, other states have good reason to build up their arms, interpret ambiguous actions as aggressive, strike pre-emptively, and guard their resources jealously. My subsequent discussion of a variety of views concerning how the incidence of dominators in the state system might be reduced has not given much grounds for optimism. The nature or internal structure of some or all of the units which make up the state system may in various ways make the occurrence of war likely – lack of democracy, a capitalist economic structure, strong national identifications, or the concentration of sovereignty may each be contributory causes of war.

The truth about which aspects of the nature of states or their internal structures make them prone to war or peace-loving is no doubt complex,

---

[55] This does not constitute an argument against the idea that dispersing sovereignty in various ways would, in principle, be ideal, but it does raise doubts about whether such a proposal is viable in practice.

and the factors I have considered are unlikely to be exhaustive. But even if we came into possession of that truth, there would be the further question of whether and how states could undergo the transformations which it implies are required to make them peace-loving. Here there are limits to the measures which other states are entitled to take in their effort to make dominators peace-loving. In the previous chapter I argued that there should be a presumption against intervention (except on grounds of self-defence), which can only legitimately be overridden in some cases when states are committing serious moral crimes against their own citizens (see Chapter 8, sections 2–3). Aside from these cases, conflicts between allowing political communities to retain their own character and promoting liberal ideals of global community should be resolved in favour of the former. This means that although states can intervene on grounds of self-defence, or come to the aid of other states which have been attacked by dominators, they are not entitled to intervene solely on the grounds that some state has a nature, or internal structure, which makes it prone to war, unless, perhaps, it poses a clear and specific threat to international peace and security. (In some cases, forms of interference which fall short of intervention, such as diplomatic pressure or even sanctions, may be justified, but that is all.)

These limits to intervention do not, however, give reason to conclude that liberal ideals of global community are unachievable *to any significant degree*. The structure of the state system does not always constitute a significant obstacle to peace. In the absence of good evidence that any of the powerful states is a dominator, and where there is no reason to think that the incidence of dominators amongst the other states is high, states can afford to be more relaxed without making themselves vulnerable – even more so when there is an ethos of cooperation. And the other potential contributory causes of war that I have considered, such as lack of democracy, a capitalist economic structure and the concentration of sovereignty, are unlikely to be of the kind which makes mutual help or significant periods of peace impossible.

Conclusion

This book began with the observation that the term 'community' is employed in a variety of different contexts for a variety of different purposes, and that we do not possess a clear view of its different uses. In response I introduced a number of distinctions with the hope of disentangling some of the different strands of the notion. I contrasted what I called the ordinary concept of community with the moralized concept, distinguished between levels and kinds of community, and between aspects and degrees of community. The structure provided by these distinctions was employed to make sense of our talk about community and to understand the purposes which it serves.

The distinction between levels and kinds of community also enabled us to focus an important question which the debate between liberals and communitarians has shown that we need to take seriously, viz. what kind of community, if any, is ideal at the level of the state and what steps may the state legitimately take to promote it? I began by considering the dominant liberal answer to that question. The dominant liberal conception of political community maintains that we should aspire to a community in which citizens identify with their major institutions because they each converge on the principles that underlie them. In its contractualist form at least, this represented a version of the moralized concept of community, for citizens are presumed to be mutually concerned (they have a non-instrumental desire to justify their institutions to one another), and their relations with one another are presented as just (their institutions are structured by principles which no one can reasonably reject, and the impossibility of reasonable rejection is taken to be a constitutive property of just principles).

The republican challenge which I considered to the dominant liberal conception argued for a more robust community at the level of the state. According to this challenge, a community of citizens must be united in some important way by the good of citizenship. This led to an improved version of the moralized notion of what it is for citizens to constitute a community – according to the republican conception, citizens constitute a community only if they fulfil their special obligations to one another, and in that way realize the good of citizenship. But an appreciation of the difficulties of realizing either the republican conception or dominant liberal conception of political community – in particular, the fear that both require greater homogeneity than we are entitled to expect in modern democratic states – motivated us to distinguish between the ideal in principle and the ideal in practice. Even if (say) the republican conception represents an ideal political community in principle, it is likely to be unrealizable in practice and there may be better ideals with which to regulate and inform institutions and policy making. (Of course, the fact that some conception is unrealizable in practice does not mean that it is not a genuine ideal. To think that unrealizability in practice undermines an ideal is to fall prey to 'sour grapes' reasoning – to suppose that just because the grapes are out of reach, they cannot be sweet and juicy.)

Working with a similar distinction, Aristotle argued in the *Politics* that the ideal state in principle is an aristocracy, rule of the truly excellent, but in practice the ideal for most states is polity, a mixed constitution containing elements of democracy and oligarchy. Aristotle's argument illustrates a point emphasized more recently by Robert Goodin: that when the best is unachievable, the second best may differ radically from it. In consequence, the best in principle should not always be a regulative ideal, for pursuing it even indirectly may lead us away from the second best.

In the case of political community, I suggested that the best in practice is likely to be an inclusive political community. An inclusive political community is a polity to which the vast majority of citizens have a sense of belonging. It is governed by liberal institutions (broadly understood) but may contain significant illiberal minorities. They nevertheless identify with the major institutions and practices and feel at home in them, partly because they have their own reasons for valuing them, and partly because they have a voice in the running of the polity. Although inclusive political community is an ideal in practice, it is not quite a version of the moralized concept of community. Members of such a community need not be mutually concerned. They are, however, likely to develop a sense of sharing a common fate as a result of being part of a society to which they all have a sense of belonging, and this may in some circumstances lead to the development of mutual concern.

The problem of how an inclusive political community might be realized has many dimensions to it. In this book, I have focused on the difficulties it encounters in the face of deep cultural diversity, including the presence of minorities who reject liberal principles. There are other difficulties, no less important, which have other sources. The homeless and the unemployed, and those facing prejudice of various kinds, are just as likely to lack a sense of belonging to the polity in which they live. Perhaps liberal institutions, when they are running properly, are inconsistent with the existence of homeless people, or with the existence of prejudice (at least when it is of the kind which manifests itself in discrimination). But if so, that confirms just how difficult it is for them to run properly.

Inclusive political community is, in ordinary circumstances, the most to which a polity can reasonably aspire. In many circumstances even that is way beyond reach, however, for it requires a 'culture', that is, a set of traditions and practices, which can support liberal institutions. The common habit of referring to the citizens of states as political communities stands in need of justification. If, however, we interpret 'community' in its most undemanding way, to mean simply a group of people who share some values, a way of life, identify to some degree with their institutions, and acknowledge each other as members, then this will draw in a number of polities with non-liberal institutions. It is community in this sense which threatens to come into conflict with liberal visions of community at the global level, understood as ideals in the moralized sense.

Since political communities in the ordinary sense may be oppressive or fail to protect some of their citizens, leaving them alone to run their own affairs can stand in the way of promoting global community, for global community in the moralized sense requires the absence of systematic injustice between individuals. Although a principle of non-intervention gives too much ground to political community when it is understood in the undemanding way described earlier, there are good reasons for thinking that permitting widespread humanitarian intervention would be at best counterproductive and at worst result in greater injustice. A limited practice of humanitarian intervention, which legitimized intervention only in grave cases of injustice (to stop mass murder, enslavement or deportation, or to stop the institutional use of rape or torture), is more sensitive to the difficulties and dangers of intervention, and represents the best that can be done (along this dimension) towards realizing a liberal conception of global community. The direct pursuit of global justice in many circumstances is likely to be self-defeating. Again, the appropriate regulative ideal – stopping the worst human rights abuses, perhaps in conjunction with the alleviation of the worst poverty – may be rather different from the ideal in principle, even if this time it is on the same continuum.

There are many more conflicts between kinds of community, and between levels of community, than I have discussed in this book. For instance, I have said nothing about the way in which communities at the transnational level can come into conflict with community at the level of the state, but perhaps promote a liberal ideal of global community in the process. I do not mean to suggest that conflicts of other sorts are unimportant. But they are beyond the scope of this book which has focused instead on two other important sorts of conflict: between political community in the moralized sense and communities in the ordinary sense below the level of the state; and between political communities in the ordinary sense and liberal ideals of global community in the moralized sense.

Bibliography

Acton, Lord, 'Nationalism', in J. Figgis and R. Laurence (eds.), *The History of Freedom and Other Essays* (London: Macmillan, 1922)

Allison, G., 'Conceptual Models and the Cuban Missile Crisis', *American Political Science Review*, vol. 63, 1969

Anderson, B., *Imagined Communities: Reflections on the Origin and Spread of Nationalism*, revd edn (London: Verso, 1991)

Appiah, K. A., 'Identity, Authenticity, Survival: Multicultural Societies and Social Reproduction' in A. Gutmann (ed.), *Multiculturalism: Examining the Politics of Recognition* (Princeton, NJ: Princeton University Press, 1994)

Archard, D., 'The Marxist Ethic of Self-realization: Individuality and Community' in J. D. G. Evans (ed.), *Moral Philosophy and Contemporary Problems* (Cambridge: Cambridge University Press, 1987)

'Autonomy, Character and Situation', in D. E. Milligan and W. Watts Miller (eds.), *Liberalism, Citizenship and Autonomy* (Aldershot: Avebury, 1992)

Children: Rights and Childhood (London: Routledge, 1993)

Augustine, St., *City of God*, trans. H. Bettenson (Harmondsworth: Penguin, 1984)

Baker, J., *Arguing for Equality* (London: Verso, 1987)

Ball, T., *Transforming Political Discourse* (Oxford: Blackwell, 1988)

Barker, E., *National Character and the Factors in its Formation* (London: Methuen, 1927)

Barry, B., 'The Obscurities of Power', *Government and Opposition*, vol. 10, 1975

'Self-Government Revisited', in D. Miller and L. Siedentop (eds.), *The Nature of Political Theory* (Oxford: Oxford University Press, 1983)

'Political Accommodation and Consociational Democracy', in *Democracy, Power and Justice: Essays in Political Theory* (Oxford: Clarendon Press, 1989)

Theories of Justice (Hemel Hempstead: Harvester-Wheatsheaf, 1989)

Justice as Impartiality (Oxford: Oxford University Press, 1995)

'Review of W. Kymlicka, *Multicultural Citizenship*', *Ethics*, vol. 107, 1996

'Statism and Nationalism: A Cosmopolitan Critique', in I. Shapiro and L. Brilmayer (eds.), *NOMOS*, vol. 41, *Global Justice* (New York: New York University Press, 1999)

Bauer, J., and D. Bell (eds.), *The East Asian Challenge for Human Rights* (Cambridge: Cambridge University Press, 1999)

Beitz C., *Political Theory and International Relations* (Princeton, NJ: Princeton University Press, 1979)

'The Reagan Doctrine in Nicaragua', in S. Luper-Foy (ed.), *Problems of International Justice* (Boulder, CO: Westview Press, 1988)

Bell, D., *Communitarianism and its Critics* (Oxford: Oxford University Press, 1993)

Bellamy, R., 'Citizenship and Rights', in R. Bellamy (ed.), *Theories and Concepts of Politics: An Introduction* (Manchester: Manchester University Press, 1993)

'The Constitution of Europe: Rights or Democracy?', in R. Bellamy, V. Bufacchi and D. Castiglione (eds.), *Democracy and Constitutional Culture in the Union of Europe* (London: Lothian Foundation Press, 1995)

Benn, S., *A Theory of Freedom* (Oxford: Oxford University Press, 1988)

Benner, E., *Really Existing Nationalisms: A Post-Communist View from Marx and Engels* (Oxford: Oxford University Press, 1995)

Berlin, I., 'Benjamin Disraeli, Karl Marx and the Search for Identity', in H. Hardy (ed.), *Against the Current* (Oxford: Oxford University Press, 1980)

Blum, L., *Friendship, Altruism and Morality* (London: Routledge and Kegan Paul, 1980)

Brewin, C., 'Liberal States and International Obligations', *Millennium: Journal of International Studies*, vol. 17, 1988

Brown, C., 'International Political Theory and the Idea of World Community' in K. Booth and S. Smith (eds.), *International Relations Theory Today* (Cambridge: Polity, 1995)

Brudney, D., 'Community and Completion' in A. Reath, B. Herman and C. Korsgaard (eds.), *Reclaiming the History of Ethics: Essays for John Rawls* (Cambridge: Cambridge University Press, 1997)

Bubeck, D., 'A Feminist Approach to Citizenship', EUI Working Paper EUF No. 95/1

Buber, M., *Paths in Utopia* (Boston: Beacon Press, 1958)

Buchanan, A., 'Assessing the Communitarian Critique of Liberalism', *Ethics*, vol. 99, 1989, 852–82

Secession: The Morality of Political Divorce from Fort Sumter to Lithuania and Quebec (Boulder, CO: Westview, 1991)

Bull, H. (ed.), *Intervention in World Politics* (Oxford: Oxford University Press, 1984)

Callan, E., *Creating Citizens: Political Education and Liberal Democracy* (Oxford: Oxford University Press, 1997)

Camilleri, J. A. and J. Falk, *The End of Sovereignty? The Politics of a Shrinking and Fragmenting World* (Aldershot: Edward Elgar, 1992)

Caney, S., 'Liberalism and Communitarianism: a Misconceived Debate', *Political Studies*, vol. 40, 1992

'Impartiality and Liberal Neutrality', *Utilitas*, vol. 8, 1996

'Individuals, Nations and Obligations', in S. Caney, D. George, and P. Jones (eds.), *National Rights and International Obligations* (Oxford: Westview, 1996)

'Cosmopolitanism, Realism and the National Interest', in G. Parry and H. Steiner (eds.), *Freedom and Trade* (London: Routledge, 1997)

Canovan, M., *Nationhood and Political Theory* (Cheltenham: Edward Elgar, 1996)

Charvet, J., 'What is Nationality, and Is There a Moral Right to National Self-Determination?', in S. Caney, D. George, and P. Jones (eds.), *National Rights, International Obligations* (Oxford: Westview, 1996)

Cicero, *On the Commonwealth*, trans. by G. H. Sabine and S. B. Smith (New York: Macmillan, 1976)

Clayton, M., 'White on Autonomy, Neutrality and Well-Being', *Journal of Philosophy of Education*, Vol. 27, 1993

'Educating Liberals: An Argument about Political Neutrality, Equality of Opportunity, and Parental Autonomy' (D.Phil thesis, Faculty of Social Studies, University of Oxford, 1997)

Cohen, G. A., *History, Labour and Freedom: Themes from Marx* (Oxford: Oxford University Press, 1988)

'Incentives, Inequality, and Community', in G. B. Peterson (ed.), *The Tanner Lectures on Human Values, Vol. 13* (Salt Lake City, UT: University of Utah Press, 1992)

Self-Ownership, Freedom, and Equality (Cambridge: Cambridge University Press, 1995)

Cohen, J., 'Deliberation and Democratic Legitimacy', in A. Hamlin and P. Pettit (eds.), *The Good Polity: Normative Analysis of the State* (Oxford: Blackwell, 1989)

'Moral Pluralism and Political Consensus' in D. Copp, J. Hampton and J. Roemer (eds.), *The Idea of Democracy* (Cambridge: Cambridge University Press, 1993)

Cohen, M., 'Moral Skepticism and International Relations', in C. Beitz, M. Cohen, T. Scanlon and A. J. Simmons (eds.), *International Ethics* (Princeton, NJ: Princeton University Press, 1985)

Connolly, W., *The Terms of Political Discourse*, 2nd edn (Oxford: Martin Robertson, 1983)

Cooper, D., 'Multicultural Education', in J. North (ed.), *The GCSE: An Examination* (London: Claridge, 1987)

Crisp, R., 'Values, Reasons and the Environment', in R. Attfield and A. Belsey (eds.), *Philosophy and the Natural Environment* (Cambridge: Cambridge University Press, 1994)

'Raz on Well-Being', *Oxford Journal of Legal Studies*, vol. 17, 1997

Crittenden, J., *Beyond Individualism: Reconstituting the Liberal Self* (New York: Oxford University Press, 1992)

D'Agostino, F., *Free Public Reason: Making It Up As We Go* (New York: Oxford University Press, 1996)

Dagger, R., 'Rights, Boundaries, and the Bond of Community: A Qualified Defense of Moral Parochialism', *American Political Science Review*, vol. 79, 1985

Civic Virtues: Rights, Citizenship, and Republican Liberalism (Oxford: Oxford University Press, 1997)

Dancy, J., *Moral Reasons* (Oxford: Blackwell, 1993)

'Value and Intrinsic Value' (unpublished paper)

De Schryver, R., 'The Belgian Revolution and the Emergence of Belgium's Biculturalism', in A. Lijphart (ed.), *Conflict and Coexistence in Belgium: The Dynamics of a Culturally Divided Society* (Berkeley, CA: Institute of International Studies, University of California, 1981)

Delphy, C., and D. Leonard, *Familiar Exploitation* (Cambridge: Polity, 1992)

Doyle, M., 'Kant, Liberal Legacies and Foreign Affairs', *Philosophy and Public Affairs*, vol. 12, 1983

Dworkin, R., *A Matter of Principle* (Oxford: Oxford University Press, 1985)
Law's Empire (London: Fontana, 1986)

Etzioni, A., *The Spirit of Community* (New York, 1993)

Feinberg, J., 'The Child's Right to an Open Future', in W. Aiken and H. LaFollette (eds.), *Whose Child? Children's Rights, Parental Authority and State Power* (Totowa, NJ: Rowman and Littlefield, 1980)
The Moral Limits of the Criminal Law, vol. 4: Harmless Wrongdoing (New York: Oxford University Press, 1988)

Fitzmaurice, J., *The Politics of Belgium: A Unique Federalism* (London: Hurst and Co, 1996)

Flew, A., 'The Monstrous Regime of "Anti-Racism"', *The Salisbury Review*, vol. 7, 1989
'Education: Anti-Racist, Multi-ethnic and Multi-cultural', in I. Mahalingham and B. Carr (eds.), *Logical Foundations* (Basingstoke: Macmillan, 1991)

Forde, S., 'Classical Realism', in T. Nardin and D. Mapel (eds.), *Traditions of International Ethics* (Cambridge: Cambridge University Press, 1992)

Franck, T. M. and N. Rodley, 'After Bangladesh: The Law of Humanitarian Intervention by Force', *American Journal of International Law*, vol. 67, 1973

Frazer, E. and N. Lacey, *The Politics of Community: A Feminist Critique of the Liberal-Communitarian Debate* (Hemel Hempstead: Harvester-Wheatsheaf, 1993)
'Blind Alleys: Communitarianism', *Politics*, vol. 14, 1994

Friedman, M., 'Feminism and Modern Friendship: Dislocating the Community', *Ethics*, vol. 99, 1989

Fukuyama, F., *The End of History and the Last Man* (London: Hamish Hamilton, 1992)

Gallie, W. B., 'Essentially Contested Concepts', *Proceedings of the Aristotelian Society*, vol. 56, 1955–6

Galston, W., *Liberal Purposes: Goods, Virtues, and Diversity in the Liberal State* (Cambridge: Cambridge University Press, 1991)

Gardner, P., 'Propositional Attitudes and Multicultural Education or Believing Others Are Mistaken', in J. Horton and P. Nicholson (eds.), *Toleration: Philosophy and Practice* (Aldershot: Avebury, 1992)

Gaus, G., *Justificatory Liberalism: An Essay on Epistemology and Political Theory* (Oxford: Oxford University Press, 1996)

Gauthier, D., *Morals By Agreement* (Oxford: Oxford University Press, 1986)
'Political Contractarianism' in P. Koller and K. Puhl (eds.), *Proceedings of the 19th International Wittgenstein Symposium 1996: Current Issues in Political Philosophy* (Vienna: Holder-Pichler-Tempsky, 1997)

Gellner, E., 'Concepts and Society', in B. Wilson (ed.), *Rationality* (Oxford: Blackwell, 1970)

Genovese, E. D., *Roll, Jordan, Roll: The World the Slaves Made* (New York: Pantheon Books, 1974)

George, R. P., *Making Men Moral: Civil Liberties and Public Morality* (Oxford: Oxford University Press, 1993)

Gewirth, A., *Reason and Morality* (Chicago: University of Chicago Press, 1978)
'Ethical Universalism and Particularism', *Journal of Philosophy*, vol. 85, 1988
Gilbert, M., *Living Together: Rationality, Sociality, and Obligation* (Lanham, MD: Rowman and Littlefield, 1996)
Gleason, P., 'American Identity and Americanization' in S. Thernstrom (ed.), *The Harvard Encyclopaedia of American Ethnic Groups* (Cambridge, MA: Harvard University Press, 1980)
Glover, J., 'Nations, Identity, and Conflict' in R. McKim and J. McMahan (eds.), *The Morality of Nationalism* (New York: Oxford University Press, 1997)
Goodin, R., *Protecting the Vulnerable: A Reanalysis of Our Social Responsibilities* (Chicago: University of Chicago Press, 1985)
Reasons for Welfare: The Political Theory of the Welfare State (Princeton, NJ: Princeton University Press, 1988)
'What Is So Special about Our Fellow Countrymen?', *Ethics*, vol. 98, 1988
'Designing Constitutions: the Political Constitution of a Mixed Commonwealth', *Political Studies*, vol. 44, 1996
Graham, G., 'The Justice of Intervention', *Review of International Studies*, vol. 13, 1987
Graham, K., *The Battle of Democracy* (Brighton: Wheatsheaf, 1986)
Karl Marx, Our Contemporary (Hemel Hempstead: Harvester-Wheatsheaf, 1992)
Gray, J., *Enlightenment's Wake: Politics and Culture at the Close of the Modern Age* (London: Routledge, 1995)
Green, L., *The Authority of the State* (Oxford: Oxford University Press, 1990)
'Internal Minorities and Their Rights' in W. Kymlicka (ed.), *The Rights of Minority Cultures* (Oxford: Oxford University Press, 1995)
Green, T. H., *Lectures on the Principles of Political Obligation* (London: Longmans, Green and Co, 1941)
Gutmann, A., *Democratic Education* (Princeton, NJ: Princeton University Press, 1987)
'Civic Education and Social Diversity', *Ethics*, vol. 105, 1995
Gutmann, A., and D. Thompson, *Democracy and Disagreement* (Harvard: Harvard University Press, 1996)
Habermas, J., 'Citizenship and National Identity: Some Reflections on the Future of Europe' in R. Beiner (ed.), *Theorizing Citizenship* (Albany, NY: State University of New York Press, 1995)
Haldane, J., 'Identity, Community and the Limits of Multiculture', *Public Affairs Quarterly*, vol. 7, 1993
Halstead, J. M., *The Case for Muslim Voluntary-Aided Schools* (Cambridge: The Islamic Academy, 1986)
Education, Justice and Cultural Diversity: An Examination of the Honeyford Affair, 1984–5 (Lewes: Falmer Press, 1988)
'Ethical Dimensions of Controversial Events in Multicultural Education', in M. Leicester and M. Taylor (eds.), *Ethics, Ethnicity and Education* (London: Kogan Page, 1992)
'Voluntary apartheid? Problems of Schooling for Religious and Other Minorities in Democratic Societies', *Journal of Philosophy of Education*, vol. 29, 1995

Hardimon, M. O., *Hegel's Social Philosophy: The Project of Reconciliation* (Cambridge: Cambridge University Press, 1994)

Hardin, R., *One For All: The Logic of Group Conflict* (Princeton, NJ: Princeton University Press, 1995)

Hare, W., 'Open-mindedness in the Classroom', *Journal of the Philosophy of Education*, vol. 19, 1985

Heater, D., *World Citizenship and Government: Cosmopolitan Ideas in the History of Western Political Thought* (Basingstoke: Macmillan, 1996)

Hegel, G. W. F., *Phenomenology of Mind*, trans. by J. B. Baillie (London: George Allen and Unwin, 1931)

Held, D., 'Democracy and the New International Order', in D. Archibugi and D. Held (eds.), *Cosmopolitan Democracy: An Agenda for a New World Order* (Cambridge: Polity, 1995)

Hobbes, T., *Leviathan* (Harmondsworth: Penguin, 1968)

Hobsbawm, E., *Nations and Nationalism since 1780: Programme, Myth, Reality*, 2nd edn (Cambridge: Cambridge University Press, 1990)

Hobson, J., *Imperialism*, 3rd edn (London: George Allen and Unwin, 1938)

Holden, B., 'Democratic Theory and the Problem of Global Warming', in B. Holden (ed.), *The Ethical Dimensions of Global Change* (Basingstoke: Macmillan, 1996)

Honeyford, R., 'The Gilmore Syndrome', *The Salisbury Review*, vol. 4, 1986 *Integration or Disintegration? Towards a Non-Racist Society* (London: Claridge Press, 1988)

Honneth, A., *The Struggle for Recognition: The Moral Grammar of Social Conflicts* (Cambridge: Polity, 1995)

Horsman, M. and A. Marshall, *After the Nation-State: Citizens, Tribalism and the New World Disorder* (London: HarperCollins, 1994)

Horton, J., *Political Obligation* (Basingstoke: Macmillan, 1993)

Hurka, T., 'The Justification of National Partiality', in R. McKim and J. McMahan (eds.), *The Morality of Nationalism* (New York: Oxford University Press, 1997)

Hurley, S., *Natural Reasons: Persons and Polity* (Oxford: Oxford University Press, 1989)

Jackson, R., 'International Community Beyond the Cold War', in G. Lyons and M. Mastanduno (eds.), *Beyond Westphalia: State Sovereignty and International Intervention* (Baltimore, MD: Johns Hopkins University Press, 1995)

Jenkins, R., *Essays and Speeches* (London: Collins, 1967)

Jones, P., 'International Human Rights: Philosophical or Political?', in S. Caney, D. George, and P. Jones (eds.) *National Rights, International Obligations* (Oxford: Westview Press, 1996)

Kant, I., *Political Writings*, ed. H. Reiss (Cambridge: Cambridge University Press, 1991)

Kavka, G. S., *Hobbesian Moral and Political Theory* (Princeton, NJ: Princeton University Press, 1986)

Keat, R. N., 'Individualism and Community in Socialist Thought', in J. Mepham and D.-H. Ruben (eds.), *Issues in Marxist Philosophy*, vol. IV (Brighton: Harvester, 1981)

Khin Zaw, S., 'Locke and Multiculturalism: Toleration, Relativism, and Reason', in R. K. Fullinwider (ed.), *Public Education in a Multicultural Society: Policy, Theory, Critique* (Cambridge: Cambridge University Press, 1996)

Korsgaard, C., 'Two Distinctions in Goodness', in *Creating the Kingdom of Ends* (Cambridge: Cambridge University Press, 1996)

Krasner, S., *Structural Conflict: The Third World Against Global Capitalism* (Berkeley, CA: University of California Press, 1985)

Kripke, S., *Wittgenstein on Rules and Private Language* (Cambridge, MA: Harvard University Press, 1982)

Kukathas, C., 'Are There Any Cultural Rights?', *Political Theory*, vol. 20, 1992
'Cultural Rights Again: A Rejoinder to Kymlicka', *Political Theory*, vol. 20, 1992

Kymlicka, W., *Liberalism, Community, and Culture* (Oxford: Oxford University Press, 1989)
'The Rights of Minority Cultures: Reply to Kukathas', *Political Theory*, vol. 20, 1992
'Two Models of Pluralism and Tolerance', *Analyse und Kritik*, vol. 13, 1992
Multicultural Citizenship: A Liberal Theory of Minority Rights (Oxford: Oxford University Press, 1995)
'Social Unity in a Liberal State', *Social Philosophy and Policy*, vol. 13, 1996

Larmore, C., 'Political Liberalism', *Political Theory*, vol. 18, 1990

Leicester, M., 'Values, Cultural Conflict and Education', in M. Leicester and M. Taylor (eds.), *Ethics, Ethnicity and Education* (London: Kogan Page, 1992)

Lenin, V., *Imperialism, the Highest Stage of Capitalism: A Popular Outline* (Moscow: Progress Publishers, 1968)

Lijphart, A., *Democracy in Plural Societies: A Comparative Exploration* (New Haven, CT: Yale University Press, 1977)

Linklater, A., 'The Problem of Community in International Relations', *Alternatives*, vol. 15, 1990
'What Is a Good International Citizen?', in P. Keal (ed.), *Ethics and Foreign Policy* (St. Leonards, NSW: Allen and Unwin, 1992)
The Transformation of Political Community: Ethical Foundations of the Post-Westphalian Era (Cambridge: Polity, 1998)

Luban, D., 'The Romance of the Nation-State' in C. Beitz, M. Cohen, T. Scanlon and A. J. Simmons (eds.), *International Ethics* (Princeton, NJ: Princeton University Press, 1985)

Lukes, S., *Power: A Radical View* (London: Macmillan, 1974)

Macedo, S., *Liberal Virtues: Citizenship, Virtue, and Community in Liberal Constitutionalism* (Oxford: Oxford University Press, 1990)
'Liberal Civic Education and Religious Fundamentalism: The Case of God v. John Rawls?', *Ethics*, vol. 105, 1995

MacIntyre, A., *After Virtue: a Study in Moral Theory* (Notre Dame: University of Notre Dame Press, 1981)
Whose Justice? Which Rationality? (London: Duckworth, 1988)
'A Partial Response to My Critics' in J. Horton and S. Mendus (eds.), *After MacIntyre: Critical Perspectives on the Work of Alasdair MacIntyre* (Cambridge: Polity, 1994)

MacMurray, J., *Persons in Relation* (London: Faber and Faber, 1961)

Mapel, D., 'When is it Right to Rescue? A Response to Pasic and Weiss', *Ethics and International Affairs*, vol. 11, 1997

Margalit, A., 'The Moral Psychology of Nationalism' in R. McKim and J. McMahan (eds.), *The Morality of Nationalism* (New York: Oxford University Press, 1997)

Margalit, A. and J. Raz, 'National Self-Determination', *Journal of Philosophy*, vol. 87, 1990

Marshall, T. H., *Class, Citizenship and Social Development* (New York, 1964)

Marx, K and F. Engels, *Selected Works*, vol. 1 (Moscow: Foreign Languages Publishing House, 1962)

The Communist Manifesto (Harmondsworth, Middlesex: Penguin, 1967)

Collected Works, vol. 22 (London: Lawrence and Wishart, 1975)

Collected Works, vol. 5 (London: Lawrence and Wishart, 1976)

Mason, A., 'Liberalism and the Value of Community', *Canadian Journal of Philosophy*, vol. 23, 1993

Explaining Political Disagreement (Cambridge: Cambridge University Press, 1993)

'MacIntyre on Liberalism and Its Critics: Tradition, Incommensurability and Disagreement' in J. Horton and S. Mendus (eds.), *After MacIntyre: Critical Perspectives on the Work of Alasdair MacIntyre* (Cambridge: Polity, 1994)

'The State, National Identity, and Distributive Justice', *New Community*, vol. 21, 1995

'Two Concepts of Community', in N. Snow (ed.), *In the Company of Others: Perspectives on Family, Community and Culture* (Lanham, MD: Rowman and Littlefield, 1996)

'Review of *Multicultural Citizenship*', *Philosophical Quarterly*, vol. 47, 1997

'Special Obligations to Compatriots', *Ethics*, vol. 107, 1997

'The Public Funding of Separate Religious Schools', *Journal of Franco-British Studies*, No. 23, 1997

'Imposing Liberal Principles', in R. Bellamy and M. Hollis (eds.), *Pluralism and Liberal Neutrality* (London: Frank Cass, 1999)

'Political Community, Liberal-Nationalism, and the Ethics of Assimilationism', *Ethics*, vol. 109, 1999

Mason, A. and N. Wheeler, 'Realist Objections to Humanitarian Intervention', in B. Holden (ed.), *The Ethical Dimensions of Global Change* (Basingstoke: Macmillan, 1996)

May, L., *The Morality of Groups: Collective Responsibility, Group-Based Harm, and Corporate Rights* (Notre Dame, IN: University of Notre Dame, Press, 1987)

McCulloch, C., 'The Problem of Fellowship in Communitarian Theory: William Morris and Peter Kropotkin', *Political Studies*, vol. 32, 1984

McLaughlin, T., 'The Ethics of Separate Schools', in M. Leicester and M. Taylor (eds.), *Ethics, Ethnicity and Education* (London: Kogan Page, 1992)

McMahan, J., 'The Ethics of International Intervention', in K. Kipnis and D. Meyers (eds.), *Political Realism and International Morality* (Boulder, CO: Westview Press, 1987)

'The Limits of National Partiality' in R. McKim and J. McMahan (eds.), *The Morality of Nationalism* (Oxford: Oxford University Press, 1997)

McMahon, C., *Authority and Democracy: A General Theory of Government and Management* (Princeton, NJ: Princeton University Press, 1994)

Mendus, S, *Toleration and the Limits of Liberalism* (Basingstoke: Macmillan, 1989)

Mill, J. S., 'On Liberty', in M. Warnock (ed.), *Utilitarianism* (Glasgow: Fontana, 1962)

Considerations on Representative Government (Chicago: Henry Regnery, 1962)

'Coleridge' in J. M. Robson (ed.), *Collected Works of John Stuart Mill, vol. X, Essays on Ethics, Religion and Society* (Toronto: University of Toronto Press, 1969)

'A Few Words on Non-Intervention', in J. M. Robson (ed.), *Collected Works of John Stuart Mill, vol. 21, Essays on Equality, Law, and Education* (London: Routledge, 1984)

Miller, D., 'Socialism and Toleration', in S. Mendus (ed.), *Justifying Toleration: Conceptual and Historical Perspectives* (Cambridge: Cambridge University Press, 1988)

'In What Sense Must Socialism Be Communitarian?', *Social Philosophy and Policy*, vol. 6, 1989

Market, State, and Community: Theoretical Foundations of Market Socialism (Oxford: Oxford University Press, 1989)

'Citizenship and Pluralism', *Political Studies*, vol. 43, 1995

'Reflections on British National Identity', *New Community*, vol. 21, 1995

On Nationality (Oxford: Oxford University Press, 1995)

Modgil, S., G. Verma, K. Mallick and C. Modgil (eds.), *Multicultural Education: the Interminable Debate* (Lewes: Falmer Press, 1986)

Modood, T., 'On Not Being White in Britain: Discrimination, Diversity and Commonality', in M. Leicester and M. Taylor (eds.), *Ethics, Ethnicity and Education* (London: Kogan Page, 1992)

Not Easy Being British (London: Trentham, 1992)

'Establishment, Multiculturalism and British Citizenship', *The Political Quarterly*, vol. 65, 1994

Monroe, K., M. Barton and U. Klingmann, 'Altruism and the Theory of Rational Action: Rescuers of Jews in Nazi Europe', *Ethics*, vol. 101, 1990

Moon, J. D., *Constructing Community: Moral Pluralism and Tragic Conflicts* (Princeton, NJ: Princeton University Press, 1993)

Moore, A. and R. Crisp, 'Welfarism in Moral Theory', *Australasian Journal of Philosophy*, vol. 74, 1996

Morgenthau, H., *Politics Among Nations: The Struggle for Power and Peace*, 2nd edn (New York: Alfred Knopf, 1954)

Morton, A. L. (ed.), *The Political Writings of William Morris* (London: Lawrence and Wishart, 1979)

Mulhall, S. and A. Swift, *Liberals and Communitarians*, revd edn (Oxford: Blackwell, 1996)

Nagel, T., *Equality and Partiality* (New York: Oxford University Press, 1991)

Narveson, J., *The Libertarian Idea* (Philadelphia, PA: Temple University Press, 1988)

'Collective Rights?', *Canadian Journal of Law and Jurisprudence*, vol. 4, 1991

Natsios, A., 'NGOs and the Humanitarian Impulse', *Ethics and International Affairs*, vol. 11, 1997

Niebuhr, R., *Christian Realism and Political Problems* (New York: Charles Scribner's Sons, 1945)

Nisbet, R., *The Sociological Tradition* (London: Heinemann, 1967)

Nozick, R., *Anarchy, State, and Utopia* (Oxford: Blackwell, 1974)

Nussbaum, M., 'Patriotism and Cosmopolitanism' in J. Cohen (ed.), *For Love of Country: Defining the Limits of Patriotism* (Boston: Beacon Press, 1996)

Parekh, B., 'The Concept of Multicultural Education', in S. Modgil, G. Verma, K. Mallick and C. Modgil (eds.), *Multicultural Education: the Interminable Debate* (Lewes: Falmer Press, 1986)

'The Cultural Particularity of Liberal Democracy', *Political Studies*, vol. 40, 1992

'A Misconceived Discourse on Political Obligation', *Political Studies*, vol. 41, 1993

'Decolonizing Liberalism', in A. Shtromas (ed.), *The End of 'Isms'? Reflections on the Fate of Ideological Politics after Communism's Collapse* (Oxford: Blackwell, 1994)

'Minority Practices and Principles of Toleration', *International Migration Review*, vol. 30, 1996

'Towards the Just World Order: The Aims and Limits of Humanitarian Intervention', *Times Literary Supplement*, 26 September 1997

Park, H. E. and H. A. Miller, *Old World Traits Transplanted* (New York: Harper, 1921)

Pettit, P., *The Common Mind: An Essay on Psychology, Society, and Politics* (Oxford: Oxford University Press, 1993)

Republicanism: A Theory of Freedom and Government (Oxford: Oxford University Press, 1997)

Phillips, A., 'Democracy and Difference: Some Problems for Feminist Theory', in W. Kymlicka (ed.), *The Rights of Minority Cultures* (Oxford: Oxford University Press, 1995)

The Politics of Presence (Oxford: Oxford University Press, 1995)

Plant, R., *Community and Ideology: An Essay in Applied Social Philosophy* (London: Routledge and Kegan Paul, 1974)

'Community: Concept, Conception, and Ideology', *Politics and Society*, vol. 8, 1978

'Citizenship and Rights', in R. Plant and N. Barry, *Citizenship and Rights in Thatcher's Britain: Two Views* (London: IEA Health and Welfare Unit, 1990)

Plant, R., H. Lesser, and P. Taylor-Gooby, *Political Philosophy and Social Welfare* (London: Routledge and Kegan Paul, 1980)

Pogge, T., *Realizing Rawls* (Ithaca, NY: Cornell University Press, 1989)

'Cosmopolitanism and Sovereignty', *Ethics*, vol. 103, 1992

Poulter, S., *English Law and Ethnic Minority Customs* (London: Butterworths, 1986)

'Cultural Pluralism and its Limits: A Legal Perspective', in B. Parekh (ed.), *Britain: a Plural Society* (London: CRE, 1990)

Ramsbotham, O. and T. Woodhouse, *Humanitarian Intervention in Contemporary Conflict: A Reconceptualization* (Cambridge: Polity, 1996)

Rawls, J., 'Legal Obligation and the Duty of Fair Play', in S. Hook (ed.), *Law and Philosophy* (New York: New York University Press, 1964)

A Theory of Justice (Cambridge, MA: Harvard University Press, 1971)

'The Law of Peoples' in H. Shute and S. Hurley (eds.), *On Human Rights: The Oxford Amnesty Lectures* (New York: Basic Books, 1993)

Political Liberalism (New York: Columbia University Press, 1993, pbk. edn 1996)

Raz, J., 'Promises and Obligations', in P. Hacker and J. Raz (eds.), *Law, Morality, and Society: Essays in Honour of H. L. A. Hart* (Oxford: Oxford University Press, 1977)

The Morality of Freedom (Oxford: Oxford University Press, 1986)

'Liberating Duties', *Law and Philosophy*, vol. 8, 1989

'Multiculturalism: A Liberal Perspective', in *Ethics in the Public Domain* (Oxford: Oxford University Press, 1994)

Regan, D., 'Authority and Value: Reflections on Raz's *The Morality of Freedom*', *Southern California Law Review*, vol. 62, 1989

Rorty, A. O., 'The Hidden Politics of Cultural Identification', *Political Theory*, vol. 22, 1994

Rorty, R., *Contingency, Irony, and Solidarity* (Cambridge: Cambridge University Press, 1989)

Russett, B., *Grasping the Democratic Peace: Principles for a Post-Cold War World* (Princeton, NJ: Princeton University Press, 1993)

Ryan, A., 'The Liberal Community', in J. W. Chapman and I. Shapiro (eds.), *NOMOS*, vol. 35, *Democratic Community* (New York: New York University Press, 1993)

Sandel, M., *Liberalism and the Limits of Justice* (Cambridge: Cambridge University Press, 1982)

'The Procedural Republic and the Unencumbered Self', in S. Avineri and A. de-Shalit (eds.), *Communitarianism and Individualism* (Oxford: Oxford University Press, 1992)

Scanlon, T., 'Contractualism and Utilitarianism', in A. Sen and B. Williams (eds.), *Utilitarianism and Beyond* (Cambridge: Cambridge University Press, 1982)

Scheffler, S., 'Families, Nations and Strangers', The Lindley Lecture, University of Kansas, 1994

Scheman, N., 'On Sympathy', *The Monist*, vol. 62, 1979

Schwarzenbach, S., 'On Civic Friendship', *Ethics*, vol. 107, 1996

Scruton, R., 'In Defence of the Nation' in *The Philosopher on Dover Beach* (Manchester: Carcanet, 1990)

Selbourne, D., *The Principle of Duty* (London: Sinclair-Stevenson, 1994)

Singer, P., *Practical Ethics*, 2nd edn (Cambridge: Cambridge University Press, 1993)

Skinner, Q., 'The Idea of Negative Liberty: Philosophical and Historical Perspectives', in R. Rorty, J. B. Schneewind and Q. Skinner (eds.), *Philosophy in History* (Cambridge: Cambridge University Press, 1984)

Slater, J. and T. Nardin, 'Non-Intervention and Human Rights', *Journal of Politics*, vol. 48, 1986

Spinner, J., *The Boundaries of Citizenship: Race, Ethnicity and Nationality in the Liberal State* (Baltimore: Johns Hopkins Univesity Press, 1994)

Steinberg, J., *Why Switzerland?*, 2nd edn (Cambridge: Cambridge University Press, 1996)

Stengers, J., 'Belgian National Sentiments' in A. Lijphart (ed.), *Conflict and Coexistence in Belgium: The Dynamics of a Culturally Divided Society* (Berkeley, CA: Institute of International Studies, University of California, 1981)

Suganami, H., *On the Causes of War* (Oxford: Oxford University Press, 1996)

Swann *et al.*, *Education for All: The Report of the Committee of Inquiry into the Education of Children from Ethnic Minority Groups* (London: HMSO, 1985)

Swidler, A. (ed.), *Human Rights in Religious Traditions* (New York: Pilgrim Press, 1982)

Sylvan, R., 'Is There a Need for a New, an Environmental, Ethic?', in M. E. Zimmerman (ed.), *Environmental Philosophy: From Animal Rights to Radical Ecology* (Englewood Cliffs, NJ: Prentice Hall, 1993)

Tamir, Y., *Liberal Nationalism* (Princeton, NJ: Princeton University Press, 1993)
'Reconstructing the Landscape of Imagination' in S. Caney, D. George, and P. Jones (eds.), *National Rights, International Obligations* (Oxford: Westview, 1996)
'Hands off Clitoridectomy: What Our Revulsion Reveals About Ourselves', *Boston Review*, vol. 21, Summer 1996

Taylor, C., 'Atomism' in *Philosophical Arguments: Volume 2* (Cambridge: Cambridge University Press, 1985)
Sources of the Self: The Making of the Modern Identity (Cambridge: Cambridge University Press, 1989)
'Shared and Divergent Values', in *Reconciling the Solitudes: Essays on Canadian Federalism and Nationalism*, ed. G. Laforest (Montreal: McGill-Queen's University Press, 1993)
'The Politics of Recognition', in A. Gutmann (ed.), *Examining the Politics of Recognition* (Princeton, NJ: Princeton University Press, 1994)
'Cross-Purposes: The Liberal-Communitarian Debate', in *Philosophical Arguments* (Cambridge, MA: Harvard University Press, 1995)
'Conditions of an Unforced Consensus on Human Rights', in J. Bauer and D. Bell (eds.), *The East Asian Challenge for Human Rights* (Cambridge: Cambridge University Press, 1999)

Taylor, M., *Community, Anarchy and Liberty* (Cambridge: Cambridge University Press, 1982)

Ten, C. L., 'Multiculturalism and the Value of Diversity', in C. Kukathas (ed.), *Multicultural Citizens: The Philosophy and Politics of Identity* (St. Leonards, NSW: Centre for Independent Studies, 1993)

Thomas, C., 'The Pragmatic Case Against Intervention', in I. Forbes and M. Hoffman (eds.), *Political Theory, International Relations and the Ethics of Intervention*

Thompson, J., *Justice and World Order: A Philosophical Inquiry* (London: Routledge, 1992)

Tönnies, F., *Community and Association*, trans. C. P. Loomis (London: Routledge and Kegan Paul, 1955)

Troyna, B., 'Multiracial Education: Just Another Brick in the Wall?', *New Community*, vol. 10, 1982–3

'Beyond Multiculturalism: Towards the Enactment of Anti-Racist Education in Policy Provision and Pedagogy', *Oxford Review of Education*, vol. 13, 1987

Tully, J., *Strange Multiplicity: Constitutionalism in an Age of Diversity* (Cambridge: Cambridge University Press, 1995)

Urquart, B., 'For a UN Volunteer Force', *New York Review of Books*, 10 June, 1993

Viroli, M., *For Love of Country: An Essay on Patriotism and Nationalism* (Oxford: Oxford University Press, 1995)

Waldron, J., 'A Right-Based Critique of Constitutional Rights', *Oxford Journal of Legal Studies*, vol. 13, 1993

'Theoretical Foundations of Liberalism' in *Liberal Rights: Collected Papers 1981– 91* (Cambridge: Cambridge University Press, 1993)

'Special Ties and Natural Duties', *Philosophy and Public Affairs*, vol. 22, 1993

'Minority Cultures and the Cosmopolitan Alternative', in W. Kymlicka (ed.), *The Rights of Minority Cultures* (Oxford: Oxford University Press, 1995)

Waltz, K., *Man, the State and War: A Theoretical Analysis* (New York: Columbia University Press, 1959)

Theory of International Politics (Reading, MA: Addison Wesley, 1979)

Walzer, M., *Just and Unjust Wars* (Harmondsworth, Middlesex: Penguin, 1978)

Spheres of Justice: A Defence of Pluralism and Equality (Oxford: Martin Robertson, 1983)

'The Moral Standing of States: A Response to Four Critics', in C. Beitz, M. Cohen, T. Scanlon and A. J. Simmons (eds.), *International Ethics* (Princeton, NJ: Princeton University Press, 1985)

'Justice Here and Now', in F. Lucash (ed.), *Justice and Equality Here and Now* (Ithaca, NY: Cornell University Press, 1986)

'What Does It Mean to Be an American?', *Social Research*, vol. 57, 1990

'Education, Democratic Citizenship and Multiculturalism', *Journal of Philosophy of Education*, vol. 29, 1995

'The Politics of Rescue', *Social Research*, vol. 62, 1995

On Toleration (New Haven, CT: Yale University Press, 1997)

Weiss, P., and M. Friedman (eds.), *Feminism and Community* (Philadelphia, PA: Temple University Press, 1995)

Weiss, T. G., 'UN Responses in the Former Yugoslavia: Moral and Operational Choices', *Ethics and International Affairs*, vol. 8, 1994

Wheeler, N. and K. Booth, 'The Security Dilemma' in J. Baylis and N. Rengger (eds.), *Dilemmas of World Politics: International Issues in a Changing World* (Oxford: Oxford University Press, 1992)

Williams, B., *Moral Luck: Collected Papers 1973–1980* (Cambridge: Cambridge University Press, 1981)

'Identity and Identities', in H. Harris (ed.), *Identity: Lectures Based on Herbert Spencer Lectures Given in the University of Oxford* (Oxford: Oxford University Press, 1995)

'Is International Rescue a Moral Issue?', *Social Research*, vol. 62, 1995

Young, I., 'The Ideal of Community and the Politics of Difference', in L.
    Nicholson (ed.), *Feminism/Postmodernism* (London: Routledge, 1990)
    Justice and the Politics of Difference (Princeton, NJ: Princeton University Press,
    1990)
Zec, P., 'Multicultural Education: What Kind of Relativism is Possible?', *Journal
    of the Philosophy of Education*, vol. 14, 1980

Index

Lightning Source UK Ltd.
Milton Keynes UK
UKHW03f0423290318
320227UK00001B/59/P